Facets
African-American
Video Guide

Compiled by Patrick Ogle

Facets Multimedia, Inc./Academy Chicago Publishers
Chicago

© 1994 Facets Multimedia Inc.

Published by:

Facets Multimedia, Inc.
1517 W. Fullerton Avenue
Chicago, IL 60614

Printed and bound in the U.S.A.

Distributed to the trade by:

Academy Chicago Publishers
363 W. Erie Street
Chicago, IL 60610

Library of Congress Cataloging-in-Publication Data

Ogle, Patrick.
  Facets African-American video guide/Facets Multimedia, Inc.,
compiled by Patrick Ogle.

    p. cm.
  Includes indexes.
  ISBN 0-89733-402-7 : $12.95

  1. Afro-Americans in motion pictures.   2. Afro-American entertainers
3. Motion pictures--Catalogs.   4. Video recordings--Catalogs.   5.
Documentary films--Catalogs.   I. Facets Multimedia (Chicago, Ill.) II. Title.
III. Title: African-American video guide.
PN1995.9.N4M38   1994
016.79143'75'08996073--dc20

Contents

Upfront i

How and Where to Find Videos and Laser Disks in this Book iii

The Facets African-American Video Guide

Classic African-American Cinema 1
Recent African-American Feature Films 27
Blaxploitation Films 89
Foreign Feature Films 99
Children's and Family Films 111
Non-Fiction Films 121
The Civil Rights Movement 151
Documentaries About Africa 157

Music Dance and Comedy

Music from Africa 169
Gospel 171
Popular Music 181
Reggae 186
Soul 187
Blues 187
Jazz 193
Classical and Opera 206
Dance 208
Comedy 211

Director Index 215
Major Performers Index 221
Title Index 222

Acknowledgments

This book was edited by Marissa Reyes, Milos Stehlik, Hope Nathan and Anita Miller. Our sincere appreciation to Shirley Riley-Davis, for much of the original research during which the book took shape, to Jordan Miller of Academy Chicago Publishers, and to Kevin Durkin for editorial assistance with the music section.

Our thanks for use of stills from the films featured in this book to Essenay Entertainment, Facets Multimedia, Inc., History on Video, Interama, Inc., Island Pictures, Janus Films, Kino International, David Koff, LIVE Entertainment, Inc., Miramax Films, Monterey Movie Company, Museum of Contemporary Art, Museum of Modern Art Film Stills Archive, Mypheduh Films, Inc., New Line Cinema (Patti Bodner), New Yorker Films (Jose Lopez), Public Media, Inc., Rhapsody Films, Inc., Samuel Goldwyn Company, Twentieth Century-Fox, Universal City Studios, Inc., Universal Pictures.

Upfront

Since the era of silent films, a little-known but extensive, rich and varied American cinema has grown parallel with mainstream Hollywood films: the African-American cinema. In recent years, this has blossomed with the arrival of young, talented filmmakers who have singular, powerful visions and stories to tell that reflect their own African-American experience.

The commercial breakthroughs of filmmakers like Spike Lee, Robert Townsend, Michael Schultz and John Singleton build on the African-American filmmaking heritage which spans from the silent era to Hollywood's golden years. It builds too on the major influence of African-American music on European and American cinema.

Now this rich heritage can be discovered, thanks to the medium of home video. All the hundreds of feature films, documentaries, children's and educational and filmed or videotaped concerts are available for home viewing on video cassette or laser disk.

Audiences for African-American cinema are continually growing. African American independent filmmakers have become a major force in defining a new American cinema: their voices are strong, clear and original. Directors like Charles Burnett, Julie Dash, Charles Lane, Melvin Van Peebles, the Hughes Brothers, have not only broken new artistic ground, they have defied box office odds. Perhaps the best example is Julie Dash's "Daughters of the Dust," which started in one New York theater and in spite of its very different narrative sense, went on to become a major national success.

Too, an increasing number of African-American filmmakers are able to realize larger-budget films and African-American films are gaining broader distribution. This evolution of African-American cinema is reflected in the films which are described in the Facets African-American Video Guide: we progress from features which "dared" to have a "token" African-American character to films in which the filmmaker is free to explore African-American issues. Although our focus in this book is on the African-American cinema, we have included the relatively few African films or European films with African content which are available on home video. This remains one of the last challenges for the home video market to tackle.

There are many documentaries, films and videos on African-American issues which are distributed through the educational channels and which can be rented for public or educational screenings. We have not included these here because they are not readily accessible to the consumer. Certainly, in the future, as these "non-fiction" films gain greater acceptance within the home video marketplace, more and more of them will become available in video stores at home video prices.

Our approach has been cinematic; we have focused on each tape's artistic values.

We have made no attempt to trace the entire contribution of African-Americans to the movies. Our intention has been to document those films which contain a substantial African-American theme and significant participation by African-American artists. We have included a section on the "blaxploitation" films of the 1970's, a short-lived phenomenon of mostly white-made, white-financed action films: these represent an important transition period for increased African American participation in American cinema. They were a significant training ground for African-American actors and directors, in much the same way that Roger Corman's films offered training for a number of current "hot" American filmmakers.

It is refreshing to note the number of contemporary African-American filmmakers who are producing a growing body of work. These include American independents Julie Dash, Charles Burnett, Charles Lane, Jamaa Fanaka, and Haile Gerima.

We welcome your comments and hope this Guide will help you to spend many happy hours enjoying the accomplishments of these dozens of talented filmmakers.

Film Credits

We have provided director, year and country of release, and the running time of each film or tape based on best-available information. In some cases, as in a number of classic films and in concert music videos, full credits for productions are often impossible to get. In these cases we've provided as much information as is available.

Where To Buy or Rent Tapes

An increasing number of video stores throughout the country are venturing outside the mainstream mentality and stock independent features and documentaries.

If your video store is not one of these progressive outlets, you can purchase any tape or laser disk in this book which is currently in print directly from Facets Video. To order, within the United States call toll-free at 800-331-6197 or FAX at 312-929-5437. Otherwise, call 312-281-9075. Or write: Facets Video, 1517 West Fullerton Avenue, Chicago, Illinois 60614. The "S" numbers at the end of each video description in this book refer to Facets Video's sales order numbers.

Facets Video also offers a rent-by-mail service within the continental United States. For rent-by-mail membership information, call 800-5-FACETS (800-532-2387), FAX at 312-929-5437 or write Facets Video Rentals, 1517 West Fullerton Avenue, Chicago, Illinois 60614.

Prices

The prices listed in this book were current at the time of publication. However, video and laser disk prices are volatile and do change at the drop of a hat. Fortunately, this most often means that they are substantially reduced.

Out of Print Tapes and Disks

Much like the volatile price changes of home video and laser disks, tapes and disks go in and out of print with increasing frequency. Licensing rights expire, video companies shift direction or go out of business. Many tapes which go out of print later reappear on another label, often in a better (enhanced) version. Video stores which purchased copies of the out-of-print tape before it went out of print are and continue to rent those tapes.

Format

Tapes in BETA format: Although BETA is *still* around and has its ardent core of often vocal supporters, it is very difficult to rent or buy tapes in BETA format. If you are determined to stay only with the BETA format, it's a good idea to join one of the BETA collector's clubs.

Laser Disk Availability: An increasing number of titles are available on laser disk, often in "enhanced" versions (widescreen, additional material like director's notes or comments added). Unfortunately, some laser disk manufacturers actually "press" disks only when they get enough orders to warrant the pressing. This means that if you're trying to purchase other-than-mainstream titles, you may have to wait a while to get the laser disk you want. Hopefully this situation will improve with time as the superior image and sound quality of laser disks gains popularity, and as laser disk prices drop.

Classic African-American Cinema

The Beulah Show, Vol. 1

This tape contains two episodes of the 50s television series about the lovable maid Beulah, played in the first episode by Hattie McDaniel, who originated the role on radio. Ernest Whitman (*Green Pastures, Cabin in the Sky*) also appears. The second episode features Ethel Waters (*Cabin in the Sky, Member of the Wedding*) as Beulah. Special guest appearances by Butterfly McQueen and Dooley Wilson. USA, 1951, 60 mins.

VHS: S21389. $24.95.

The Beulah Show, Vol. 2

Louise Beavers appears as the last of the Beulahs. She portrays a maid who seems to run the household. The role is an early appearance of African-American film stereotypes on television. Beavers, as well as her predecessors Ethel Waters and Hattie McDaniel, were such solid character actors that the show remains enjoyable today. Ernest Whitman also appears. USA, 1951, 115 mins.

VHS: S21390. $24.95.

Beware

A young man returns to his alma mater, Ware College, to save it from its unscrupulous namesake Benjamin Ware III. In the process he sweeps his old college sweetheart off her feet. The film is a well-made, well-acted musical drama. Features Louis Jordan, Frank Wilson, Emory Richardson and Valerie Black.

VHS: S21419. $24.95.

Bud Pollard, USA, 1946, 60 mins.

The Big Timers

An all-Black cast film featuring "Moms" Mabley and Stepin Fetchit. Bud Pollard directs, USA.

VHS: S21411. $24.95.

The Birth of a Nation

The first full length American film and probably the most openly and avowedly racist American film, *Birth of A Nation* is often considered to be both a technical "diamond" and a moral lump of coal. It is, however, much more than that. D.W. Griffith's views about the inferiority of African-Americans and the nobility of the Southern cause were hardly a minority opinion. President Woodrow Wilson commented that the film was "history written with lightning". Thus the film shows a great deal about the attitudes that African-Americans of the day had to deal with. The film also brought a storm of protest, led by the NAACP, and was successfully banned in many cities. Black actors were used in the film in extra roles that helped shape stereotypes which would appear in U.S. films for over half a century. The basic plot revolves around two families, one Northern, one Southern, and their respective fortunes during the Civil War. Reconstruction is seen as a turning over of Southern affairs to racially inferior Blacks. With Lillian Gish, Mae Marsh, Miriam Cooper and filmmaker Raoul Walsh. Includes a 30-minute documentary on the making of the film.

VHS: S18433. $39.95.
Laser: LD70883. $49.95.

D.W. Griffith, USA, 1914, 187 mins.

Black King

Also titled *Harlem Hot Shot* and produced by an independent white-run film company, *Black King* satirizes the "Back to Africa" movement begun by shipping entrepreneur Marcus Garvey. The lead character is a con man more interested in cash than cultural identity who hits upon a way to profit from his culture's longing for its roots. Not entirely unsympathetic and certainly not a mean-spirited film. Screenplay by Donald Heywood.

VHS: S07041. $24.95.

Donald Heywood, USA, 1932, 72 mins.

Black Like Me

A white reporter, John Howard Griffin, travelled to the South disguised as a Black man and wrote a book about his experiences. This film version is an early 60s attempt to confront the problem of racism by standing in the shoes of the oppressed—if only for a short time. Stars James Whitmore and Roscoe Lee Browne.

VHS: S06585. $19.95

Carl Lerner, USA, 1964, 107 mins.

The Birth of a Nation
(Kino International)

Blackboard Jungle

Glenn Ford is a teacher trying to teach and to survive in the New York City schools. One of his students, Gregory Miller (Sidney Poitier), particularly opposes and taunts him. Miller is an early African-American character willing to openly and loudly attack the system. Yet in the end he comes to the teacher's aid when it counts. A strong performance by Poitier is accentuated by the other actors including Vic Morrow, Paul Mazursky, Jamie Farr and Anne Francis.

VHS: S11215. $19.95.

Richard Brooks, USA, 1955, 101 mins.

Blood of Jesus

A religiously suspect husband accidentally shoots his pious wife. As he anguishes and discovers his own dormant faith his wife confronts the powers of good and evil in the next world. She chooses God over Satan, comes back to life and is greeted upon her return by a musical finale and a repentant spouse. Directed by Spencer Williams, Jr., who also appears.

VHS: S07042. $24.95.

Spencer Williams, Jr., USA, 1941, 68 mins.

Boardinghouse Blues

"Moms" Mabley can't pay the rent and the landlord is about to throw her and all the entertainers in her boarding house out into the street. It all works out in the long run and the stunning Lila (Marie Cooke) is spared the indignity of the "rent couch". Naturally all the boarding house talent takes part in the show which concludes the film. Guest appearances by Lucky Millinder's band, Bull Moose Jackson, Una Mae Carlisle add to the fun.

VHS: S07044. $34.95.

Josh Binney, USA, 1948, 90 mins.

Body and Soul

Actor, lawyer, writer, athlete and an early voice against racism in the United States, Paul Robeson appeared on the screen for the first time in this Oscar Micheaux-directed silent film. The plot became a victim of the censors but it is basically the tale of a wayward preacher who is transformed into a detective then finally into a perfect husband via a bad dream by the film's heroine. Robeson's presence (despite the intrusion of the censors) brings a certain continuity to the film.

VHS: S10260. $24.95.

Oscar Micheaux, USA, 1925, 75 mins.

Boy! What A Girl!

What are the odds that the show will go on when the producers only have half the money for it? The plot may only be secondary, but if the show is good enough, who cares? Legendary jazz drummer Gene Krupa makes a guest appearance. With Tim Moore, Elwood Smith, Duke Williams, Al Jackson, Sheila Guyse.

VHS: S07045. $34.95.

Arthur Leonard, USA, 1946, 70 mins.

Broadway Rhythm

Father and son producers battle for the same star in this variation of a Jerome Kern/Oscar Hammerstein II musical. Features Lena Horne, pianist Hazel Scott and Eddie "Rochester" Anderson. Music by Tommy Dorsey and his Orchestra.

VHS: S18558. $19.98.

Roy Del Ruth, USA, 1944, 114 mins.

Broken Strings

Often overlooked actor Clarence Muse stars as a Black concert violinist who injures his hand. He encourages his son to take up where he left off but the son prefers swing to classical. Muse co-wrote the screenplay and gave the character a subtle dignity often denied African-American actors of the day. Possibly the best performance of Muse's long career which included roles in *Showboat*, *Heaven Can Wait* and *Gone With The Wind*. Also features Cyril Lewis, William Washington, Tommie More.

VHS: S07051. $34.95.

Bernard B. Ray, USA, 1940, 70 mins.

Bronze Buckaroo

Filmed at a Black dude ranch in California, this film is a musical western. Bob Blake, the hero, and his sidekick, Dusty, set out to apprehend the men responsible for the death of Blake's father. Features Herbert Jeffries, Lucius Brooks, Clarence Brooks, Artie Young and Flournoy E. Miller.

VHS: S21415. $24.95.

Richard C. Kahn, USA, 1939, 57 mins.

Burlesque in Harlem

The great African-American comedian Pigmeat Markham stars in this dance/musical burlesque. An all-Black cast of dancers, strippers and musicians back him up. 60 mins.

VHS: S21391. $24.95.

Cabin in the Sky

Often criticized for its stereotyping, *Cabin in the Sky* nonetheless features memorable musical numbers and performances by a cast including Eddie Anderson ("Rochester" of *The Jack Benny Show* fame), Lena Horne and Louis Armstrong. The plot centers on a good man (Anderson) who is killed after being led astray. He becomes part of a bet between demons and angels. Lena Horne plays the seductress while Ethel Waters plays the wife and savior.

VHS: S01747. $19.98.
Laser: LD70538. $34.98.

Vincente Minelli, USA, 1943, 99 mins.

Carmen Jones

Dorothy Dandrige plays Carmen, a woman caught between two men and her own unorthodox nature in this film based on the Bizet opera *Carmen*. The men, one a pretty boy and the other a tough sergeant, are portrayed by Harry Belafonte and Brock Peters. Dandridge lures Joe (Belafonte) into deserting from the army and then leaves him for the two-fisted Sgt. Brown (Peters). The supporting cast is every bit as impressive as the main actors and includes Pearl Bailey, Joe Adams and Diahann Carroll in her first film role. Dandridge became the first African-American nominated for a Best Actress Academy Award. The film won a Golden Globe for Best Musical/Comedy in 1955.

VHS: S21385. $19.98.

Otto Preminger, USA, 1954, 105 mins.

Check and Double Check

Amos 'n' Andy appear in their only feature film. The black-faced white actors Gosden and Correll play Uncle Tom in the streets of New York and in a haunted house. An example of the 30s view of African-Americans and an example of the death throes of this offshoot of the once-popular minstrel show. Duke Ellington and his Orchestra briefly appear.

VHS: S13992. $19.98.

Melville Brown, USA, 1930, 77 mins.

China Gate

Nat "King" Cole appears as Goldie, a Foreign Legionnaire, who wants peace and understanding. The plot concerns a group of soldiers on a mission to destroy a communist ammunition dump in Vietnam. Cole is not his usual cool, calm and collected self, but he gets to sing a few songs. Also features Gene Berry and Angie Dickinson.

VHS: S09623. $19.95.

Samuel Fuller, USA, 1957, 97 mins.

The Connection

Shot in a documentary style, *The Connection* shows a group of junkies waiting for their dealer. The film broke new ground by taking a look at a neglected segment of society. Shirley Clarke won the Critics Prize at Cannes for her now-classic *cinema verite* feature. The cast includes Roscoe Lee Brown and Carl Lee as the dealer, "Cowboy".

VHS: S00265. $29.95.

Shirley Clarke, USA, 1961, 105 mins.

Death of a Gunfighter

Lena Horne plays the love interest of Sheriff Richard Widmark in this pessimistic Western.

VHS: Currently out of print. May be available for rental in some video stores.

Robert Totten/Don Siegel, USA, 1969, 100 mins.

Defiant Ones

A Black and a white prisoner escape from a chain gang in the South. Neither man much cares for his companion and is wary of him because of the color of his skin. But their situation forces them to work together for their mutual benefit. After meeting a lonely woman who helps them cut the chain one man gives up his freedom to save the other. Sidney Poitier and Tony Curtis were both nominated for Oscars for their performances and the film won Oscars for Best Screenplay and Best Cinematography. Lon Chaney, Jr., Theodore Bikel, Claude Akins and Cara Williams are all part of the large supporting cast.

VHS: S09157. $19.95.
Laser: LD71687. $34.98.

Stanley Kramer, USA, 1958, 97 mins.

Devil's Daughter

In an era in which African-American actors were routinely compared to famous white performers, Nina Mae McKinney was labelled the "Black Garbo". Sibling rivalry, voodoo, and McKinney's naughty (for the 30s) "Blood Dance" mix in one of the many all-Black musicals produced in the 30s and 40s. With Jack Carter and Ida James.

VHS: S07046. $34.95.
Laser: CLV. LD71981. $29.98.

Arthur Leonard, USA, 1939, 60 mins.

Dirty Gertie From Harlem

A showgirl flees from her jealous boyfriend to Trinidad where she becomes involved with her boss, the owner of a hotel. As all good things must end, her boyfriend shows up to spoil things. Based loosely on a W. Somerset Maugham story, *Dirty Gertie From Harlem* features director Spencer Williams, Jr. (*Blood of Jesus*, *Go Down Death*), Francine Everett and Don Wilson.

VHS: S07048. $34.95.

Spencer Williams, Jr., USA, 1946, 60 mins.

Double Deal

An innocent man is framed by his thieving rival because of jealousy over a woman. The rival has robbed a jewelry store and set the hero up. Musical numbers are performed as characters doublecross one another. With Monte Hawley, Jeni Le Gon, Edward Thompson, Florence O'Brien.

VHS: S07049. $34.95.

Arthur Dreifuss, USA, 1939, 60 mins.

Duke Is Tops

Lena Horne, in her film debut, stars opposite Ralph Cooper in this "swing music sensation". Horne plays a successful singer who very nearly loses her man because his career as a producer is on the skids. However, they are happily reunited in a rousing finale. With Ralph Cooper, Lawrence Criner, Monte Hawley, Vernon McCalla and Edward Thompson.

VHS: S07047. $24.95.

William Nolte, USA, 1938, 80 mins.

Emperor Jones

Paul Robeson did not play Brutus Jones as a sympathetic character in this film based on Eugene O'Neill's play. Brutus Jones was both power-mad and a murderer. He was a type of African-American character not previously seen in film. He assumes control of situations, blackmailing his boss or maneuvering his gullible white partner into virtual servitude before taking over the island to which he has fled. Brutus Jones is a character who shows that power and the desire for it corrupts both Black and white. Probably Robeson's finest role. With Dudley Digges, Frank Wilson and Fredi Washington. On the same program is the documentary short, *Paul Robeson: Tribute to an Artist*, directed by Scott Turrell.

VHS: S02627. $19.95.

Dudley Murphy, USA, 1933, 72 mins.

Gang War

Two gangs go head to head over a criminal enterprise: the control of a city's juke box business. Ralph Cooper and Lawrence Criner are the competing hoods but the town isn't big enough for both of them. Features Gladys Snyder and Mantan Moreland.

VHS: S21430. $24.95.

Leo Popkin, USA, 1940, 60 mins.

Girl from Chicago

Alonzo Smith, a Black secret service agent, falls in love with Norma, a Mississippi school teacher. He is then obliged to assist Norma's friend Mary in New York City. Mary has fallen in with a bad crowd causing the noble Alonzo to be accused of murder. Micheaux frequently showed African-Americans in positions of authority and respectability, in contrast to Hollywood stereotypes. Despite criticisms that these characters were unrealistic, they were a source of pride to the Black community.

VHS: S07054. $24.95.

Oscar Micheaux, USA, 1932, 69 mins.

Emperor Jones
(Janus Films)

Girl in Room 20

A small-town girl moves to New York City to "make it" as a singer. Her dreams are more difficult to realize than she had ever imagined. Features Geraldine Brock, Judy Jones and Spencer Williams, Jr., who also directs the film.

VHS: S20544. $19.95

Spencer Williams, Jr., USA, 194?, 60 mins.

Go Down Death

Inspired by a James Weldon Johnson poem, this morality tale was directed by the veteran producer of Black cast films of the 30s and 40s, Spencer Williams, Jr. Similar to Williams's earlier effort, *The Blood of Jesus*, it is an attempt to deal with Black religious heritage. Myrna Hemmings is featured as the angelic and tragic preacher, Sister Caroline. Jim, a bar owner, is tortured by his conscience for his part in Caroline's death when she is wrongly accused of immorality.

VHS: S07043. $24.95.

Spencer Williams, Jr., USA, 1944, 50 mins.

God's Step Children

Oscar Micheaux's film deals with a light-skinned African-American orphan who refuses to acknowledge her race. She winds up in a convent after being disruptive in her all-Black school. Eventually she marries a dark-skinned man. A serious and moving film featuring Alice B. Russell, Carmen Newsome, Jacqueline Lewis and Ethel Moses.

VHS: S21471. $24.95.

Oscar Micheaux, USA, 1937, 65 mins.

Good-Bye, My Lady

Sidney Poitier has a supporting role in this timeless tearjerker about a boy and the puppy which becomes his best friend. The film also deals with the problems of Louisiana sharecroppers. Louise Beavers appears in a supporting role. With Brandon de Wilde, Walter Brennan and Phil Harris.

VHS: S11612. $59.98.

William Wellman, USA, 1956, 95 mins.

The Green Pastures

Upon its initial release, this film was boycotted by Southern theater owners because it used an all-Black cast to recreate Biblical tales in a Black idiom. Today the film is reviled as racist stereotyping at its worst. The film is based upon Marc Connelly's Pulitzer prize-winning play, and tells various Biblical stories in what is represented as traditional Black style. With Rex Ingram, Oscar Polk, Eddie Anderson and Frank Wilson.

VHS: S02528. $19.98.

William Keighley/Marc Connelly, USA, 1936, 90 mins.

Guess Who's Coming to Dinner

Two older couples, one Black and one white, must come to terms with their children's interracial relationship and impending marriage. Neither couple is pleased and both bring up varying reasons for their disapproval. A controversial film in 1967 for which Katharine Hepburn won an Academy Award for Best Actress. The film also won for Best Screenplay. Stanley Kramer directed Hepburn and Spencer Tracy's last film together. Katharine Houghton and Sidney Poitier play the young couple. With Beah Richards, Cecil Kellaway and Roy E. Glenn, Sr.

VHS: S13316. $14.98.

Stanley Kramer, USA, 1967, 108 mins.

Hallelujah!

A naive young farmer becomes a preacher but that doesn't protect him from temptation in King Vidor's vibrant, colorful musical. The film is a heartfelt attempt, notably because of the excellent cast and the Deep South locations which capture a piece of African-American culture. The basic plot is similar to many films that would follow. In the end, both the temptress and tempted are saved while traditional spirituals are performed along with Irving Berlin's "Waiting at the End of the Road" and "Swannee Shuffle". With Daniel L. Haynes, Nina Mae McKinney and William Fountaine.

VHS: S18504. $19.98.

King Vidor, USA, 1929, 90 mins.

Harlem on the Prairie

Herbert Jeffries and Mantan Moreland head the cast of this first all-Black western. The plot centers on gold, love and making sure the bad guys get theirs. There are also musical numbers. Features F.E. Miller and Connie Harris.

VHS: S21470. $24.95.

Sam Newfield, USA, 1938, 54 mins.

Harlem Rides the Range

A radium mine belongs to the hero's (Herb Jeffries) girlfriend and he struggles to outwit the villainous swindler (Lucius Brooks). An all-Black cast (and crew) made this western musical. Also featuring Clarence Brooks, Artie Young and Spencer Williams, Jr.

VHS: S07053. $24.95.

Richard C. Kahn, USA, 1939, 58 mins.

Home of the Brave

One of the first U.S. films to directly deal with racism, *Home of the Brave* features James Edwards as "Moss", a Black soldier who faces the bigotry of his white fellow soldiers during World War II. The story is told through a series of flashbacks as Moss recounts the ordeal of his life to a doctor after he has finally broken down. An important early film which shows the effects of racism but is optimistic about the possibility of overcoming prejudice. With Lloyd Bridges, Steve Brodie, Frank Lovejoy and Jeff Corey.

VHS: S04252. $19.98.
Laser: CLV. LD71990. $29.98.

Mark Robson, USA, 1949, 86 mins.

Imitation of Life

In this remake of the 1934 film starring Fredi Washington, Susan Kohner, a white actress, plays the light-skinned Black woman who turns her back on her mother to pass for white. Douglas Sirk's last film features Juanita Moore as the rejected mother who becomes a maid for an actress played by Lana Turner.

VHS: S00611. $14.95.

Douglas Sirk, USA, 1959, 124 mins.

In the Heat of the Night

Sidney Poitier portrays Virgil Tibbs, a Philadelphia police detective who is passing through a Southern town. While Tibbs is there, a wealthy business-man is murdered and Tibbs becomes involved in solving the case. Racial tension rises. Rod Steiger is the redneck sheriff who at first wants no help from Tibbs but eventually relents. Winner of five Oscars including Best Picture and Best Actor (Steiger). Music score by Quincy Jones.

VHS: S03621. $19.95.

Norman Jewison, USA, 1967, 110 mins.

Intruder in the Dust

Juano Hernandez is a Black man accused of shooting a white man in the back in this adaptation of William Faulkner's novel. Hernandez delivers a portrait of a proud and unyielding man who asks for no gifts and shows little fear even in the face of a lynch mob. To prove his innocence, he enlists the aid of a young white boy (he earlier rescued from a fall into a creek). The film (and book) is as much about the young man's dealing with his gratitude and respect for an African-American as it is about the gathering of whites for a lynching. Shot largely in Faulkner's hometown of Oxford, Mississippi. With Claude Jarman, Jr. and David Brian.

VHS: S18505. $19.98.

Clarence Brown, USA, 1949, 87 mins.

The Jackie Robinson Story

Robinson appears as himself in this story of his climb from the Negro leagues to the Majors. Robinson, the first African-American to play in Major League baseball is supported by a cast including Ruby Dee (as Robinson's wife) and Louise Beavers. The baseball player performs surprisingly well.

VHS: S06334. $19.95.

Alfred Green, USA, 1950, 76 mins.

Jericho

Paul Robeson flees from pre-World War II France after being wrongfully con-victed. Arriving in North Africa, he becomes a desert sheik after rescuing a stranded caravan. He then becomes involved in a romance with a desert princess before his previous accuser arrives to return him to France. It is interesting to note that white actor Wallace Ford is Robeson's sidekick in the film.

VHS: S02162. $24.95.

Thorton Freeland, Great Britain, 1937, 75 mins.

The Joe Louis Story

This partially fictionalized retelling of Joe Louis' life features actual footage from some of his greatest fights. Included are bouts with Max Baer, Primo Carnera and others. Features Coley Wallace, Paul Stewart and Hilda Simms.

VHS: S06336. $19.95.

Robert Gordon, USA, 1953, 88 mins.

Judge Priest

Stepin Fetchit is featured alongside Will Rogers in John Ford's classic. Rogers is funny and touching as the aging judge, while Stepin Fetchit takes the more politically incorrect part. Though many might cringe, his performance has to be looked at in the context of 1934. Neither he nor many others saw anything wrong with his performances, just as today many see nothing wrong with African-Americans cast only as killers or tough cops.

VHS: S03012. $14.95.

John Ford, USA, 1934, 84 mins.

Juke Joint

Bad News Johnson and July Jones arrive in Hollywood with 25 cents between them. But they manage to convince Mama Lou Holiday that they are actors, so she takes them on as boarders. The film is partially a musical featuring an all-Black cast. With Spencer Williams, Jr., July Jones, Inez Newman, Melody Duncan, Katherine Moore.

VHS: S07050. $29.95.

Spencer Williams, Jr., USA, 1947, 70 mins.

Junction 88

An early all-Black musical featuring Bob Howard and Pigmeat Markham.

VHS: S21429. $24.95.

USA, 1940, 60 mins.

Keep Punching

A fighter is destroyed when he is seduced by the high life and a fast woman. The fast woman is Mae Johnson, who later starred in *The Defilers*, and the boxer is played by Henry Armstrong. Canada Lee, the fatigued minister in *Cry, the Beloved Country* also appears. An all-Black cast film.

VHS: S06858. $34.95.

John Clein, USA, 1939, 80 mins.

Killer Diller

This all-Black musical features a magician whose role links together the musical numbers in the film. The Nat "King" Cole Trio put in an impressive performance and are joined by Jackie "Moms" Mabley, Dusty Fletcher, Andy Kirk and Orchestra, and others.

VHS: S07056. $34.95.

Josh Binney, USA, 1948, 80 mins.

King Solomon's Mines

Paul Robeson appears in a supporting role in this adaptation of H. Rider Haggard's novel. Cedric Hardwicke plays an adventurer searching for the legendary diamond mines and Robeson is along for the ride as African guide Umbopa, a Mashona chief who disguises his identity. A first-rate adventure film with plenty of the fantastic and full of "vicious natives" and other villains.

VHS: S00682. $39.95.

Robert Stevenson, Great Britain, 1937, 80 mins.

Lilies of the Field

Sidney Poitier is a vagabond handyman who reluctantly winds up helping immigrant nuns build a chapel. He also helps the sisters learn English. Lilia Skala is the Mother Superior with whom Poitier develops a close friendship. Poitier won an Oscar for Best Actor. Features Lisa Mann, Isa Crino, and Stanley Adams.

VHS: S13390. $19.98.
Laser: LD72124. $34.98.

Ralph Nelson, USA, 1963, 93 mins.

Look Out Sister

This film is a musical satire of Westerns featuring Louis Jordan and an all-Black cast. Also features Monte Hawley (*Tall, Tan and Terrific*) and Suzette Harbin.

VHS: S21428. $24.95.

Bud Pollard, USA, 1948, 64 mins.

Lucky Ghost

Mantan Moreland is the hero of this stereotype-riddled follow-up to *Mr. Washington Goes to Town*. Moreland was, however, one of the most continually employed Black actors of the 40s. As always his performance is spirited. Other Moreland films include *Juke Joint* and *Harlem on the Prairie*.

VHS: S15481. $29.95.

Jed Buell, USA, 1941.

Lying Lips

Elsee, a nightclub singer, is sent to prison for the murder of her aunt. Her boyfriend, Benjamin, attempts to prove her innocence. Assisting Benjamin is Detective Wanzer, played by Robert Earl Jones. Appearing in a bit part is Juano Hernandez (later to star in *Intruder in the Dust*). A prime example of Micheaux's use of Hollywood genres and characterizations in so-called "race films". Edna Mae Harris stars.

VHS: S00786. $24.95.

Oscar Micheaux, USA, 1939, 60 mins.

A Man Called Adam

Sammy Davis, Jr. is a jazz musician trying to come to terms with the death of his wife and child. This is made all the more difficult by the fact that he was responsible for the accident that killed them. Davis must also face racism as well as his own self-censure. With Ossie Davis, Cicely Tyson, Louis Armstrong, Peter Lawford, and Mel Torme.

VHS: S17883. $14.95.

Leo Penn, USA, 1966, 102 mins.

Marching On

Spencer Williams, Jr. directs this docu-drama about the all-Black 25th Infantry. He shows the harsh reality of segregation but also makes it clear that the African-American soldier during World War II was as patriotic and dedicated as his white counterparts. Spencer Williams, Jr. directs, USA.

VHS: S21410. $24.95.

Mark Of The Hawk

Sidney Poitier stars as a man put on trial for murder in colonial Africa. In the beginning he sides with the liberation movement but in the end makes a speech that is positive about colonialism as a whole. The cast includes Eartha Kitt who performs "This Man is Mine". Also featured is Juano Hernandez (*Intruder in the Dust*).

VHS: S21412. $24.95.

Michael Audley, Great Britain, 1958, 83 mins.

Miracle in Harlem

A gang tries to take a piece of the action at a Harlem candy shop. The gang leader winds up dead and it appears the shop owner's daughter had a hand in the killing. A landmark all-Black gangster film featuring one of the day's biggest African-American stars, Stepin Fetchit.

VHS: S21417. $19.95.

Jack Kemp, USA, 1948, 69 mins.

Mistaken Identity

This mystery musical with an all-Black cast is set against the background of a big city nightclub. It features the famed production sequence "I'm A Bangi from Ubangi". Features Nelly Hill (*Murder with Music*) and George Oliver. USA, 1941, 60 mins.

VHS: S16182. $29.95.

Moon Over Harlem

A musical gangster film, *Moon Over Harlem*, tells the story of a widow who unwittingly falls for a charismatic gangster involved in the numbers racket. The music is the high point of the film and it features a 60 piece orchestra and clarinetist Sidney Bechet.

VHS: S02163. $24.95.

Edgar G. Ulmer, USA, 1939, 67 mins.

Murder In Harlem

Clarence Brooks (*Harlem Rides the Range, Bronze Buckaroo*) stars in this story of a night watchman accused of murder. When he finds the body of a white woman in the chemical factory he guards, he must prove his innocence in court. Also stars Laura Bowman, Dorothy Van Engle, Andrew Bishop and Alec Lovejoy. A provocative murder mystery from the director of *Girl From Chicago* and *Lying Lips*.

VHS: S21388. $24.95.

Oscar Micheaux, USA, 1935, 102 mins.

Murder on Lennox Ave

An all-Black cast is featured in this gangster film. Mamie Smith appears in one of the musical numbers and is supported by a cast that includes Alec Lovejoy and Edna Mae Harris.

VHS: S21413. $24.95.

Arthur Dreifus, USA, 1941, 65 mins.

Native Son

Richard Wright wrote the screenplay and stars in this adaptation of his novel as a young Black man hired to chauffer a rich white girl. When he accidentally kills her, he flees. Wright was some three decades too old for the part but the film is an early attempt to put African-American literature on the screen.

VHS: S03682. $24.95.

Pierre Chenal, Argentina, 1951, 91 mins.

Nothing But a Man

An impressive collaboration between director Michael Roemer (*The Plot Against Harry*) and cinematographer/writer Robert Young (*The Ballad of Gregorio Cortez*) about racial attitudes in the South during the 1960s. Ivan Dixon plays a dignified railroad worker whose desire to lead a normal life with a beautiful schoolteacher (jazz virtuoso Abbey Lincoln) is unhinged by racial politics and discrimination. The Motown soundtrack features Stevie Wonder, Mary Wells and Martha and the Vandellas. With Julius Harris, Gloria Foster, Martin Priest, Leonard Parker, Yaphet Kotto and Stanley Greene.

VHS: S20283. $89.95.

Michael Roemer, USA, 1964, 92 mins.

Panama Hattie

Cole Porter's Broadway musical about a nightclub owner in Panama is notable for Lena Horne singing "Just One of Those Things." With Ann Sothern and Red Skelton.

VHS: S15428. $19.98.

Norman Z. McLeod, USA, 1942, 79 mins.

Paradise in Harlem

The star of Micheaux's *Lying Lips*, Edna Mae Harris, is featured with Frank Wilson in this gangster/musical. Like many of the so-called "race" films, this one is short on plot but long on talent. A prime example of a film in which actors elevate their material.

VHS: S08458. $29.95.

Joseph Seiden, USA, 1939-40, 83 mins.

Paris Blues

Two expatriate jazz musicians (Paul Newman and Sidney Poitier) are caught up in the Parisian nightlife on the Left Bank. Joanne Woodward and Diahann Carroll play their respective romantic interests. The score is by Duke Ellington. Special appearance by Louis Armstrong. With Serge Reggiani.

VHS: S19492. $19.98.

Martin Ritt, USA, 1961, 98 mins.

Patch of Blue

A young blind girl, on her first day out of the house in 13 years, meets a kind stranger. The friendship blossoms and she falls in love—never knowing or caring that the man is Black while she is white. The film is a call for "color blindness". Shelley Winters won a best supporting Oscar for her role as the meanspirited prostitute mother. With Ivan Dixon and Wallace Ford. Based on the story "Be Ready with Bells and Drums" by Elizabeth Kata.

VHS: S12530. $19.98.

Guy Green, USA, 1965, 105 mins.

The Pawnbroker

A Jewish pawnbroker (Rod Steiger) in Harlem is unable to shake memories of the Holocaust. The African-American characters surrounding him with their various plights serve to emphasize his own disillusionment with life.

Thelma Oliver and Juano Hernandez turn in tragic and beautiful performances. Also features Brock Peters, Jaime Sanchez, Geraldine Fitgerald and Raymond St. Jacques in a small role.

VHS: S01004. $19.98

Sidney Lumet, USA, 1965, 116 mins.

Pinky

An African-American nurse (played by white actress Jeanne Crain) passes for white in the north but visits the South where she is confronted with this denial of her heritage. She sees the error of her ways and remains in the South to work for her people. The film is one of a number of optimistic efforts at dealing with America's racism in the 40s and 50s. The excellent supporting cast includes Ethel Waters, Nina Mae McKinney and Frederick O'Neal.

VHS: S21300. $19.98.

Elia Kazan, USA, 1949, 102 mins.

Quiet One

A classic documentary-drama, winner of awards at Venice and Edinburgh, and one of the most penetrating studies of juvenile delinquency ever filmed. The film is the story of a Black youth who grows up in Harlem without the love of his parents and, rejected, falls into delinquency. Sidney Meyers, the director, was apparently influenced by Italian neo-realism and the commentary, written by James Agee, is spoken by Gary Merrill. "A most moving, important and memorable film" (Paul Rotha).

VHS: S06879. $39.95.

Sidney Meyers/Janet Loeb, USA, 1948, 67 mins.

The Scar of Shame
(Museum of
Contemporary Art)

Sanders of the River

A British officer in colonial Africa, known affectionately as "Sandi" by the natives, quells a revolt and rescues the wife of the chief. Paul Robeson is Bosambo, a chief loyal to Sanders but disturbed by marauding slave traders. Nina Mae McKinney (*Hallelujah!*) stars opposite Robeson. The performances and personalities involved in the picture save it from being mere pro-colonial propaganda.

VHS: S02765. $29.95.

Zoltan Korda, Great Britain, 1935, 85 mins.

The Scar of Shame

A concert pianist from a middle class family falls for a young woman from the wrong side of the tracks. He hides his wife from his judgmental mother and when his wife discovers this, she vows to leave him. An argument between the wife's father, his racketeering friend and the husband ends with the wife being shot and disfigured. The husband goes to prison, escapes and finds a more acceptable mate. The disfigured wife then kills herself. The film can be seen as an early examination of social divisions between African-Americans and the typecasting of those with a darker complexion. Produced by the Colored Players Film Corporation of Philadelphia.

VHS: S15388. $24.95.

Frank Peregini, USA, 1927, 90 mins.

The Scar of Shame
(Smithsonian/Library of Congress)

Included in this restored video version of *Scar of Shame* is the short experimental musical *Sissle and Blake* which features the music of Nobel Sissle and Eubie Blake. From the Smithsonian Institution and the Library of Congress.

VHS: S21266. $34.95.

Frank Peregini, USA, 1927, 105 mins.

Sepia Cinderella

A songwriter leaves the woman he loves to pursue his career and the high life. Eventually he discovers there is more to life than a place in society and returns to his singer/girlfriend. An all-Black film featuring Sheila Guyse and Rubel Blakely. Freddie Bartholemew appears as himself.

VHS: S06913. $29.95.

Arthur Leonard, USA, 1947, 67 mins.

Sergeant Rutledge

Former L.A. Ram Woody Strode stars as a Black cavalryman wrongly accused of raping a white woman. He is dignified while on trial and is eventually able to demonstrate both his courage and his innocence. Strode would later appear in *Spartacus* and *The Professionals*. The film is probably director John Ford's best film featuring African-Americans.

VHS: S18609. $19.98.

John Ford, USA, 1960, 118 mins.

Show Boat

Hattie McDaniel is the tough Queenie and Paul Robeson is Joe in this remake of the Kern/Hammerstein musical. Their characters rise above stereotyping and Robeson's musical performance is the best in the picture. The plot revolves around singer "Julie" who is revealed to have "Negro blood". Her husband is understanding, but she is nonetheless destroyed. The subject is treated with sympathy. With Irene Dunne, Allan Jones, Helen Morgan, and Charles Winninger.

Laser: CAV, 3 discs, Criterion. LD70459. $124.95.
Laser: CLV, 1 disc, Criterion. LD70460. $49.95.

James Whale, USA, 1936, 110 mins.

The Slender Thread

Sydney Pollack's (*Out of Africa*) first film features Sidney Poitier as a volunteer at a crisis center. One of his callers is Anne Bancroft who has taken an overdose of sleeping pills. Poitier must somehow keep her on the phone until she can be located. Music by Quincy Jones. Also stars Steven Hill and Telly Savalas.

VHS: S16457. $14.95.

Sydney Pollack, USA, 1965, 98 mins.

Son of Ingagi

Spencer Williams, Jr. directs and stars in this all-Black cast horror film. The plot revolves around a kidnapping and hidden gold but does have a happy ending.

VHS: S06912. $34.95.

Spencer Williams, Jr., USA, 1940, 70 mins.

Song of Freedom

As with many of Paul Robeson's films, *Song of Freedom* was made abroad. Robeson plays an English laborer who returns to Africa to discover his heritage. This film is, in many ways, a precursor to later films in which African-Americans go in search of their past. Robeson also sings many of his best-known songs.

VHS: S01231. $24.95.

J. Elder Wills, Great Britain, 1936, 70 mins.

Spirit of Youth

Joe Louis plays Joe Thomas, a poor Black fighter who climbs to the top of the boxing world. Louis's performance is augmented by a fine supporting cast including Mantan Moreland, Clarence Muse and Edna Mae Harris.

VHS: S07059. $34.95.

Harry Fraser, USA, 1937, 70 mins.

Stormy Weather

Following the success of *Cabin in the Sky*, Black entertainers were enlisted for another all-Black musical that features Lena Horne, Cab Calloway, Fats Waller and Bill Robinson. Waller performs "Ain't Misbehavin'" and Lena Horne chimes in with the legendary title track. Features *Casablanca*'s Dooley Wilson, Bill Robinson and Cab Calloway.

VHS: S02828. $19.98.

Andrew Stone, USA, 1943, 78 mins.

Sunday Sinners

A musical feature with lyrics and music by Donald Heywood, a writer and composer who was prominently associated with independent Black films from 1932 onwards. An all-Black cast is featured. With Mamie Smith, Alec Lovejoy, Edna Mae Harris.

VHS: S07055. $34.95.

Arthur Dreifuss, USA, 1941, 65 mins.

Swing

Oscar Micheaux was in the director's chair for this tribute to African-American music. Featured are songs performed from Alabama to Harlem, with the Tyler Twins performing the dance numbers, and also featuring Cora Green, Hazel Diaz, Carmen Newsome and Alec Lovejoy.

VHS: S07057. $34.95.

Oscar Micheaux, USA, 1938, 80 mins.

Tall, Tan and Terrific

Mantan Moreland (*Lucky Ghost*) portrays a detective out to clear the name of a Harlem club owner, Handsome Harry, (Monte Hawley) who is accused of murder. Francine Everett stars as Miss Tall, a waitress at the club and the object of Harry's affections.

VHS: S21416. $24.95.

Bud Pollard, USA, 1946, 60 mins.

Tamango

John Berry (*Claudine*), who was blacklisted during the Communist witch hunts of the fifties, directs this frenetic melodrama with a curious affinity for racial and class exploitation. Curt Jurgens plays a Dutch slave trader in love with a beautiful Black woman (Dorothy Dandridge) who is trying to suppress a slave revolt led by "Tamango" (Alex Cressan). Dandridge is at her melancholy best and Jurgens is convincing as the compromised villain. At the time of its theatrical release, no one would distribute the film in the United States due to its content (and possibly its director). With Jean Servais, Roger Hanin and Guy Mairesse.

VHS: S18254. $29.95.

John Berry, USA, 1959, 98 mins.

To Kill a Mockingbird

Based on Harper Lee's novel, this film is the story of a small town Southern lawyer, Atticus Finch (Gregory Peck) who defends a Black man (Brock Peters) accused of raping a white woman. Finch tries to explain the situation to his children and their friends, and most of the film is told from the point of view of Finch's young daughter. Peck won a Golden Globe and an Academy Award for his portrayal of the soft-spoken attorney, and Horton Foote's screenplay also won an Oscar.

VHS: S02640. $19.95.
Laser: LD70089. $39.98.

Robert Mulligan, USA, 1962, 129 mins.

To Sir, With Love

Sidney Poitier plays Mark Thackery, a novice teacher who is assigned to a slum school in London's East End where he faces disinterested students. The tables are turned from Poitier's earlier role in *Blackboard Jungle* where he was cast as the salvageable delinquent. By teaching his class what is important in life he manages to have an impact. With Judy Geeson, Christian Roberts, and Lulu (who sings the title song).

VHS: S01355. $19.95.

James Clavell, Great Britain, 1967, 105 mins.

Two-Gun Man From Harlem

A bogus preacher from Harlem travels to the old West. As you might suspect from the title, he brings along a couple of guns just in case. Features Herbert Jeffries, Marguerite Whitten and Mantan Moreland.

VHS: S21414. $24.95.

Richard C. Kahn, USA, 1938, 60 mins.

Uncle Tom's Cabin (1903 & 1914)

Uncle Tom's Cabin, originally an antebellum attack on the institution of slavery, was often perverted to show an idealized "happy" slave. Nonetheless both the 1903 and the 1914 versions of this story are an important part of African-American cinema. The 1914 version features Sam Lucas, along with other Black stage actors, in one of the first "leading" roles for an African-American. Both of these films demonstrate the prevalent attitudes of early American cinema toward those of African descent. The 1903 version was restored from Library of Congress paper prints. USA, directed by William R. Daly, 54 mins.

VHS: S15482. $29.95.

Veiled Aristocrats

Lorenzo Tucker (the "Black Valentino") stars in this story of a lawyer who returns home to find that his light-skinned sister is about to marry a dark-skinned man. His mother has picked a more suitable candidate. Director Oscar Micheaux once again tackles the issue of dark-skinned versus light-skinned African-Americans. Features Laura Bowman.

VHS: S21468. $24.95.

Oscar Micheaux, USA, 1932, 50 mins.

Way Down South

Bobby Breen portrays a young white man who inherits his father's plantation. He battles with a vicious overseer who is appointed caretaker of the land. Clarence Muse stars as Uncle Caton in this melodrama which also features musical numbers. The script was co-written by Clarence Muse and Langston Hughes.

VHS: S21431. $24.95.

Bernard Vorhaus, USA, 1939, 62 mins.

Within Our Gates

Oscar Micheaux's second film is often seen as a reaction to D. W. Griffith's *Birth of a Nation*. In fact the film was a graphic depiction of the virulent racism of the day rather than simply a response to one film. A sharecropper is blamed for a murder and faces an angry mob. Micheaux included a lynching scene that startled many. Part of the Smithsonian Video/Library of Congress collection.

VHS: S21262 $34.95

Oscar Micheaux, USA, 1920.

Recent African-American Feature Films

48 Hours

A violent prison break and subsequent murders lead hardened cop Jack Cates (Nick Nolte) to spring convicted felon Reggie Hammond (Eddie Murphy) from prison on a bogus two-day furlough. Cates needs help solving the crimes while Hammond is mainly interested in his share of the haul from the robbery of a drug dealer. It doesn't sound like a comedy but, of course, it is. An important African-American film for the introduction of Eddie Murphy, clearly one of the biggest stars of the 80s. Murphy's character also shows an African-American male who reacts with intelligence and wit to the constant racist barrage aimed at him by Cates—and others.

VHS: S02354. $19.95.

Walter Hill, USA, 1982, 97 mins.

Adios Amigos

Fred Williamson directs and Richard Pryor stars in this mid-seventies family Western. Pryor is a con man travelling the West and is joined by a cast that includes James Brown, Thalmus Rasulala and Fred Williamson.

VHS: S21418. $19.95.

Fred Williamson, USA, 1975, 87 mins.

Almos' a Man

LeVar Burton portrays a young man virtually enslaved as a sharecropper. Not able to make enough to pay his debts, he is tied to the land he works. Based on a short story by Richard Wright, *Almos' a Man* also features Madge Sinclair and Robert Doqui.

VHS: S01956. $24.95.

Stan Lathan, USA, 1977, 52 mins.

Another 48 Hours

After seven years, Eddie Murphy is released from jail in order to help San Francisco cop Nick Nolte solve a case and to save himself from a manslaughter charge. Lots of action in this sequel that also stars Brion James and Kevin Tighe.

VHS: S21476. $19.95.

Walter Hill, USA, 1990, 96 mins.

Another You

Richard Pryor and Gene Wilder are paired in this comedy in which Pryor, on parole, has to do community service by caring for Wilder, who has just been released from a sanitarium. The two immediately get mixed up in a scam.

VHS: S21477. $19.95.

Maurice Phillips, USA, 1991, 98 mins.

Ashes and Embers

Directed by Ethiopian-born filmmaker Haile Gerima, this award-winning film tells the story of a bitter Vietnam veteran trying to come to terms with the war and with the racial tensions in America. This ex-GI leans on the strengths of friends and family in order to find his way. Gerima currently teaches at Howard University. His other films include *Bush Mama*, *Harvest 3000 Years* and *Child of Resistance*.

VHS: S13411. $59.95.

Haile Gerima, USA, 1983, 120 mins.

Assault at West Point

A Black West Point cadet claims to have been assaulted in a racial incident. When his story does not check out, it is he who is charged. The differences between civilian ideas about justice and the military's "code of honor" become the focus of the ensuing trial. Stars Samuel L. Jackson, Sam Waterston, John Glover and Seth Gilliam as the cadet, Johnson Whittaker. Based upon a true story.

VHS: S21141. $92.98.

Harry Moses, USA, 1994, 98 mins.

Autobiography of Miss Jane Pittman

Cicely Tyson stars in this fictional account of a 110-year old former slave and her view of the treatment of African-Americans from slavery days until the begining of the `Civil Rights movement. Based upon the book by Ernest J. Gaines, this made-for-TV drama earned nine Emmys including Best Actress for Tyson. Features Odetta, Joseph Tremice and Richard Dysart.

VHS: S00076. $19.95.

John Korty, USA, 1974, 110 mins.

Bagdad Cafe ·

A German tourist leaves her husband on the road and winds up at an isolated truck stop run by a harassed Black owner. The two are at odds with each other but eventually wind up friends. Director Percy Adlon uses ordinary objects like a coffee dispenser to show how people from completely different backgrounds can come to understand and even like one another. The cast includes Marianne Sagebrecht (*Sugarbaby*) and C.C. Pounder as the harassed manager. Jack Palance also appears as an eccentric artist.

VHS: S07965. $14.98.

Percy Adlon, USA, 1988, 91 mins.

Beat Street

Afrika Bambaata and the Soul Sonic Force, Grand Master Melle Mel and the Furious Five along with salsa king Ruben Blades provide the music in this break dance docudrama. Features Rae Dawn Chong, Leon Grant, Saundra Santiago and Kadeem Hardison.

VHS: S21458. $14.98.

Stan Latham, USA, 1984, 106 mins.

Betrayed

Radical racists plan terrorist attacks across the United States as an FBI agent (Debra Winger) goes undercover to thwart the plot. African-Americans are at the center of the film's action but remain peripheral as actual characters. An example of Hollywood films dealing with racial prejudice but having no main characters that are Black. Nonetheless the film is a provocative dramatic look at white racist groups in the U.S. heartland.

VHS: S09919. $19.98.

Constantin Costa-Gavras, USA, 1988, 107 mins.

Beverly Hills Cop

Eddie Murphy is funny and electrifying as the fast-talking Detroit cop who begins to unofficially investigate the death of a friend which leads him to Beverly Hills. With Judge Reinhold and John Ashton.

VHS: S01839. $19.95.

Martin Brest, USA, 1984, 105 mins.

Beverly Hills Cop 2

Eddie Murphy is back to help out his L.A. buddies and is fast on the track of an illegal arms dealer (Juergen Prochnow) and his hit lady (Brigitte Nielsen) in this sequel.

VHS: S21478. $19.95.

Tony Scott, USA, 1987, 102 mins.

The Big Dis

A Black soldier on leave is looking for what the soldier or sailor on leave is always looking for in the movies: sex. In this case the young Romeo has a rude awakening. He's dissed by every woman he moves in on. This first work by Gordon Erikson and John O'Brien is a comedy reminiscent of the early 70s films of Melvin Van Peebles.

VHS: S17104. $59.95.

Gordon Eriksen/John O'Brien, USA, 1989, 88 mins.

The Bingo Long Traveling All-Stars & Motor Kings

John Badham's film is adapted from Chicago writer William Brashler's novel about a militant group of barnstorming baseball players who broke off from the Negro Leagues to play the Southern circuit. Set in 1939, with a medley of period music, the film takes an observant, trenchant look at competition, social interaction and racial dynamics. With Billy Dee Williams, James Earl Jones, Richard Pryor, Rico Dawson and Stan Shaw.

VHS: S05370. $49.95.

John Badham, USA, 1976, 111 mins.

Bird

Forest Whitaker is Charlie "Bird" Parker in Clint Eastwood's homage to one of jazz's greatest musicians. The film is more than simple praise of a great man. Parker's often troubled life, as well as his music, are explored in depth. Diane Venora plays Chan Parker, Parker's wife, as a woman both loving and patient with an often stormy relationship. Whitaker won the Best Actor award at the Cannes Film Festival and the film was nominated for an Academy Award for Best Achievement in Sound.

VHS: S09321. $19.98.
Laser: LD70526. $29.98.

Clint Eastwood, USA, 1988, 160 mins.

Black Brigade

Billy Dee Williams and Richard Pryor star in this World War II film. They are part of an all-Black unit, dropped behind Nazi lines on a sabotage mission, and are not expected to return. Features Stephen Boyd. USA, 1969, 90 mins.

VHS: S21438. $14.95.

Blue Chips

The NBA's Shaquille O'Neal is featured in this film about ethics and college basketball. Nick Nolte stars as a winning college coach whose team doesn't match his expectations. He takes the low road and essentially buys the team. The film deals with the pressure on a coach to keep winning and on young men to "succeed" in any way they can. Features Anfernee Hardaway, Mary McDonald and Alfre Woodard.

VHS: S21381. $92.98.

William Friedkin, USA, 1994, 107 mins.

Blue Collar

Paul Schrader directed this powerful first feature which stars Richard Pryor, Harvey Keitel and Yaphet Kotto as Detroit production line auto workers who are being ripped off not only by the management, but by their own union. When they break into the union offices, they discover documents that link the union with organized crime.

VHS: S04661. $69.95.

Paul Schrader, USA, 1978, 114 mins.

Boomerang

Eddie Murphy's first romantic comedy shows him portraying a womanizing advertising executive. The first object of his affections (Robin Givens) is too much for him because of her aggressive approach, so he turns to a "nicer" woman (Halle Berry). The cast includes David Allen Grier, Martin Lawrence, Grace Jones, Eartha Kitt, Chris Rock, Tisha Campbell, John Witherspoon and Melvin Van Peebles.

VHS: S21448. $19.95.

Reginald Hudlin, USA, 1992, 118 mins.

Bopha!

Morgan Freeman's directorial debut casts Danny Glover as a South African police officer torn between his duty, his conscience, and his family. A look at a man whose job is, at least in part, to defend the system that enslaves him and his people.

VHS: S20614. $95.98.

Morgan Freeman, USA, 1993, 120 mins.

Boyz N The Hood

Two young men, one a promising athlete, the other a talented student, try to survive the troubles of South Central Los Angeles. Cuba Gooding, Jr. stars while Laurence Fishburne has a supporting role as his thoughtful business-man father. Ice Cube steals the film as a misanthropic, violent, yet likeable gang member. Twenty-three-year-old John Singleton was the first African-American director nominated for an Academy Award and the youngest person ever nominated in the Best Director category.

VHS: S15671. $19.95.
Laser: LD71181. $49.95.

John Singleton, USA, 1991, 107 mins.

Breakin'

A musical/break dance film with a limited plot but a lot of great dancing. The film was one of the earliest to capture the spine-crushing athleticism of break dancing. Features Lucinda Dickey, Adolpho "Shabba Doo" Quinones and Michael "Boogaloo Shrimp" Chambers.

VHS: S21408. $79.95.

Joel Silberg, USA, 1984, 87 mins.

Breakin' II: Electric Boogaloo

The cast of the first film returns to put on a show to save an urban community center. Virtually a return to films of the 30s in its earnestness and lack of plot. The dancing is again the focus.

VHS: S21407. $79.95.

Sam Firstenberg, USA, 1984, 94 mins.

Brewster's Millions

Richard Pryor has to spend 30 million dollars in order to inherit 300 million dollars. He indulges in every sort of extravagance along the way to his goal. Features the late John Candy and Lonette McKee (*Sparkle, Round Midnight*).

VHS: S21451. $19.95.

Walter Hill, USA, 1985, 101 mins.

The Brother From Another Planet

John Sayles (*Matewan, City of Hope*) directs this comedy about a runaway slave from outer space. He lands in New York City where he finds both sympathy and corruption. Joe Morton (*City of Hope, Terminator II*) stars as the alien and director Sayles appears as an extraterrestrial bounty hunter. Features Dee Dee Bridgewater, Ren Woods and Steve James.

VHS: Currently out of print. May be available for rental in some video stores.

John Sayles, USA, 1984, 104 mins.

Brother John

A mystical film about an angel who returns to the small Alabama town of his birth shortly before the death of his aunt. Sidney Poitier stars as John Kane, the angel, and is able to see the future and speak virtually every language. A Black strike is about to hit the city and his presence leads to the suspicion that he is involved. Paul Winfield and Will Geer turn in fine supporting performances. Music by Quincy Jones.

VHS: S06711. $14.95.

James Goldstone, USA, 1972, 94 mins.

Buck and the Preacher

Sidney Poitier's first feature as director. Poitier also plays a wagonmaster on the long trek out West as the wagon train is attacked by white nightriders and encounters a group of slaves freed at the end of the Civil War. With Harry Belafonte as a hustler preacher and Ruby Dee.

VHS: S21479. $19.95.

Sidney Poitier, USA, 1971, 103 mins.

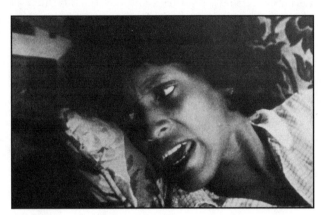

Bush Mama
(Mypheduh Films, Inc.)

Bush Mama

Alternating easily between past and present, dream and reality, Haile Gerima tells the moving story of a mother on welfare who is trying to raise her daughter on her own. Her man is in jail on a trumped-up charge and she is left with no means of support—either emotional or financial. Humor is mixed with violence and fantasy as she copes with her situation.

VHS: S15644. $59.95.

Haile Gerima, USA, 1976, 100 mins.

The Bushbaby

A woman plans to smuggle her pet lemur to the West, but instead loses the creature. She enlists the help of her father's former employee, Temba (Louis Gossett, Jr.) in the search for "Bushbaby". The authorities believe she has been kidnapped by Temba and pursue. Filmed in Tanzania (never mind that lemurs only inhabit the island of Madagascar). As usual, a fine performance from Louis Gossett, Jr.

VHS: S19034. $19.98.

John Trent, Great Britain, 1970, 100 mins.

Bustin' Loose

Richard Pryor stars as a con artist enlisted to drive a group of orphans across the country. Cicely Tyson co-stars in this comedy. The film captures Pryor, on whose idea the film is based, at the height of his comic power.

VHS: S21449. $14.98.

Oz Scott, USA, 1981, 94 mins.

California Suite

Herbert Ross directs this Neil Simon comedy which consists of four sketches about guests in a Hollywood hotel. Richard Pryor and Bill Cosby are paired as two friends constantly at odds with each other in one of the episodes. Based on the Broadway hit play.

VHS: Currently out of print. May be available for rental in some video stores.

Herbert Ross, USA, 1978, 103 mins.

Candyman

Clive Barker's short story "The Forbidden" moves from Liverpool to Chicago, with Virginia Madsen as a doctoral candidate who inadvertently unleashes the spirit of "Candyman", a mythological 19th century Black serial killer with a hook for his left hand who was brutally murdered by white racists. Cinematography by Anthony B. Richmond. Music by Philip Glass. With Tony Todd (as Candyman), Xander Berkeley and Kasi Lemmons.

VHS: S18323. $94.95.

Bernard Rose, USA, 1992, 108 mins.

Car Wash

African-American director Michael Schultz (*Cooley High*) put together a fine group of comics for this look at the "fascinating" world of car washers. The plot centers on a day at work at a car wash—and on all of the strange characters who file through in their dirty autos. Features Richard Pryor, Franklyn Ajaye, The Pointer Sisters, Antono Fargas, Bill Duke, Tracy Reed, Ivan Dixon and Melanie Mayron.

VHS: S07800. $59.95.

Michael Schultz, USA, 1976, 97 mins.

Carbon Copy

George Segal plays a secretly Jewish successful corporate executive whose illegitimate Black son (Denzel Washington) suddenly shows up and reveals Segal for what he is. Directed by Michael Schultz (*Car Wash*).

VHS: S21480. $14.95.

Michael Schultz, USA, 1981, 91 mins.

Chameleon Street

This film is the story of a man driven to impersonate others both for profit and attention. Beginning with a comically failed extortion bid and moving to impersonations of journalists, physicians, and others, Doug Street reacts to the pressures and financial strain of his life. Too moral to deal drugs, he turns to various half-baked schemes to make money and improve his self esteem. Based on a true story, *Chameleon Street*, asks the question: "Have 400 years of conditioning turned African-Americans into chameleons in a white dominated society?" With Paula McGee, Anthony Ennis and Daven Kiley.

VHS: S17244. $19.95.

Wendell B. Harris, Jr., USA, 1989, 95 mins.

City of Hope

Vincent Spano (*Alive*) and Joe Morton (*Brother from Another Planet, Terminator II*) head a massive cast in John Sayles's take on the conditions of urban life. Spano is the son of a labor boss who hands out patronage while Morton plays a politician caught between the radicalism of the district he represents and the reality of City Hall. Numerous subplots weave in and out of the film including a bogus child molestation charge aimed at a white professor by a Black child. All the plots are pulled together in the end.

VHS. S16087. $92.95.
Laser: LD71573. $39.95.

John Sayles, USA, 1991, 130 mins.

Clara's Heart

Whoopi Goldberg is Clara, the nurturing housekeeper for a family of middle class suburbanites. The family, and in particular the son (Neil Patrick Harris), are not a sympathetic bunch. Yet Clara takes an interest in the boy and eventually helps to make him a more caring person. Goldberg's performance as the patient Jamaican domestic is compelling despite her being forced into an almost stereotypical role. With Kathleen Quinlan, Michael Ontkean, Beverley Todd and Spalding Gray. A sensitive drama with lots of Jamaican music.

VHS: S09167. $14.95.

Robert Mulligan, USA, 1988, 108 mins.

Clarence and Angel

Clarence and his family arrive in New York City from South Carolina. The twelve-year-old's problems in adjusting to his new environment are compounded by his difficulties at school. It seems that the young man cannot read. Angel, a kung-fu enthusiast and fellow classmate, helps the troubled boy learn to read. Features Darren Brown, Marc Cardova, Cynthia McPherson and Leroy Smith.

VHS: S07131. $59.95.

Robert Gardner, USA, 1980, 75 mins.

The Color Purple

An excellent cast including Whoopi Goldberg, Danny Glover, Adolph Caesar and Oprah Winfrey are featured in this optimistic turn on Alice Walker's book. Goldberg is Celie, a young woman abused by her stepfather and then by her husband (Glover) in a loveless marriage. She finds strength with the arrival of Shug Avery, her husband's mistress, and eventually with the return of her children, taken from her at their birth. Perhaps more sugary than Walker intended, but the film and performances are first rate.

VHS: S03551. $19.98.
Laser: CAV. LD70545. $59.98.
Laser: CLV. LD70546. $29.98.

Steven Spielberg, USA, 1985, 154 mins.

City of Hope
(The Samuel
Goldwyn Company)

Colors

Gang members serve as the backdrop for police officers played by Robert Duvall and Sean Penn. Although the film lacks major roles for African-Americans, *Colors* depicts police-gang relations in Los Angeles. Dennis Hopper's direction and Robert Duvall's performance as the veteran officer bring life to the picture. With Maria Conchita Alonso & Trinidad Silva.

VHS: S07786. $19.98.

Dennis Hopper, USA, 1988, 120 mins.

Coming to America

Eddie Murphy plays His Royal Highness Akeem, Crown Prince of Zamunda who runs away from an arranged marriage and lands in Queens (New York) where he finds a job as a cleaner in a hamburger joint and encounters the sophisticated Shari Headley. Murphy displays a brilliant sense of comic timing. With James Earl Jones, Arsenio Hall, Madge Sinclair.

VHS: S08358. $14.95.

John Landis, USA, 1988, 117 mins.

Conrack

The islands off the Carolina coast, one of the first areas where slaves were freed, is the setting for this film—one hundred years after emancipation. *Conrack*, based on the true story of Pat Conroy, deals with a white teacher who is trying to educate Black youths living on these islands. Jon Voight teaches the children using common sense rather than a rigid curriculum. The film also introduces Madge Sinclair and features Paul Winfield. Based on Conroy's book *The Water is Wide*.

VHS: S01856. $59.98.

Martin Ritt, USA, 1974, 107 mins.

Cooley High

A coming of age film from the director of *Car Wash* and *Krush Groove*, *Cooley High* is the story of members from the graduating class of 1964. The anxieties, hopes, failures, embarrassments and joys of adolescence are the subject and seldom do they seem more real in cinema. A humorous film with a serious side and a part of African-American movie history. Glynn Turman, Lawrence Hilton-Jacobs and *Saturday Night Live* regular Garret Morris in an early film role are supported by a soundtrack of Motown's greatest.

VHS: S13765. $79.98.

Michael Schultz, USA, 1975, 107 mins.

Cotton Comes to Harlem

Ossie Davis directed this high-energy adaptation of a Chester Himes novel. A preacher leading a "Back to Africa" movement is suspected of being a swindler by two detectives, "Grave Digger Jones" (Godfrey Cambridge) and "Coffin Ed Johnson" (Raymond St. Jacques). The characters set old stereotypes on their ears with good humor. Includes Calvin Lockhart, Judy Pace, Cleavon Little and Redd Foxx.

VHS: S17976. $14.95.

Ossie Davis, USA, 1970, 97 mins.

The Court Martial of Jackie Robinson

Baseball idol Jackie Robinson's stint in the army was marked by an event not often mentioned when his name comes up; he was brought before the courts martial for insubordination. Robinson experienced a great deal of racism while in the army and eventually stood up by refusing to move to the back of a bus. Andre Braugher portrays Robinson and is supported by a cast which includes Ruby Dee, Daniel Stern and Bruce Dern.

VHS: S13556. $79.98.

Larry Peerce, USA, 1990, 93 mins.

Cry Freedom

The story of Donald Woods (Kevin Kline), who became friends with Black activist Stephen Biko (Denzel Washington). Biko was murdered while in the custody of the South African police. Woods brought Biko's story to the world after fleeing the country.

VHS: S06820. $14.98.
Laser: LD70021. $39.98.

Richard Attenborough, USA, 1987, 157 mins.

Daughters of the Dust

Isolated descendants of West African slaves (the Gullah) are thinking about leaving their home on the Georgia coastal islands. They gather for a last picnic as a very divergent group ranging from a former prostitute to a missionary. The time period is 1902 and the film seems like a "farewell" to a vanished way of life. It is also the story of resourceful, intelligent women. A beautiful film, both visually and content-wise from first-time feature director Julie Dash. With Cora Lee Day, Alva Rogers, Barbara O, Turla Hoosier and Kaycee Moore.

VHS: S16913. $79.95.

Julie Dash, USA, 1991, 113 mins.

*Daughters
of the Dust*
(Kino International)

Dawn of the Dead (Director's Cut)

The zombies have returned to feast on the flesh of the living in George Romero's second installment of his "Dead" films. Veteran horror actor Ken Foree (*From Beyond, Texas Chainsaw Massacre III*) plays another strong, smart African-American character—much more resourceful and intelligent than his white counterparts because he survives. Romero, as in *Night of the Living Dead*, makes a not-so-subtle point about race relations and consumerism. In the end, after pointedly rejecting suicide, only the Black man and a white woman remain alive.

VHS: S04563. $14.98.

George A. Romero, USA, 1978, 131 mins.

Dead Man Out

Danny Glover is a psychiatrist brought in to evaluate the sanity of a condemned prisoner. Should he find the man sane he will likely be put to death for his crimes. Ruben Blades is the vicious prisoner in this examination of the issues of sanity and capital punishment. Originally shot for HBO.

VHS: S10614. $89.99.
Laser: LD70005. $39.95.

Richard Pearce, USA, 1988, 87 mins.

Deadly Drifter

A violent urban revolutionary, now less than enthusiastic about his cause, turns his talents to even more negative ends. Danny Glover is the disaffected revolutionary who winds up trapped in his own trail of destruction. 83 mins.

VHS: S18817. $29.95

Deep Cover

Laurence Fishburne's first major role is as an undercover cop from the Midwest imported to infiltrate a West Coast drug ring. Jeff Goldblum plays a lawyer who becomes Fishburne's "partner" in drug dealing.

VHS: S21481. $19.95.

Bill Duke, USA, 1992, 106 mins.

Demolition Man

This sci-fi thriller and action adventure features Sylvester Stallone and Wesley Snipes. When a dangerous 20th-century man is re-animated in the not-too-distant future, the stage is set for a classic struggle between two men. They square off amidst a treasure trove of special effects and over-the-top futuristic scenery.

VHS: S20682. $95.98.
Laser: LD72378. $34.98.

Marco Brambilla, USA, 1993, 115 mins.

Disorderlies

The Fat Boys are the stars of this Three Stooges-like comedy about an incompetent hospital staff. As you might expect, they also perform a number of songs. The film is an enjoyable combination of rap music and sheer idiocy.

VHS: S21400. $19.98.

Michael Schultz, USA, 1987, 86 mins.

Distinguished Gentleman

Eddie Murphy portrays a con man who makes his way into the Congress. Once there, he develops a sense of responsibility. Murphy shows he can still get a laugh with just a look. Features Lane Smith, Sheryl Lee Ralph, Joe Don Baker and Charles Dutton.

VHS: S21447. $94.95.

Jonathan Lynn, USA, 1992, 122 mins.

Don't Look Back: The Story of Leroy "Satchel" Paige

Leroy "Satchel" Paige was one of the greatest pitchers in the Negro League and possibly the best there ever was. He fought for the day when the Major Leagues would be desegregated. Eventually he would see that day. Stars Louis Gossett, Jr., Beverly Todd, Ossie Davis and Cleavon Little.

VHS: S21387. $79.99.

Richard A. Colla, USA, 1981, 98 mins.

Do The Right Thing

Tensions and temperatures rise in Spike Lee's comedy drama about race relations in New York City. Danny Aiello is the owner of a Bedford-Stuyvesant pizza parlor which he runs with the help of his two sons. A few local residents boycott the pizza place because there are only photos of Italians on the walls. Small conflicts between characters escalate to the point where a young man is killed for playing a radio too loud. The film leaves the audience wondering exactly who "did the right thing". The action moves from humor to deadly seriousness with disarming speed. The cast includes Ossie Davis, Ruby Dee, Rosie Perez and John Turturro as Aiello's racist son.

VHS: S11445. $19.95.
Laser: LD70023. $39.98.

Spike Lee, USA, 1989, 120 mins.

Driving Miss Daisy

Morgan Freeman stars as the long-suffering chauffer of an elderly Jewish woman in Georgia. He accepts her small abuses as she accepts his good will and accommodation. Yet in the end she realizes that her put-upon servant is, and has been, her only friend. Freeman's role has often been labeled a stereotype but it is clearly more than that. When asked at the last moment, in a thoughtless way, to attend a speech by Martin Luther King, Jr. he refuses

and sits outside on principle. Jessica Tandy won an Academy Award for Best
Actress and the film won for Best Picture. Also featured are Esther Rolle and
Dan Aykroyd.

VHS: S12524. $19.98.
Laser: LD70562. $24.98.

Bruce Beresford, USA, 1989, 99 mins.

For Us, the Living:
The Story of
Medgar Evers
(Xenon Home Video)

A Dry White Season

Another film about South Africa in which most of the major characters are
white. Donald Sutherland is a school teacher whose gardener's son is arrested for no reason. It might seem that the character is a bit of a fool but the
government of South Africa labelled most detainees as Communists, terror-
ists or both. Sutherland's character knows the young man is neither and is
perplexed to the point of ruining his own life in an attempt to find justice.
Set in 1976, the film is grounded in the period of extreme bloodshed surrounding the Soweto riots. Zakes Mokae is the activist cab driver and Marlon
Brando appears briefly as a cynical and reluctant liberal lawyer.

VHS: S11785. $19.98.
Laser: LD70957. $39.98.

Euzhan Palcy, USA, 1989, 97 mins.

Fame

A multi-ethnic group of teenagers try to succeed at New York's High School
for the Performing Arts. A musical drama starring Irene Cara. The film won
Academy Awards for Best Song ("Fame") and Best Original Score.

VHS: S05952. $19.98.

Alan Parker, USA, 1980, 133 mins.

The Father Clements Story

Louis Gossett, Jr. is Father Clements in this true story of the activist Chicago priest. Clements works on Chicago's West Side where he becomes concerned over a youth's welfare and resolves to help. He tries to provide the young man with a reason to live in the midst of poverty and despair but his methods bring objections from higher-ups in the diocese. With Louis Gossett, Jr., Malcolm-Jamal Warner and Carroll O'Connor.

VHS: S17910. $19.98.

Ed Sherin, USA, 1987, 100 mins.

Firehouse

Richard Roundtree stars in this drama about a Black rookie fireman who takes over for a retiring veteran. It turns out that he is the only African-American at the station. Racial tensions flare.

VHS: S18820. $19.95.

Alex March, USA, 1972, 73 mins.

The Five Heartbeats

Robert Townsend's follow-up to *Hollywood Shuffle* is a more serious film which follows the career of an African-American musical group, The Five Hearbeats. The group's highs and lows as well as their music are chronicled. Features Townsend, Tressa Thomas, Michael Wright, Harry J. Lennix and Diahann Carroll.

VHS: S21433. $19.98.

Robert Townsend, USA, 1991, 120 mins.

For Us, the Living: The Story of Medgar Evers

In 1958, a Civil Rights leader emerged in Mississippi who changed the course of Black history. His amazing courage, his lifelong struggle for equal rights and his painfully tragic death are recounted here with an extraordinary cast including Howard Rollins, Jr., Irene Cara, Margaret Avery and Roscoe Lee Brown.

VHS: S06960. $19.95

Michael Schultz, USA, 1988, 84 mins.

Free, White, and 21

A Black hotel owner is accused of raping a white Civil Rights protester in this pseudo-documentary. Stars Frederick O'Neal as the hotel owner and features Annalena Lund, George Edgely, and John Hicks.

VHS: Currently out of print. May be available for rental in some stores.

Larry Buchanan, USA, 1962, 104 mins.

Freedom Man

Ossie Davis stars in this dramatization of the true story of Benjamin Banneker, who worked with the Underground Railroad and saved runaway slaves from bounty hunters. His writings advocated the abolition of slavery and helped educate Thomas Jefferson about the capabilities of Black Americans. A self-taught writer, mathematician, astronomer, clockmaker and surveyor, he helped design the city of Washington, D.C. A forgotten and important part of American history. Recommended by The National Education Association.

VHS: S09328. $29.95.

Bob Walsh/Leroy Morais, USA, 1989, 61 mins.

Freedom Road

This made-for-TV movie stars Muhammad Ali as an ex-slave who becomes a U.S. Senator during the Reconstruction Years after the Civil War. Narration by Ossie Davis and adapted from the Howard Fast novel, with Kris Kristofferson, Ron O'Neal, Barbara O. Jones and Edward Herrmann. Director Jan Kadar's last film.

VHS: S00465. $69.95.

Jan Kadar, USA, 1979, 186 mins.

Ghost

The story of a murdered man who returns from beyond to save his beloved. Whoopi Goldberg is featured in the role that won her an Academy Award and a Golden Globe. She is the medium who helps Patrick Swayze warn Demi Moore of impending danger.

VHS: S13653. $14.95.

Jerry Zucker, USA, 1990, 127 mins.

Ghost Dad

Bill Cosby dies in a cab accident and has only a couple of days to get his finances in order to provide for his children in this family comedy. With Kimberly Russell and Denise Nicholas.

VHS: S21482. $19.98.

Sidney Poitier, USA, 1990, 84 mins.

Glory

Glory spans the story of the 54th Massachusetts Regiment from its birth to the near destruction of the unit in an almost suicidal assault. Matthew Broderick stars as 25-year-old Colonel Robert Gould Shaw, the commanding officer of the 54th Massachusetts Regiment, but the film does not simply focus on the white colonel. He is portrayed in the context of the men he commands. Morgan Freeman is the former grave digger-turned non-commissioned officer and Denzel Washington (who won an Oscar for his performance) is a bitter and rebellious former slave. Probably the most accurate Civil War drama ever made. Academy Awards for sound and cinematography.

VHS: S12846. $14.95.

Edward Zwick, USA, 1989, 122 mins.

Go Tell It on the Mountain

James Baldwin's autobiographical novel about the African-American experience follows a family's migration from the rural South to Harlem. At the center of the film is a young man who struggles to understand and earn the approval of his stern, moody stepfather. With Paul Winfield, James Bond III, Olivia Cole, Rosalind Cash, Ruby Dee, Linda Hopkins and Alfre Woodard.

VHS: S20385. $69.95.

Stan Lathan, USA, 1984, 97 mins.

The Golden Child

In many ways this is Murphy's remake of Chaplin's *The Kid*, except that instead of rescuing a child from the authorities he must rescue a child from the powers of hell. A detective/kung-fu comedy reviled by some as a throw away. However, it's full of action and humor and features an excellent villain played by Charles Dance. Murphy's interacial romance in the picture is not exploitative but is shown as perfectly natural.

VHS: S21394. $14.95.

Michael Ritchie, USA, 1986, 96 mins.

Graffiti Bridge

Prince returns as "The Kid" to face his old nemesis from *Purple Rain*, Morris Day. Once again the two battle over a woman (Ingrid Chavez). The focus of the film is the music.

VHS: S21437. $14.95.

Prince, USA, 1990, 90 mins.

Greased Lightning

Richard Pryor plays Wendell Scott, the first U.S. African-American stock car driver. The bulk of this biographic film was apparently directed by Melvin Van Peebles, but completed by and credited to Michael Schultz. With Pam Grier, Cleavon Little, Richie Havens, Beau Bridges.

VHS: S21483. $19.98.

Melvin Van Peebles/Michael Schultz, USA, 1977, 96 mins.

Great White Hope

Jack Johnson was the first Black heavyweight champion of the world and he paid the price for his notoriety. James Earl Jones plays Jack Jefferson, a character conspiciously similar to Jack Johnson. Forced to flee trumped-up charges, Jefferson winds up in Europe playing in pathetic versions of *Uncle Tom's Cabin* and hounded by the authorities. His only hope for returning to America is to fight the "Great White Hope" (and lose) thus giving the legitimate title back to a white man. Current NEA Chair Jane Alexander stars in her first role as his lover. Both were nominated for Academy Awards. Also in the cast are Robert Webber, Hal Holbrook, R.G. Armstrong, Beah Richards, Moses Gunn, Marlene Whitfield and Chester Morris.

VHS: Currently out of print. May be available for rental in some video stores.

Martin Ritt, USA, 1970, 102 mins.

Half Slave, Half Free, Part 1

Originally released as *Solomon Northrup's Odyssey*, this video deals with the kidnapping and enslavement of a free Black man. It is based on a true story which shows how tenuous freedom was even for emancipated Blacks before the Civil War. Taken from Northrup's memoirs describing his 12 years as a slave. Directed by the creator of *Shaft*. With Avery Brooks and Mason Adams.

VHS: S01532. $59.95.

Gordon Parks, USA, 1985, 100 mins.

Half Slave, Half Free, Part 2: Charlotte Forten's Mission

Melba Moore stars in this second part of the PBS drama as a Black woman who, during the Civil War, sets out to prove that Blacks are the equals of whites. She journeys to a Union-occupied Georgia coastal island and proceeds to teach the inhabitants—freed slaves—to read. The story is based upon fact. Also features Moses Gunn.

VHS: S14609. $59.95.

Barry Crane, USA, 1985, 120 mins.

Hangin' with the Homeboys

What is there to do in the South Bronx on a Friday night? Go to Manhattan! Four friends from the South Bronx, two Black and two Puerto Rican, do just that as they complain humorously about their various situations. But none of them seem to show much interest in actually changing the problems they talk about. Written and directed by Joseph B. Vasquez, the film captures a realistic slice of life. With John Leguizama, Mario Joyner, Doug E. Doug and Nestor Serrano.

VHS: S15822. $19.95.

Joseph B. Vasquez, USA, 1991, 88 mins.

Harlem Nights

Black nightclub owners Richard Pryor and Eddie Murphy team up against the mob and the law in this action comedy. Curiously, Pryor is cast as the more cautious and learned of the two men. Murphy also directed an all-star cast that includes Redd Foxx (with his usual acidic wit), Danny Aiello (*Do the Right Thing*), Della Reese, Jasmine Guy and Arsenio Hall.

VHS: S21446. $19.95.

Eddie Murphy, USA, 1989, 118 mins.

Heaven Is a Playground

Michael Warren, *Hill Street Blues* alumnus and former USC basketball player, stars as a Chicago basketball talent scout. D.B. Sweeney is the white lawyer who has moved to the city determined to help a group of young men. Warren allows him to help if he will coach a team of beginners and help with the legal affairs of a young star (L.A. Lakers' Bo Kimble). Both men strive to keep the youths away from drugs and crime by helping them focus on getting to college through discipline and sports. Based on a book by Rick Telander. With Victor Love, Richard Jordan and Janet Julian.

VHS: S15926. $19.95.

Randall Fried, USA, 1991, 111 mins.

A Hero Ain't Nothin' But a Sandwich

Larry B. Scott is a thirteen-year old who is not overjoyed with his mother's (Cicely Tyson) live-in lover (Paul Winfield). Things become worse when the young man turns to drugs. Set in Watts, the film is based upon Alice Childress's book of the same title.

VHS: S14280. $19.95.

Ralph Nelson, USA, 1978, 107 mins.

Hit!

A revenge action movie which stars Richard Pryor, Billy Dee Williams and Paul Hampton. Williams is the federal agent who springs into action after his daughter overdoses. He puts together his own revenge squad in order to get nine heroin dealers in Marseilles.

VHS: S21484. $19.95.

Sidney J. Furie, USA, 1973, 134 mins.

Hollywood Shuffle

Robert Townsend takes on the stereotyping of Black actors in Hollywood films. The story revolves around a young man who wants to be an actor but is stuck in a nowhere job at "Winky-Dinky Dog". When he finally lands a part, it is in a blaxploitation film full of platform shoes and enormous afros. In a series of hilarious daydreams he works out his dilemma—should he accept the demeaning role or find work "at the post office"?

VHS: Currently out of print. May be available for rental in some video stores.

Robert Townsend, USA, 1987, 82 mins.

House Party

Grounded by his father, a teenager must sneak out to join the festivities at the party of the year. Rappers Kid 'N Play star in this musical comedy which spoofs everything from the police to halitosis. Especially memorable are the jail scene and the supporting performance of the late comedian Robin Harris (*Bebe's Kids, Mo' Better Blues*).

VHS: S12749. $19.98.

Reginald Hudlin, USA, 1990, 100 mins.

House Party 2: The Pajama Jam

The stars of *House Party* are back and in college. In order to raise tuition Kid 'N Play (Christopher Reid and Christopher Martin) put together a fundraiser. Needless to say, it does not turn out exactly as planned. Features Tisha Campbell, Iman, Queen Latifah and Martin Lawrence.

VHS: S21395. $19.95.

Doug McHenry/George Jackson, USA, 1991, 94 mins.

House Party 3

Kid 'N Play return for a third *House Party*. This time Kid is on his way to the altar and Play takes it upon himself to plan the bachelor party of all time. The fiance, Veda, becomes suspicious of Kid's party plans and the result is more madcap hijinx like that featured in the first two installments. The film also introduces female rappers TLC. Features Christopher Reid and Christopher Martin (aka Kid 'N Play), Tisha Campbell, Bernie Mac and Michael Colyar.

VHS: S21386. $95.95.

Eric Meza, USA, 1994, 93 mins.

House Party
(New Line Cinema)

How U Like Me Now

A young man on the south side of Chicago deals with his social-climbing girlfriend. She is overly ambitious while he lacks drive. A sort of romantic comedy with a great script. Features Darnell Williams, Salli Richardson, Daniel Gardner and Raymond Whitefield.

VHS: S21445. $92.95.

Daryll Roberts, USA, 1992, 109 mins.

Huckleberry Finn

Mark Twain's book about a young boy and the runaway slave he befriends is interpreted as a musical. Jeff East is Huck Finn while Paul Winfield, in a slightly peculiar but interesting performance, is the runaway slave Jim. Odessa Cleveland appears as Jim's wife and Roberta Flack sings the theme song. Score by Richard and Robert Sherman. With Harvey Korman, David Wayne and Arthur O'Connell.

VHS: S19031. $14.95.
Laser: LD72123. $34.98.

J. Lee Thompson, USA, 1974, 118 mins.

I Know Why the Caged Bird Sings

An eloquent film based on poet Maya Angelou's memories of the hardships, private joys and public pleasures of growing up in the Depression-era South. Ostracized by the social and racial caste systems of the period, Angelou finds self-expression and fulfillment through writing. Written by Leonora Thuna, Ralph B. Woolsey and Angelou. With Diahann Carroll, Esther Rolle, Ruby Dee, Paul Benjamin, Roger E. Mosley and Constance Good (who plays Angelou as a young girl).

VHS: S19890. $19.98.

Fielder Cook, USA, 1979, 100 mins.

Illusions

Nineteen-forty-two Hollywood is recreated in a fable of an ambitious Black woman studio executive, who passes for white and rises to the top of a wartime movie studio. Included in the compilation *Fact Is Stranger Than Fiction*.

VHS: S06513. $59.95

Julie Dash, USA, 1983, 34 mins.

I'm Gonna Git You Sucka

Keenan Ivory Wayans' directorial debut is both a parody and an homage to the blaxploitation films of the seventies. When the neighborhood is threatened, Wayans assembles virtually every "baaad" man from those seventies films to come to the rescue. Bernie Casey, Isaac Hayes, Jim Brown and

Antonio Fargas all put in appearances. Hilarious takes on stereotypes ranging from the early days of film through the present, including "Ghetto
Olympics" and a really mean twist on the old "Mammy" character. Also features John Vernon, Damon Wayans and Steve James.

VHS: S09397. $19.95.
Laser: LD72137. $34.98.

Keenan Ivory Wayans, USA, 1988, 85 mins.

The Jesse Owens Story

Dorian Harewood plays the famous Black track star who won four gold
medals at the 1936 Berlin Olympics. Owens's victory at these Olympics was
a slap in the face to the Nazis and their "master race" madness. The life of
Owens is profiled from his college days to his later exploitation. The cast
includes George Stanford Brown, LeVar Burton, Debbi Morgan, Tom Bosley,
Ronny Cox, George Kennedy and Ben Vereen.

VHS: S10826. $29.95.

Richard Irving, USA, 1984, 174 mins.

Jesus Christ, Superstar

The lead in Tim Rice and Andrew Lloyd Webber's play is actually Judas and
the film version features African-American actor Carl Anderson in the role.
A rock opera loosely based upon the Gospels, this version has considerable
sympathy for the wayward apostle. After all, without him and his betrayal,
the story could have never come to its necessary conclusion. Ted Neeley
appears as Jesus while Yvonne Elliman is Mary Magdalene.

VHS: S04920. $29.95.
Laser: Letterboxed, chapter search. LD71579. $34.98.

Norman Jewison, USA, 1973, 103 mins.

Joe's Bed-Stuy Barbershop: We Cut Heads

Set in a neighborhood barbershop, Spike Lee's first film has the same point-
ed humor as his later efforts. Lee displays remarkable powers of observation
in capturing the lives of assorted characters for whom this Bedford-
Stuyvesant barbershop is a focal point.

VHS: Currently out of print. May be available for rental in some video stores.

Spike Lee, USA, 1983, 60 mins.

Joey Breaker

A smooth-talking agent (Richard Edson) who lives in the fast lane has his priorities and indeed his world view dramatically altered when he's drawn to a beautiful and mysterious young Jamaican woman (Cedella Marley). Winner of top prize at the Santa Barbara International Film Festival. With Erik King, Gina Gershon, Phillip Seymour Hoffman and Fred Fondren.

VHS: S19204. $92.95.

Steven Starr, USA, 1993, 92 mins.

Jo Jo Dancer, Your Life is Calling

Richard Pryor directs this autobiographical (and self-indulgent) film about a comic reviewing his career from a hospital bed. The film is far heavier than any of Pryor's previous films, but still retains a sense of humor.

VHS: S21472. $14.95.

Richard Pryor, USA, 1986, 97 mins.

The Josephine Baker Story

Josephine Baker (Lynn Whitfield) was born poor, but achieved fame and fortune in France through her sizzlingly exotic and erotic singing and dancing performances. She starred in numerous films and was active with the French resistance during World War II. Her beauty and ambition ensured that she will always be remembered as the first, and possibly most loved, truly international star.

VHS: S14630. $19.98.

Brian Gibson, USA, 1990, 129 mins.

Juice

Cinematographer Ernest Dickerson's (*Do the Right Thing, Jungle Fever*) directorial debut deals with inner city crime and the search for respect by urban youth. A young D.J. called "Q" is talked into committing a robbery and winds up involved in a murder. The cast includes Omar Epps, Jermaine Hopkins, Tupac Shakur and Samuel L. Jackson.

VHS: S21444. $19.95.

Ernest R. Dickerson, USA, 1992, 95 mins.

Jungle Fever

Spike Lee's film, with its view of interracial romance as basically unnatural, features Wesley Snipes, a successful architect attracted to Annabella Sciora, his white temporary secretary. The relationship intrudes on all aspects of his life, making those around him uncomfortable. Lee makes his point with humor and a cast that includes Ossie Davis, Ruby Dee, John Turturro, Lonette McKee, Anthony Quinn, Spike Lee and Samuel L. Jackson, who won a special award at Cannes for his performance as Snipes's drug-addicted brother. Songs by Stevie Wonder.

VHS: S15412. $19.98.
Laser: LD71405. $39.98.

Spike Lee, USA, 1991, 132 mins.

Jungle Fever
(Universal Pictures)

Just Another Girl on the I.R.T.

A 17-year-old African-American woman (Ariyan Johnson) from Brooklyn is the focus of Leslie Harris's directorial debut. The title character is ambitious and streetwise, with plans to attend college and study medicine. She is independent and has her own ideas as to what constitutes education and what is relevant in her life. Plans go awry when she discovers that she is pregnant and then frivolously spends the money she intended to use for an abortion. Winner of the Special Jury Prize at the Sundance Film Festival. With Kevin Thigpen, Jerard Washington and Ebony Jerido.

VHS: S19024. $92.98.

Leslie Harris, USA, 1992, 90 mins.

The Killing Floor

A soldier returning from World War I wants something more out of life. Formerly a sharecropper, he moves to Chicago and becomes involved in the labor movement. Times become tougher and tougher until racial tension flares up and results in the bloody Chicago race riot of 1919. A powerful film produced for American Playhouse and shot on location against the backdrop of the Chicago stock yards. The film has a remarkable documentary feel, and features strong performances from Damien Leake, Alfre Woodard, Moses Gunn, Clarence Felder and Bill Bremer.

VHS: S10894. $19.95.

William Duke, USA, 1987, 118 mins.

King

Paul Winfield stars along with Cicely Tyson and Ossie Davis in this sensitive and powerful five-hour mini-series which recreates the life and struggle of Dr. Martin Luther King, Jr. With Howard Rollins, William Jordan and Cliff De Young. three-tape set. Abby Mann, USA, 270 mins.

VHS: S20472. $59.98.

Kiss Shot

Whoopi Goldberg is a single mother trying her hardest to make it on her own. She supports her daughter in a most unusual fashion: as a pool shark. Dennis Franz (*NYPD Blue, Hill Street Blues*) appears along with Teddy Wilson and Dorian Harewood. The film's director is Jerry London, the director of *The Dick Van Dyke Show*.

VHS: S16881. $19.95.

Jerry London, USA, 1992, 88 mins.

The Klansman

Racial strife in rural Alabama pits local blacks against the Ku Klux Klan. A white woman is raped, and an eccentric "Southern Gentleman" lives a fantasy life in the past. O.J. Simpson, Lola Falana, Richard Burton and Lee Marvin star. Charles Fuller co-wrote the script.

VHS: S13703. $19.95.

Terence Young, USA, 1974, 112 mins.

Krush Groove

Blair Underwood (*LA Law*, *Posse*) stars in the first all-rap musical. Musicians featured include Kurtis Blow, The Fat Boys and Sheila E.

VHS: S21404. $14.95.

Michael Schultz, USA, 1985, 95 mins.

Lady Sings the Blues

Based loosely on Billie Holiday's autobiography, this film deals with her climb to fame and her battle with drugs. Diana Ross stars as the fictionalized Holiday in a performance that earned her a Best Actress Academy Award nomination. The cast also includes Billy Dee Williams as her love interest, Louis McKay and Richard Pryor as "Piano Man".

VHS: S10836. $29.95.

Sidney J. Furie, USA, 1972, 144 mins.

Last Dragon

Motown's Berry Gordy produced this musical kung-fu film featuring pop singer Vanity. The plot involves a young kung-fu enthusiast portrayed by Taimak, who fights the evil "Sho-Nuff, Shogun of Harlem". Never mind the mixed-up cultural references—this is primarily a musical. Music by Stevie Wonder, Smokey Robinson, The Temptations and Debarge.

VHS: S21398. $79.98.

Michael Schultz, USA, 1985, 108 mins.

Leadbelly

The life of Huddie Ledbetter, the legendary musician who became a master of the 12-string guitar and served time on Texas and Louisiana chain gangs is recreated by Gordon Parks and stars Roger Mosley. The dynamic musical score includes the classics "Rock Island Line" and "Goodnight Irene." With James Brodhead, John McDonald.

VHS: Currently out of print. May be available for rental in some video stores.

Gordon Parks, USA, 1976, 127 mins.

Lean on Me

Morgan Freeman stars in this true story of Joe Clark, the baseball-bat-wielding, hard-nosed principal of a New Jersey high school. Clark, in real life as in the film, took tough measures to curb delinquency and drugs in order to improve education at his school. His methods were not unanimously applauded but he is shown here as a man with his heart in the right place. Also features Beverly Todd, Robert Guillaume, and Lynne Thigpen.

VHS: S10436. $14.95.

John G. Avildsen, USA, 1989, 109 mins.

The Learning Tree

A Black teenager comes of age in 1920s Kansas in this film based upon the autobiographical book by director Gordon Parks. The trials encountered by the young man call to mind the difficulties faced not only by African-American youths at the time but also by American youth in general. Parks would later become an acclaimed photo journalist. With Kyle Johnson as Newt and Dana Elcar as the Sheriff.

VHS: S03572. $19.98.

Gordon Parks, USA, 1969, 107 mins.

Lethal Weapon

Danny Glover and Mel Gibson are unlikely partners in this violent action film. Glover portrays a family man who has just had his fiftieth birthday. Gibson, his new partner, is a burnt-out and possibly suicidal former special forces commando. The two stumble across a vicious gang of drug dealers.

VHS: S05970. $19.98.

Richard Donner, USA, 1987, 100 mins.

Lethal Weapon II

This sequel finds the two mismatched partners teamed with Joe Pesci as an accountant who is informing on the mob. The "mob" in this case has a connection with South African diplomats who moonlight as drug smugglers.

VHS: S11576. $19.98.

Richard Donner, USA, 1989, 113 mins.

Lethal Weapon III

As could be expected, Murtaugh's (Danny Glover) last week on the police force does not end with only a gold watch. He and partner Riggs (Mel Gibson) uncover a crooked ex-cop who is selling confiscated firearms. The film is non-stop action from begining to end, with comic relief provided by Joe Pesci who reprises his role from *Lethal Weapon II*.

VHS: S21402. $19.98.

Richard Donner, USA, 1992, 118 mins.

Let's Do It Again

Sidney Poitier and Bill Cosby reprise their roles in this sequel to *Uptown Saturday Night*. The two men fleece a couple of gamblers in order to build a lodge hall. Features Ossie Davis, Jimmy Walker, John Amos, Denise Nicholas and Calvin Lockhart.

VHS: S21459. $19.98.

Sidney Poitier, USA, 1975, 113 mins.

The Liberation Of L.B. Jones

Legendary director William Wyler's last film is the story of an African-American undertaker who finds that his wife is having an affair with a white police officer. The film is set in the South and approaches the connections between racism and sex. Watch for the memorable small role of Yaphet Kotto. Stars Roscoe Lee Browne and Lola Falana.

VHS: Currently out of print. May be available for rental in some video stores.

William Wyler, USA, 1970, 101 mins.

The Life and Times of Deacon A.L. Wiley

Actor and writer Gregory Alan-Williams stars in the oral history of a strong African-American father and preacher, Deacon A.L. Wiley. Alan-Williams based this intimate portrait on the interviews Zora Neale Hurston conducted with former slaves in the 30s.

VHS: S21856. $29.95

The Long Walk Home

A maid (Whoopi Goldberg) supports the Montgomery bus boycott called by Rev. Martin Luther King, Jr. Unfortunately she still has to get to work and must walk the entire distance. When her new employer (Sissy Spacek) finds out, she helps by driving her to and from work as much as she is able. Her

---

motives are as much selfish as altruistic; she wants her maid to get to work on time. But in the long run she becomes more socially conscious and eventually winds up in conflict with her husband (Dwight Schultz) who must decide between his family and his racist attitudes.

VHS: S14504. $14.98.

Richard Pearce, USA, 1989, 95 mins.

Love to All, Lorraine

Lorraine Hansberry wrote the acclaimed play *A Raisin in the Sun* before she was thirty and died, tragically, at the age of thirty-four. This film is an adaptation for video of a one-woman play depicting Hansberry's life, work and struggle with poor health. Directed by Woodie King, Jr. and Elizabeth Van Dyke.

VHS: S20853. $59.95.

Love Your Mama

A mother on the south side of Chicago faces her husband's alcoholism, her daughter's pregnancy and her son's criminal activity. She tries to hold her family together despite these problems. Carol Hall is the strong but suffering mother in this film directed and financed by Chicago day care center operator Ruby Oliver. The film is also known as *Leola*. With Audrey Morgan, Andre Robinson, Earnest Raymond and Kearo Johnson.

VHS: S19633. $89.95.

Ruby Oliver, USA, 1989, 94 mins.

Mad Max Beyond Thunderdome

Tina Turner is Auntie Entity, the deadly Queen of Barter Town in the third installment of the *Mad Max* series. Mel Gibson plays Mad Max, who is forced into gladiatorial combat and then tossed out into the desert by Turner. Eventually he leads her on a destructive cross-country chase. Turner's first acting role.

VHS: S00793. $14.95.
Laser: LD70619. $34.98.

George Miller, Australia, 1985, 107 mins.

Made in America

Ted Danson and Whoopi Goldberg star in this comedy about a mix-up at a sperm bank. When Goldberg's artificially inseminated child wants to know who her father is, she finds that he's an uncouth used car salesman.

VHS: S21399. $95.99.

Richard Benjamin, USA, 1993, 109 mins.

Mahogany

Diana Ross is a secretary thrown into the heights of the international fashion scene. She trades Chicago for Rome but then must choose between her new career and her man, Brian (Billy Dee Williams). Ross plays one of the few African-American female characters of the time who actually have a choice between a career and their man. Motown's Berry Gordy directs a cast that includes Tony Perkins, Beah Richards, Jean-Pierre Aumont and Nina Foch.

VHS: S10831. $14.95.

Berry Gordy, USA, 1976, 109 mins.

Malcolm X

Spike Lee chose the life of Malcolm X for his first epic. He used the *Autobiography of Malcolm X (as told to Alex Haley)* as his source. The film follows the life of the religious and political leader from his years as a porter and small-time thief to his assassination in 1964. Malcolm's embrace of Islam and his ascension as a brilliant orator and black leader is covered as well as his fateful trip to Mecca. It was after this journey that he finally broke away from his mentor and Nation of Islam leader, Elijah Muhammad. Denzel Washington, nominated for an Oscar, leads a cast that includes Spike Lee, Angela Bassett and Al Freeman, Jr. as Elijah Muhammed. Appearing in cameos are the Rev. Al Sharpton as a street preacher, Christopher Plummer as a prison pastor and Nelson Mandela as a school teacher. Music by Terence Blanchard.

VHS: S18855. $24.98.
Laser: Letterboxed. LD71884. $39.98.

Spike Lee, USA, 1992, 201 mins.

Man and Boy

A family film which stars Bill Cosby as a Civil War veteran who, together with his son, takes off after the thief who stole their horse. With Gloria Foster, Leif Erickson.

VHS: S21486. $59.98.

E. W. Swackhamer, USA, 1972, 98 mins.

Mandela

An HBO film on the life and times of South African President Nelson Mandela. Danny Glover and Alfre Woodard star as Nelson and Winnie, a courageous married couple dedicated to opposing the apartheid system of South Africa. A stirring dramatic reenactment of the life of a man who endured nearly three decades in prison for his beliefs. The film was made well before anyone thought Mandela would be released, let alone elected President.

VHS: S06394. $79.99.

Philip Saville, USA, 1987, 135 mins.

Matewan

John Sayles' film charts the events that presage the final action of the so-called "Matewan Massacre", an extremely violent labor confrontation in the 1920s. Rural West Virginia coal country is the setting for this bitter strike. The mine owners bring in thugs and prospective scab workers consisting of Southern blacks and Italian immigrants. Their plan falls through when the scabs join the strike. James Earl Jones appears as the leader of the Black miners. With Chris Cooper and Mary McDonnell.

VHS: S06028. $19.98.
Laser: LD71135. $29.98.

John Sayles, USA, 1987, 132 mins.

Menace II Society

Possibly the best recent drama about the disintegration of life in the inner city. Violence and hopelessness are examined not only as the result of current conditions but as a legacy of the second-class citizenship afforded African-Americans. Although this picture was marketed as a "gangsta" film, the characters elevate it to a higher level. With Jada Pinkett, Vonte Sweet, MC Eiht, Ryan Williams, Too $hort, Samuel L. Jackson, Charles Dutton and Bill Duke.

VHS: S19937. $94.95.

The Hughes Brothers, USA, 1993, 97 mins.

Meteor Man

A meteor crashes to Earth, endowing a man with super powers which he uses for the good of mankind. An upbeat, largely non-violent superhero film starring director Robert Townsend.

VHS: S21409. $95.99.

Robert Townsend, USA, 1993, 99 mins.

The Mighty Quinn

Denzel Washington stars as Quinn, an island police chief caught between the demands of friendship, his failed marriage and murderous intrigue. Robert Townsend is Maubee, a quasi-legendary character of dubious occupation who has come up with a large number of "10,000 dollar bills". Hot on Maubee's trail is a vicious CIA agent (M. Emmet Walsh). Reggae music and comedy abound, with supporting performances by Esther Rolle and Sheryl Lee Ralph as Quinn's wife.

VHS: S11203. $89.98.

Carl Schenkel, USA, 1989, 98 mins.

Mississippi Burning

This film received seven Oscar nominations and one award (Best Cinematography). Gene Hackman and Willem Dafoe head an FBI investigative team looking to uncover the circumstances surrounding three missing Civil Rights workers. A powerfully acted (albeit historically dubious) portrayal of the FBI's role in the Civil Rights movement. With Frances McDormand and Brad Dourif.

VHS: S09573. $19.98.

Alan Parker, USA, 1988, 127 mins.

Mississippi Masala

A twist on earlier films about interracial relationships, this is the story of an Indian woman and an African-American who become involved with each other. Neither of their families approve. Denzel Washington is the ambitious carpet cleaner and Sarita Choudhury is the object of his affection. Set, as the title would suggest, in Mississippi, the film is a humorous look at the attitudes of the "New South". Directed by Mira Nair whose work includes *Salaam Bombay*. Also features Charles Dutton.

VHS: S17070. $92.95.
Laser: LD72200. $34.95.

Mira Nair, USA, 1991, 110 mins.

Mister Johnson

Mr. Johnson (Maynard Eziashi) is an ambitious clerk with questionable accounting methods in Bruce Beresford's story set during the days of British colonialism. The plot centers on the building of a road and the new district officer (Pierce Brosnan) who is perplexed as to how this can be accomplished with the resources available to him. But with the assistance of Mr. Johnson the job is done. The film points to the difficulty of simple human interaction and the waste of human potential that typified colonialism. With Edward Woodward and Denis Quilley. Based on the novel by Joyce Cary.

VHS: S15407. $89.98.

Bruce Beresford, USA, 1991, 105 mins.

Mister Johnson
(LIVE Entertainment, Inc.)

Mo' Better Blues

Bleek Gilliam (Denzel Washington) is a self-serving jazz trumpeter who divides his time between two women. The story follows his dalliances and his career maneuverings to the point where he is no longer able to play. The story is partly based upon the life of Spike Lee's father Bill who wrote the score. Music by the Branford Marsalis Quartet; the late Robin Harris is featured as a jazz club comedian. With Spike Lee, Cynda Williams, Joie Lee, Ruben Blades, John Turturro and Wesley Snipes as Bleek's friend/rival.

VHS: S13291. $19.95.

Spike Lee, USA, 1990, 129 mins.

Mo' Money

Daman Wayans stars in this comedy about a con man who goes straight—for a while. When he begins work at a credit card company he reverts to his old ways. He then gets sucked into more dangerous scams. This comedy also stars Marlon Wayans and Stacey Dash.

VHS: S21442. $19.95.

Peter MacDonald, USA, 1992, 97 mins.

Mother, Jugs and Speed

A funny comedy-thriller about an L.A. ambulance service that's in hot competition with a rival company. Bill Cosby gets some funny lines. With Harvey Keitel, Raquel Welch, Larry Hagman.

VHS: S21487. $19.95.

Peter Yates, USA, 1976, 98 mins.

Mo' Better Blues
(Universal Pictures)

Mountains Of The Moon

An epic film about the European effort to find the source of the Nile. The travels of "explorers" Richard Burton and John Haning Speke are detailed as they cross Africa in the name of the Empire. The film contains excellent location footage and is an accurate look at early European penetration of Africa.

VHS: S12479. $14.98.

Bob Rafelson, USA, 1990, 140 mins.

Moving

Richard Pryor has just lost his engineering job but has the chance of a lifetime if he can only move 2,000 miles to Boise, Idaho. Predictably, the move is full of comic obstacles. With Beverly Todd and Randy Quaid.

VHS: S21452. $19.98.

Alan Metter, USA, 1988, 89 mins.

Native Son

A second version of Wright's book, this film is a more professional effort than Wright's own, but tones down the harshness of the original. Features Oprah Winfrey.

VHS: S05330. $14.98.

Jerrold Freedman, USA, 1986, 111 mins.

New Jack City

A drug lord is pursued by an interacial police duo in this violent drama. Wesley Snipes portrays the drug dealer and the "Salt and Pepper" team on his trail are Ice-T and Judd Nelson. The plot is simple but the acting is top notch. In addition, the supporting cast includes director Mario Van Peebles and *Saturday Night Live* alumnus Chris Rock (*CB4*).

VHS: S21405. $19.98.

Mario Van Peebles, USA, 1991, 101 mins.

Night of the Living Dead

The basic plot here is the rising of the dead and their snacking on the living. The last two survivors are a Black man and a white woman. A posse of "zombie hunters" (the film's "powers that be") kill the African-American. George A. Romero had a pessimistic view of race relations in 1968. The film comments on racism and is a landmark horror film.

VHS: S18644. $19.95.
Laser: CLV. LD72009. $29.98.

George A. Romero, USA, 1968, 96 mins.

An Officer and a Gentleman

Louis Gossett, Jr. won an Academy Award for his portrayal of a tough Marine drill sergeant. The film centers on the romance between Richard Gere as a would-be Navy pilot and Debra Winger as a factory worker but it is Gossett who steals the film.

VHS: S01586. $14.95

Taylor Hackford, USA, 1982, 126 mins.

One False Move

A grisly murder in Los Angeles leads to a nationwide man hunt involving the LAPD and a rural Arkansas sheriff. The L.A. cops know where the killers are headed but they do not know the personal connection between the accomplice, an African-American woman, and the white sheriff. Her son is the key. The big city police learn the dynamics, racial and otherwise of a small southern town. Stars Bill Paxton and Cynda Williams. With Michael Beach, Earl Beach, Jim Metzler and Billy Bob Thornton.

VHS: S17057. $89.95.
Laser: LD71541. $34.95.

Carl Franklin, USA, 1991, 103 mins.

Passenger 57

Wesley Snipes portrays John Cutter, an ex-government agent, who is coincidentally on the same plane as an evil apprehended terrorist (Bruce Payne) headed to trial in L.A. Unfortunately some of the terrorist's thugs have also sneaked aboard with plans to hijack the plane. Music by Stanley Clarke.

VHS: S21406. $19.98.

Kevin Hooks, USA, 1992, 84 mins.

Passion Fish

A white soap opera star, May-Alice (Mary McDonnell) is paralyzed in an automobile accident and returns to her home in Louisiana to recuperate. Her obnoxious behavior irritates her live-in nurse until the arrival of Chantelle (Alfre Woodard). The two women develop friendship and interdependence. They are running from their pasts and support each other's hopes for the future. Both women become involved in curious relationships: May-Alice with a childhood sweetheart, and Chantelle with a "French-talking Louisiana cowboy" played by Vondie Curtis-Hall. From the director of *Matewan* and *Brother from Another Planet*.

VHS: S18746. $94.95.

John Sayles, USA, 1992, 137 mins.

Pastime

An aging pitcher, depressed about his inevitable retirement, befriends a Black teenager assigned to his minor league team. Set in 1957, the film shows the young man treated as a leper by everyone except the pitcher who endeavors to teach him a "special pitch". There are many cameos by baseball legends including Ernie Banks, Harmon Killebrew, Bill Mazeroski, Don Newcombe and Duke Snider. With Glenn Plummer, Noble Willingham, Jeffrey Tambor, Scott Plank and Deirdre O'Connell.

VHS: S16041. $19.95.

Robin Armstrong, USA, 1991, 95 mins.

Paul Robeson

One of the many casualties of the House Un-American Activities Committee was the great actor and singer, Paul Robeson. As a voice against racism and a supporter of Communism he was branded and his career was left in shambles. James Earl Jones portrays Paul Robeson in this one-man show that is both a tribute to the man and a look at the views he held.

VHS: S06092. $39.95.

Lloyd Richards, USA, 1980, 118 mins.

Pelican Brief

Denzel Washington stars as a journalist enlisted to help a law student (Julia Roberts) who has uncovered a sinister plot. The unlikely team are opposed by an underground group within Washington's "power elite". Based on the John Grisham novel.

VHS: S21079. $102.95
Laser: LD72411. $39.98.

Alan J. Pakula, USA, 1993, 141 mins.

The People Under the Stairs

A young African-American becomes entangled in an attempt to rob a bizarre couple. His accomplices are murdered and he is left in the house alone. Eventually he finds the house is peopled by the crazed, almost zombified offspring of the couple. As the plot moves along we find that the evil couple are also the ones responsible for the deplorable conditions of his neighborhood.

VHS: S21393. $19.98.

Wes Craven, USA, 1991, 102 mins.

Philadelphia

Tom Hanks won an Academy Award for Best Actor for his portrayal of a lawyer dying of AIDS. Denzel Washington is cast as his attorney, a man who must come to terms with his own prejudices in order to right an injustice.

This is a film similar to the so-called "problem films" of the 40s and 50s. These generally dealt—sometimes poorly—with the "problem" of African-Americans. In this case the "problem" becomes AIDS and it is fitting that an African-American was cast in the role of defender.

VHS: S21120. $99.95.
Laser: LD72416. $39.95.

Jonathan Demme, USA, 1993, 125 mins.

A Piece of the Action

Sidney Poitier and Bill Cosby are paired in this film about two con men put to work at a community center. A police officer (James Earl Jones) blackmails the two into becoming more productive citizens. Features Denise Nicholas, Hope Clarke, and Tracy Reed.

VHS: S21434. $19.98.

Sidney Poitier, USA, 1977, 135 mins.

Pipe Dreams

Gladys Knight makes her acting debut in this story set against the building of the Alaskan pipeline. The soundtrack is full of songs by Gladys Knight and the Pips. With Stephen Verona, Barry Hankerson, Bruce French.

VHS: S21488. $19.95.

Stephen Verona, USA, 1976, 89 mins.

Pippin

Ben Vereen and William Katt star in this filmed version of the Broadway smash, a colorful, bright pastiche of the romantic epic, designed and choreographed by the brilliant Bob Fosse (*Cabaret*, *All That Jazz*).

VHS: S04867. $29.95.

Bob Fosse, USA, 1981, 120 mins.

Poetic Justice

John Singleton's follow-up to *Boyz N the Hood* features Janet Jackson as a poet and hairdresser who is trying to cope with the senseless murder of her boyfriend. Jackson reluctantly joins a friend on a trip from South-Central Los Angeles to Oakland in a mail truck. Along the way, she develops a complicated relationship with an ambitious music producer and postal delivery man (Tupac Shakur). The soundtrack includes numbers by Babyface, Tony!

Toni! Tone!, Naughty by Nature and The Dogg Pound. The poetry spoken by Jackson was written by Maya Angelou. With Tyra Ferrell, Regina King and Joe Torry.

VHS: S20221. $94.95.
Laser: LD72331. $34.95.

John Singleton, USA, 1993, 109 mins.

Posse

Five Spanish Civil War veterans stationed in Cuba who rebel against their racist colonel (Billy Zane), seize an illegal gold shipment and flee to the American frontier. The Colonel is naturally upset. Together with his henchmen, he pursues the escapees. The deserters settle in Freedomville, a revolutionary all-Black settlement where they are, once again, threatened by a vicious white racist. This time the offender is a local sheriff (Richard Jordan). An admirable attempt at showing that there indeed were many African-Americans in the West. The film does not, however, compromise on its main intention which is to entertain. With Mario Van Peebles, Stephen Baldwin, Charles Lane, Tiny Lister, Tone Loc, Big Daddy Kane and Blair Underwood. Special appearances by Pam Grier, Isaac Hayes, filmmaker Melvin Van Peebles, Woody Strode and the Hudlin Brothers.

VHS: S19514. $94.99.

Mario Van Peebles, USA, 1993, 109 mins.

Purdy's Station

In 1859 Jerusha Moore, a school teacher, discovered a Black farmer hiding runaway slaves at his "station" on the underground railroad. She becomes aware of the divisions in her community and must make a choice between morality and her own security.

VHS: S21323. $49.95.

Don Coonley, USA, 1990.

Purple Rain

Prince's film debut is a semi-autobiographical account of an up-and-coming musician. Tormented by family problems, he takes his frustrations out on those around him, risking his career and relationships. One of these relationships is with a young woman (Apollonia Kotero) who has her own musical ambitions. A subplot involves a bitter rivalry with another musician played humorously by Morris Day. Also features Olga Karlatos, Clarence Williams III and Jerome Benton.

VHS: S21473. $19.98.
Laser: LD70660. $24.98.

Albert Magnoli, USA, 1984, 111 mins.

Putney Swope

A Black man is accidentally elected to be the chairman of the board at a Madison Avenue ad agency in this send-up of corporate America and late 60's Black radicalism. The advertising produced by the agency changes drastically and provides most of the film's humor. The agency transforms from a firm made up of sleepy middle class whites to a group of dashiki-wearing gun-toting Black radicals. Arnold Johnson stars as Putney Swope.

VHS: Currently out of print. May be available for rental in some video stores.

Robert Downey, USA, 1969, 88 mins.

Putney Swope
(Museum of Modern Art Film Stills Archive)

Rage in Harlem

A young man (Forest Whitaker) is led astray by Robin Givens in this Harlem gangster story based on the book by Chester Himes, the author of *Cotton Comes to Harlem*. Givens plays a slick country woman hiding out in the big city with a sizable amount of gold. At first she uses Whitaker's home simply to hide but winds up relying on him. Corrupt cops and a quirky gangster with an unfortunate pet play a role. The cast includes Gregory Hines, Zakes Mokae and Danny Glover.

VHS: S15133. $19.98.
Laser: LD71673. $29.98.

Bill Duke, USA, 1991, 90 mins.

Raisin in the Sun (1971)

Sidney Poitier and Ruby Dee star in this story of a family moving from the South side of Chicago to a mostly white suburb and the individual problems each family member must face with their big change. Poitier's character is angry that the only job he can get is as a chauffeur—a job that he calls "no kind of job at all". The film is based on Lorraine Hansberry's play and also features Claudia McNeil and Louis Gossett, Jr.

VHS: S01088. $14.95.

Daniel Petrie, USA, 1971, 128 mins.

Raisin in the Sun (1989)

The 25th anniversary of the famous play is honored with a production featuring Danny Glover as Walter Lee, Starletta DuPois as his wife and Esther Rolle as the widowed mother. As powerful as the original.

VHS: S12662. $69.95.

Bill Duke, USA, 1989, 171 mins.

Rappin'

Mario Van Peebles (*Posse, New Jack City*) stars in this action/musical as an ex-con trying to stay straight. He winds up in conflict with both his landlord and a gang leader. The music is the real focus of this film. Songs include "Snack Attack" and "FU 12."

VHS: S21401. $14.95.

Joel Silberg, USA, 1985, 92 mins.

The Reivers

Based upon William Faulkner's last novel, *The Reivers* is the story of a young man and two adults travelling from a small town in Mississippi to Memphis. Steve McQueen and Juano Hernandez (*Intruder in the Dust*) star.

VHS: S21403. $14.98.

Mark Rydell, USA, 1969, 107 mins.

Ricochet

Denzel Washington plays a cop who becomes a hero when he gets the bad guy (John Lithgow). Lithgow is a psycho who spends his time in prison plotting his sick revenge.

VHS: S21489. $19.98.

Russell Mulcahy, USA, 1991, 97 mins.

River Niger

The Tony Award-winning play is adapted in a production featuring Cicely Tyson and James Earl Jones. An African-American family copes with bleak prospects for the future and the injustice of social conditions in the ghetto. With Louis Gossett, Jr., Glynn Turman and Roger E. Mosley.

VHS: S18830. $29.95.

Krishna Shah, USA, 1976, 105 mins.

A Rage in Harlem
(Miramax Films)

Road to Freedom: The Vernon Johns Story

In 1953, before Blacks in the South were accustomed to talk of equal rights, Vernon Johns arrived in Alabama to preach and call for equality. His call was the starting point of the modern Civil Rights movement. James Earl Jones stars as Vernon Johns.

VHS: S21297. $89.99.

Kenneth Fink, USA, 1993, 91 mins.

Roll of Thunder, Hear My Cry

A Black family struggles to survive in Depression-era Mississippi in this television production. Set in 1933 and based on the novels of Mildred Taylor. Stars Morgan Freeman.

VHS: S09045. $14.95.

Jack Smight, USA, 1978, 110 mins.

Roots

Roots brought the experiences and suffering of the first African-Americans to prime time and remains one of the most important television events in history. The story follows a family tree, traced by descendant Alex Haley in his Pulitzer Prize-winning book. It begins in Africa with Kunta Kinte (LeVar Burton) and follows his capture by slave traders and the voyage to the New World. He and his family survive despite horrible conditions and each generation moves with hope into the future. Winner of nine Emmy Awards, the program stars Louis Gossett, Jr., Ed Asner, Olivia Cole, Henry Fonda, George Sanford Brown and Sandy Dennis.

VHS: S17435. $149.92.

David Greene, USA, 1977, 90 mins.

Roots: The Next Generations

Alex Haley's brilliant investigation of his family's origins continues where the original *Roots* left off. It is equally moving and just as important. Beginning in the years after the Civil War and continuing on to the 1970s, *Roots: The Next Generations* concludes with Haley's own remarkable life. This includes his work with Malcolm X on his autobiography and an interview with American Nazi Norman Rockwell (played by Marlon Brando). With James Earl Jones (as Haley), Al Freeman, Jr., Henry Fonda, Olivia de Havilland, Irene Cara, Dorian Harewood, Ossie Davis, Ruby Dee and Debbie Allen.

VHS: S17436. $149.92.

John Erman/Charles S. Dubin/Georg Stanford Brown/Lloyd Richards, USA, 1979, 685 mins.

Roots: The Gift

This made-for-television work picks up the fortunes of captured African warrior Kunta Kinte (LeVar Burton) and American-born slave Fiddler (Louis Gossett, Jr.). The story of their violent rebellion and heroic efforts to organize a slave rebellion and subsequent journey for freedom through the Underground Railroad is told. With cameo appearance by the late Pulitzer-Prize writer Alex Haley, whose work *Roots* set everything in motion. With Michael Learned, Avery Brooks, Kate Mulgrew and Shaun Cassidy.

VHS: S17434. $59.99.

Kevin Hooks, USA, 1988, 94 mins.

Running Scared

Gregory Hines stars with Billy Crystal in this police buddy film set in Chicago. The two begin pursuit of a drug lord just days before they are to retire to Key West. This is a moderately violent action picture.

VHS: S21396. $14.95.

Peter Hyams, USA, 1986, 106 mins.

The Saint of Fort Washington

Danny Glover and Matt Dillon play a pair of homeless men in this drama about friendship on the streets. Glover takes the learning-impaired Dillon under his wing as the two struggle to live and be accepted by society.

VHS: S20954. $95.98.
Laser: LD72417. $34.98.

Tim Hunter, USA, 1993, 104 mins.

Sarafina!

Adapted from Mbongeni Ngema's stage play, *Sarafina!* is a harsh drama containing musical and dance numbers. The cruel situation of Blacks under apartheid is juxtaposed with the power of individuals and community to stand up for themselves in even the most desperate of situations. Leleti Khumalo recreates her stage role and is supported by Whoopi Goldberg and Miriam Makeba. With John Kani and Ngema.

VHS: S18248. $94.95.

Darrell Roodt, USA, 1992, 98 mins.

School Daze

A Black Southern university is the setting for Spike Lee's second feature. Mission College's fraternities and sororities are in conflict over assimilation and the discrimination suffered by darker skinned African-Americans. Lee took the unorthodox step of making the background for these serious issues a musical. As usual, the cast is top notch and includes Larry Fishburne, Joe Seneca, Ellen Holly, Ossie Davis and Tisha Campbell. From the maker of *She's Gotta Have It*.

VHS: S07676. $14.95.

Spike Lee, USA, 1988, 114 mins.

See No Evil, Hear No Evil

The third pairing of Richard Pryor and Gene Wilder has Pryor cast as a deaf man and Wilder as a blind man. The two are being sought by the police and most of the plot revolves around their slapstick attempts to escape. Not up to their previous efforts but the chemistry between the two is still there.

VHS: S21441. $14.95.

Arthur Hiller, USA, 1989, 103 mins.

Separate But Equal

Sidney Poitier portrays Thurgood Marshall in this reenactment of an early episode in the battle for Civil Rights. Marshall, then an NAACP attorney, fought for the use of a single bus to transport black children to school. The case wound up before Chief Justice Warren of the U.S. Supreme Court, which made a landmark decision. Burt Lancaster and Richard Kiley also appear.

VHS: S14476. $19.98.
Laser: CLV. LD72029. $39.98.

George Stevens, Jr., USA, 1990, 194 mins.

Shame (The Intruder)

William Shatner stars in this Roger Corman film about race relations in the South. Corman is generally associated with low budget horror while Shatner is widely known as "Captain Kirk". But here they team up in a provocative work. Shatner is a bigot who travels through rural areas trying to marshall opposition to desegregation.

VHS: S01187. $34.95.

Roger Corman, USA, 1962, 84 mins.

She's Gotta Have It

Spike Lee's breakthrough film is the story of a free-spirited woman, Nola Darling, who is pursued by three very different men. When the men press her to choose between them, she decides on none of the above. Spike Lee turns in a hilarious performance as Mars Blackmon. Features Tracy Camila Johns, Tommy Redmond Hicks, John Canada Terell and Raye Dowell as Opal.

VHS: Currently out of print. May be available for rental in some video stores.
Laser: LD74463. $49.95.

Spike Lee, USA, 1986, 84 mins.

She's Gotta Have It
(Island Pictures)

Silver Streak

Richard Pryor teams up with Gene Wilder in this story of a white executive on vacation who winds up involved in a murder. Pryor portrays Grover, who assists Wilder in evading the police and ultimately in catching the bad guys. The film contains the classic scene where Pryor teaches Wilder to be "Black".

VHS: S21439. $14.98.

Arthur Hiller, USA, 1976, 113 mins.

Sister Act

Whoopi Goldberg is a lounge singer who witnesses a murder. As a result she must go underground and winds up hiding in a convent. She works with the choir and changes their singing style a little. The musical sequences are the highlights. With Harvey Keitel, Maggie Smith, Bill Nunn, Kathy Najimy and Mary Wickes.

VHS: S17635. $19.99.
Laser: Letterboxed. LD71824. $29.99.

Emile Ardolino, USA, 1992, 100 mins.

Sister Act II: Back in the Habit

Whoopi Goldberg received the largest paycheck ever for an actress to reprise her role as a nightclub singer and undercover nun in this sequel to the block-buster *Sister Act*. Most of her supporting cast including Maggie Smith and scene-stealing Kathy Najimy are back as well. USA, 1993.

VHS: S21432. $96.98.

Six Degrees of Separation

A young Black man endears himself to a rich white couple by pretending to be Sidney Poitier's son. This stage adaptation translates well to the screen with a fine performance by Will Smith (*The Fresh Prince of Bel Air*). The cast also includes Stockard Channing and Donald Sutherland.

VHS: S21032. $95.98.
Laser: LD72407. $34.98.

Fred Schepisi, USA, 1993, 112 mins.

The Sky Is Gray

A young Black man in Louisiana encounters prejudice on the way to the dentist in this adaptation of an Ernest Gaines short story. His realizations about racism and poverty are thrown into relief by the banal purpose of the trip. Starring Olivia Cole, James Bond III and Cleavon Little. From The American Short Story series.

VHS: S01962. $24.95.

Stan Lathan, USA, 1980, 46 mins.

A Soldier's Story

A Black sergeant is murdered on a Southern military base. Howard Rollins plays the African-American captain sent to investigate. Problems arise when the evidence incriminates white officers. The excellent cast includes Denzel Washington and Adolph Caesar as the unfortunate sergeant. Music by Herbie Hancock. Based on the play by Charles Fuller.

VHS: S01229. $14.95.

Norman Jewison, USA, 1984, 102 mins.

Some Kind of Hero

Richard Pryor is cast as a former P.O.W. returning from Vietnam. The world is no longer the place he remembers. His performance as a man dealing with newfound freedom is the saving grace in an otherwise undistinguished film.

VHS: S21450. $14.95.

Michael Pressman, USA, 1982, 97 mins.

The Sophisticated Gents

A group of childhood friends reunite their athletic club for the purpose of honoring their old coach. Each recollects how he helped guide them through their early years. Each also has a different story of what being an African-American has meant to them. A tremendous cast includes Paul Winfield, Rosey Grier, Melvin Van Peebles, Alfre Woodard, Ron O'Neal, Rosalind Cash, Denise Nicholas and Raymond St. Jacques. This teleplay was scripted by Van Peebles from John A. Williams' novel, *The Junior Bachelor Society*.

VHS: S16541. $89.95.

Harry Falk, USA, 1981, 200 mins.

Sounder

Paul Winfield portrays a sharecropper sent to prison for stealing in order to feed his family. The character is a strong African-American male figure rare in films of the time. The family perseveres through their troubles. Cicely Tyson and Paul Winfield were both nominated for Academy Awards as was the screenplay by Black writer, Lonne Elder III. Features Kevin Hooks, Carmen Mathews and Carmen Best.

VHS: S01235. $14.95.

Martin Ritt, USA, 1972, 105 mins.

Sky Is Gray
(Monterey Movie Company)

South Central

Steve Anderson's debut film is about the despair and social displacement overrunning a Los Angeles neighborhood. This film tracks one young man's odyssey from a life of violent crime to one of hope and fulfillment. With Glenn Plummer, Carl Lumbly and Byron Keith Minns.

VHS: S17890. $19.98.
Laser: LD71837. $29.98.

Steve Anderson, USA, 1992, 99 mins.

Sparkle

Three sisters form a singing group and try to make it big. One of the women, Sister (Lonette Mckee) falls for a lowlife named Satin (Tony King) while the youngest sister, Sparkle (Irene Cara), falls for a well-meaning young man, Stix (Philip Michael Thomas). Most of the film deals with Stix trying to make Sparkle a star and with the destructive relationship between Sister and Satin. Also stars Dwan Smith, Mary Alice and Dorian Harewood.

VHS: S21436. $19.98.

Sam O'Steen, USA, 1976, 98 mins.

Stir Crazy

Richard Pryor and Gene Wilder team up again in this comedy about two men convicted of a robbery they didn't commit. They wind up involved with psychotic prisoners, tough guards and an irritable warden. One of the top grossing films of 1980.

VHS: S21440. $14.95.

Sidney Poitier, USA, 1980, 111 mins.

Story of A Three Day Pass

A Black soldier gets a lecture on responsibilty from his captain while his reflection in the bathroom mirror accuses him of being an "Uncle Tom". He begins his leave with dullness and romantic failure but eventually finds love. However, interracial romance is not what his captain had in mind. Directed by Melvin Van Peebles (*Watermelon Man*).

VHS: Currently out of print. May be available for rental in some video stores.

Melvin Van Peebles, France, 1968, 87 mins.

Straight Out of Brooklyn

Downbeat and realistic, *Straight Out of Brooklyn*, shows the harsh life so often forced on inner city African-American youth. Dennis Brown has been raised in the projects of Brooklyn. His parents tell him to study hard and be patient, but he can't wait any longer. He and three of his friends plan a robbery that'll take them out of Brooklyn forever. His ill mother and alcoholic father add to the strain, as the ill-conceived plot to rob a drug runner slowly unfolds. In his first feature, 19-year-old Matty Rich directs without romanticizing crime and violence by pointing out the ultimate destruction that both can bring.

VHS: S15274. $19.98.

Matty Rich, USA, 1991, 83 mins.

Straight Out of Brooklyn
(The Samuel Goldwyn Company)

Street Wars

Jamaa Fanaka (*Penitentiary*) directs this tale about a violent struggle for power in the inner city. A high school student at an elite military school decides to avenge the murder of his drug lord brother and take over the business. He also vows to make the business legitimate—eventually.

VHS: S21392. $89.95.

Jamaa Fanaka, USA, 1994, 90 mins.

Sugar Hill

Wesley Snipes is one half of a two-brother Harlem crime syndicate. He is the half that wants out but is forced to remain. This is not simply an attempt to make the African-American *Godfather* but an effort to deal with the impetus to commit crime by basically decent people. It is also a statement about the near impossibility of walking away from a life of violence. Stars Michael Wright, Theresa Randle, Clarence Williams III and Ernie Hudson.

VHS: S21256. $96.98.

Leon Ichaso, USA, 1994, 123 mins.

Sweet Love, Bitter

Comedian Dick Gregory plays "Eagle" in this thinly disguised account of the last years in the life of Charlie "Bird" Parker. Richie "Eagle" Coles, a jazz saxophonist with a genius for friendship and self-destruction is the focus of the film. Artist Charles McPherson ghosts for Gregory on the score by Billie Holiday's pianist, Mal Waldron.

VHS: S15796. $59.95.

Herbert Danska, USA, 1966, 92 mins.

Sweet Perfection

Formerly titled *The Perfect Model*, this is the low-budget debut film of the talented Chicago director Darryl Roberts (*How U Like Me Now?*). A successful Black performer returns to his old neighborhood and falls in love with a beautiful and fiercely independent woman. She also has a younger brother in need of a male role model. This comic love story stars Stoney Jackson, Liza Cruzat and basketball player Reggie Theus.

VHS: S18835. $19.95.

Darryl Roberts, USA, 1989, 90 mins.

T Bone N Weasel

Gregory Hines and Christopher Lloyd are a pair of ne'er-do-wells in this road picture by B-movie director Lewis Teague (*Piranha*). Hines is just out of jail and Lloyd, as usual, is out of his mind as the two travel forlorn highways in pursuit of a better life. With Ned Beatty and Rip Torn. Cinematography by Thomas del Ruth. Jon Klein adapted his own play.

VHS: S18318. $89.98.

Lewis Teague, USA, 1992, 94 mins.

Talkin' Dirty After Dark

Martin Lawrence (*House Party*, Fox's *Martin*), is a struggling stand-up comedian looking to headline at "Dukies," a hot comedy venue. The owner's wife, Jedda Jones, enjoys his routines and attention, while owner John Witherspoon's eyes are set on shapely comedian Phyllis Stickney, who has his customers rolling in the aisles. The talk is definitely dirty. With Darryl Sivad, Renee Jones, Marvin Wright-Bey and Tiny Lister, Jr.

VHS: S16414. $14.95.
Laser: LD72277. $39.99.

Topper Carew, USA, 1991, 89 mins.

Tap

A film more about tap dancing and its history than Gregory Hines' character Max Washington. Washington is an ex-con and a tap dancer extraordinaire who must decide between using his talent or turning back to criminal activity. Features Sammy Davis, Jr. as "Little Mo" and a collection of tap legends like Sandman Simms and Harold Nicolas and the performing talents of Suzanne Douglas and Savion Glover. The dancing puts a great deal of joy and life into the film.

VHS: S08701. $89.95.

Nick Castle, Jr., USA, 1989, 111 mins.

They Live

John Carpenter's sci-fi thriller is about two men battling aliens who are systematically gaining control of the Earth. Wrestler Roddy Piper and Keith David (*The Thing, Platoon*) form the interracial "posse" out to destroy the creatures. Raymond St. Jacques appears as a blind preacher warning people about the invasion. The film is a comment on consumerism and divisiveness gone mad and a call for solidarity among working people against "creatures" oppressing them.

VHS: S10111. $89.95.

John Carpenter, USA, 1988, 95 mins.

To Sleep with Anger

Danny Glover stars as Harry Mention, a mysterious visitor from the deep South who comes to stay with his old friend, Gideon (Paul Butler), in South-Central Los Angeles. Harry seems to possess a malevolent power which disrupts Gideon's family both physically and spiritually. The outsider represents a link with the past and brings old ghosts back to life. He is full of folklore, lucky charms and tales of bad magic which all contribute to the thinly disguised unease. Charles Burnett (*Killer of Sheep, My Brother's Wedding*) directs a sensational cast, including Paul Butler and Mary Alice.

VHS: S13817. $19.95.
Laser: LD72255. $35.95.

Charles Burnett, USA, 1990, 105 mins.

The Toy

A flat-broke reporter must resort to becoming the "toy" of a rich millionaire's son. Richard Pryor portrays the "Toy" while Jackie Gleason is cast as the millionaire. Both turn in good performances but there is something offensive about the whole idea. It would have been more interesting had the two comedians switched roles.

VHS: S21474. $14.95.

Richard Donner, USA, 1982, 99 mins.

Trading Places

Eddie Murphy gives one of his best performances as a street hustler who is switched with preppie Dan Aykroyd. Set in Philadelphia, the film is a natural comic vehicle for Murphy. With Don Ameche, Jamie Lee Curtis, Ralph Bellamy and Denholm Elliott.

VHS: S02175. $19.95.

John Landis, USA, 1983, 116 mins.

To Sleep with Anger
(The Samuel
Goldwyn Company)

Trespass

Bill Paxton and William Sadler try to escape from a Black drug gang in an East St. Louis factory. Crack kingpin Ice-T faces off against Ice Cube in a complicated plot that uses a rap soundtrack, video, and much gratuitous violence.

VHS: S21490. $94.98.

Walter Hill, USA, 1992, 101 mins.

True Identity

Lenny Henry is cast as a struggling American actor who resorts to passing as a white hitman when he learns the secret mob past of a prominent citizen. Frank Langella (*Dracula*) orders a hit on the New York actor not knowing he has been thoroughly disguised by *Sidewalk Stories* director Charles Lane who plays his best buddy and is a theatrical make-up whiz. Henry's two main goals are to stay alive and to make it to his audition for *Othello* (out of "whiteface"). With J.T. Walsh, Anne-Marie Johnson, Michael McKean, Peggy Lipton and James Earl Jones as himself.

VHS: S16807. $19.99.

Charles Lane, USA, 1991, 93 mins.

Uncle Tom's Cabin

Star Trek: Deep Space Nine's Avery Brooks stars with Bruce Dern in this retooled version of Harriet Beecher Stowe's novel. The cast also includes Felicia Rashad and Edward Woodward as the evil Simon Legree. An interesting contrast with earlier (especially silent) versions which seem to indicate that, except for men like Legree, slavery wasn't all that bad. Here there are no qualifications or apologies for the "institution".

VHS: S19683. $9.98.

Stan Latham, USA, 1987, 110 mins.

Under the Cherry Moon

Prince stars in and directs this story of a musical gigolo on the French Riviera. His questionable lifestyle is altered when he unexpectedly falls in love with a beautiful heiress. Unfortunately her father does not approve. The music is, of course, by Prince.

VHS: S01816. $19.98.

Prince, USA, 1986, 80 mins.

Uptown Saturday Night

Sidney Poitier and Bill Cosby are cheated out of a $50,000 lottery ticket. To get the ticket back they turn to a Black gangster (Harry Belafonte) who bears a striking resemblence to Don Corleone. This comedy's supporting cast includes Lincoln Kirkpatrick, Roscoe Lee Browne, Richard Pryor, Flip Wilson and Calvin Lockhart.

VHS: S21435. $19.98.

Sidney Poitier, USA, 1974, 104 mins.

Voices of Sarafina!

This Tony-Award nominated musical concerns a South African high school class who create their own play about Nelson Mandela. Part documentary and part Broadway show, the energy is infectious and the songs touch the soul. The musical was later made into a film starring Whoopi Goldberg. The music is by Mbogeni Ngema and Hugh Masekela. Cast includes Miriam Makeba, Leleti Khumalo, Pat Miaba and Baby Cele.

VHS: S13315. $39.95.

Nigel Noble, USA, 1988, 90 mins.

The Waterdance

Overtly this is the story of a crippled writer recuperating in a hospital and his relationship with a married woman. The film also has an alternate plot of the relationship between two other patients, William Forsyth, an apparent racist, and Wesley Snipes, a ne'er-do-well attempting to straighten out his family life after he has been paralyzed. The men begin their relationship as enemies but eventually come together as a result of their shared situation. Forsyth and Snipes steal the film.

VHS: S18116. $92.95.
Laser: LD71843. $34.95.

Neal Jimenez/Michael Steinberg, USA, 1991, 110 mins.

Watermelon Man

A white bigot turns Black and has to deal with every racist's worst night-mare—he has become a "Watermelon Man". Directed by Melvin Van Peebles this is not a remake of *Black Like Me* (where the white man intentionally becomes Black). The metamorphosis here is forced, not voluntary. A change of skin color would, regrettably, change a person's life. Godfrey Cambridge and Estelle Parsons star.

VHS: S04321. $59.95.

Melvin Van Peebles, USA, 1970, 97 mins.

What's Love Got to Do With It?

Based on the autobiography of pop diva Tina Turner, this film follows her rise to stardom. It includes the controversial portrayal of her tempestuous marriage to abusive Ike Turner, and her remarkable comeback. Starring Angela Bassett and Larry Fishburne.

VHS: S20607. $96.95.
Laser: LD74456. $39.99.

Brian Gibson, USA, 1993, 118 mins.

White Men Can't Jump

Wesley Snipes and Woody Harrelson team up as a couple of hustlers who prey on pick-up basketball players who assume that white men can't jump. The film is a fast paced comedy with fine performances from Snipes and Rosie Perez as Harrelson's girlfriend. Features Tyra Ferrell, Cylk Cozart and Kadeem Hardison.

VHS: S21443. $19.98.

Ron Shelton, USA, 1992, 115 mins.

The Wilby Conspiracy

This anti-apartheid action adventure stars Sidney Poitier as Shack Twala, a Bantu revolutionary smuggling diamonds to further the struggle against apartheid. Michael Caine plays Poitier's reluctant assistant. With Persis Khambatta, Rutger Hauer, Prunella Gee and Nicol Williamson as the determined pursuer, Major Horn.

VHS: S06064. $14.95.

Ralph Nelson, USA, 1975, 105 mins.

Wild Style

This musical with style and attitude is a rumination on hip hop, street art, break dancing and rap music. The plot follows the romantic passion of Zoro (Lee Quinones), a South Bronx artist caught up in a turbulent romance with Pink (Sandra Fabara), the queen of the underground graffiti movement. Fab Five Freddy is a playfully hip impresario. With musical performances by D.J.'s Grand Master Flash, Grand Wizard Theodore, Grand Master Caz and The Cold Crush. The cast includes Patti Astor and Busy Bee.

VHS: S01463. $34.95.

Charlie Ahearn, USA, 1982, 82 mins.

The Wiz

Diana Ross takes over for Judy Garland as Dorothy in this updated version of the L. Frank Baum book. Originally a Broadway play, it translates well to the screen. The plot is the same but the music is different. Dorothy, in this version, is a Harlem school teacher taken to an Oz that is an idyllic version of New York. With Michael Jackson, Nipsey Russell and Lena Horne.

VHS: S05098. $19.98.

Sidney Lumet, USA, 1978, 133 mins.

A Woman Called Moses

This is the story of Harriet Ross Tubman, founder of the Underground Railroad, who led hundreds of slaves to freedom in the North before the Civil War. To those she helped she became known as "Moses". Cicely Tyson is brilliant in the role of Tubman.

VHS: S16561. $89.95.

Paul Wendkos, USA, 1978, 200 mins.

The Women of Brewster Place

Donna Deitch (*Desert Hearts*) directed this potent drama about a group of women (Oprah Winfrey, Cicely Tyson, Robin Givens, Jackee Kelly, Paula Kelly) who work together to get out of the ghetto. 2 cassettes.

VHS: S11588. $19.98.

Donna Deitch, USA, 1989, 180 mins.

Zebrahead

A tough Jewish high school student, Zack, falls for the wrong girl, a free spirited African-American from Brooklyn. The romance is doomed by external pressures as both teens are forced to confront the unfortunate role race can play in romance. Anthony Drazen's first film was shot in Detroit and features fine performances from N'Bushe Wright and Michael Rappaport as the young lovers. With De Shon Castle, Ron Johnson and Ray Sharkey. Music by Taj Mahal.

VHS: S18871. $94.96.

Anthony Drazen, USA, 1991, 100 mins.

Zora Is My Name!

From PBS' American Playhouse comes this funny yet stirring drama starring Ruby Dee and Louis Gossett, Jr. This is the story of Zora Neale Hurston, a Black writer and folklorist best known for her portrayals of life in the rural South of the 30s and 40s. USA, 1990, 90 mins.

VHS: S12941. $24.95.
Laser: LD71400. $39.95.

Blaxploitation Films

Avenging Disco Godfather

Rudy Ray Moore is the "Disco Godfather" in this send-up of gangster films. The film, as with most of Moore's efforts, is a mix of comedy, kung-fu, and disco music. Features Lady Reed and Carol Speed.

VHS: Currently out of print. May be available for rental in some video stores.

Rudy Ray Moore, USA, 1976, 93 mins.

Black Belt Jones

Jim Kelly, featured as one of the heroes in Bruce Lee's *Enter the Dragon*, is the star of this karate/blaxploitation film. The Mafia threatens a Watts-based self-defense school and someone has to save the day. With Gloria Hendry, Scatman Crothers, Alan Weeks and Nate Esformes.

VHS: S18928. $19.98.

Robert Clouse, USA, 1974, 87 mins.

Black Caesar

Larry Cohen directed and Fred Williamson (*M*A*S*H*, *The Legend of Nigger Charley*) stars in this inner-city gangster drama which chronicles the spectacular rise of its ambitious anti-hero. Williamson portrays an organized crime lord bent on getting his share of the profit coming from the ghetto. The film is vintage, violent blaxploitation. With Art Lund, Julius W. Harris, Gloria Hendry and D'Urville Martin.

VHS: S18929. $19.98.

Larry Cohen, USA, 1973, 96 mins.

Black Gestapo

A Black army takes over the ghetto. In the begining their aim is to help the citizens but they wind up as the oppressors. The film is a violent, crazed morality tale in which power corrupts absolutely. Features Rod Perry, Charles P. Robinson (*Night Court*), Phil Hoover and Ed Gross. USA, 1975, 89 mins.

VHS: S21462. $19.95.

The Black Godfather

Black revolutionaries come together to fight a white organized crime syndicate intent upon infecting the community with drugs and violence. Typical in many ways of the blaxploitation films of the 70s, there is plenty of violence and the bad guys lose. Jimmmy Witherspoon stars in a Penthouse production.

VHS: S18813. $29.95.

John Evans, USA, 1974, 100 mins.

Black Sister's Revenge

A Mississippi farm girl makes a move to Los Angeles and inadvertently begins a love affair with a hustler. When her new beau is arrested she has to make a number of difficult decisions. Stars Jerri Hayes and Ernest Williams II.

VHS: S18814. $19.95.

Jamaa Fanaka, USA, 1976, 100 mins.

Black Vengeance

A young singer is caught in a bizarre love triangle with the owners of a remote motel. Leslie Uggams is the charismatic singer. Her supporting cast includes Slim Pickens, Ted Cassidy, and Dub Taylor.

VHS: S18815. $29.95.

Richard Robinson, USA, 1989, 90 mins.

Bucktown

Fred Williamson and Pam Grier star in this story of a man returning to his hometown to find that all is not well. He arrives to bury his brother and winds up burying a number of others as well. Grier plays Aretha, the woman who helps him put the screws to the gang that has terrorized the town.

VHS: S21397. $59.98.

Arthur Marks, USA, 1975, 95 mins.

Cleopatra Jones

Tamara Dobson portrays Cleopatra Jones, a CIA agent/martial arts expert who uses her skills to battle a brutal gang of drug dealers. Dobson's charisma along with a quick pace make this an enjoyable action picture. With Shelley Winters, Bernie Casey, Brenda Sykes and the ubiquitous Antonio Fargas.

VHS: S18927. $19.98.

Jack Starrett, USA, 1973, 89 mins.

Cleopatra Jones and the Casino of Gold

Blaxploitation dramas often revolve around revenge, and this sequel to *Cleopatra Jones* is no exception. Like its predecessors, the film presents a battle against a powerful drug dealer. Set in Hong Kong, it features a wonderfully over-the-top performance by Stella Stevens as "The Dragon Lady". Stars Tamara Dobson as the beautiful CIA-agent Cleopatra Jones. With Tanny, Albert Popwell, Caro Kenyatta and Christopher Hunt.

VHS: S18926. $19.98.

Chuck Bail, USA, 1975, 96 mins.

Coffy

Pam Grier is Coffy, a nurse with vengeance on her mind. Her sister has become a junkie and those responsible will have to pay. *Coffy* was Grier's biggest hit and it features plenty of violence. It was classified as blaxploitation, but if the characters were white, it could easily pass for *Death Wish*. With Allen Arbus, Sid Haig, Bob Minor, Booker Bradshaw and Robert Do Qui as King George.

VHS: S07451. $19.98.

Jack Hill, USA, 1973, 91 mins.

Disco Godfather

Rudy Ray Moore mixes martial arts, rap and of course, disco in this action film. Moore portrays the owner of a disco out to topple the nation's largest producer of angel dust. USA, 93 mins.

VHS: S21461. $29.95.

Dolemite

Rudy Ray Moore (*Disco Godfather*, *Rude*) stars in this blend of karate, comedy and gangster film elements. Moore's most recognizable role as an avenging hero. With Jerry Jones and Lady Reed.

VHS: S18810. $19.95.

D'Urville Martin, USA, 1975, 88 mins.

Dolemite 2: The Human Tornado

Rudy Ray Moore's sequel to *Dolemite* is another look at the underside of disco nightlife. Moore is once again the avenging hero. Plenty of violence included.

VHS: S18823. $19.95.

Cliff Roquemore, USA, 1976, 85 mins.

Fass Black

A disco owner gets a little hot under the collar when the mob tries to move in on his night spot. Violence and music ensue in this disco-era gangster film. Music by soul artist Johnnie Taylor. Starring John Poole and Jeanne Bell.

VHS: S18819. $14.95.

D'Urville Martin, USA, 1977, 105 mins.

Foxy Brown

Pam Grier's undercover cop boyfriend is murdered by drug dealers. Naturally someone is going to pay—especially since the killers had the effrontery to do the killing on her front porch! Violence and revenge are the result with some of the bad guys losing more than their lives. Antonio Fargas plays Grier's drug dealing brother. Also featuring Terry Carter, Juanita Brown, Sid Haig, Bob Minor and Peter Brown.

VHS: S07449. $19.98.

Jack Hill, USA, 1974, 91 mins.

Friday Foster

Pam Grier is Friday Foster, a photo journalist who discovers a plot to assassinate Black politicians. Her character is based on the *Chicago Tribune* comic strip and features a bit less violence than usual. The cast includes Yaphet Kotto, Thalmus Rasulala, Eartha Kitt, Godfrey Cambridge, Scatman Crothers, Ted Lange and Jim Backus as Enos Griffith, the evil mobster pulling the strings of death.

VHS: S07447. $59.98.

Arthur Marks, USA, 1975, 89 mins.

Get Christie Love

Teresa Graves, a *Laugh-In* alumna, is the star of this blaxploitation film which revolves around bringing a drug empire to its knees. Plenty of hot pants and lots of action. Features Harry Guardino, Louise Sorel and Paul Stevens.

VHS: S18811. $19.95.

William A. Graham, USA, 1974, 100 mins.

The Guy from Harlem

A Black private eye from Harlem is on the case and he's not happy about it. Harlem's seamy underside, its atmospheric streets and dangerous environment form the setting of this violent and chilling film.

VHS: S18821. $14.95.

Rene Martinez, Jr., USA, 1977, 86 mins.

Joshua

Former football player Fred Williamson (*M*A*S*H*, *The Legend of Nigger Charley*) stars as a peace-loving man driven to revenge after the vicious murder of his mother. Originally titled *The Black Rider* and part of the last wave of blaxploitation films, *Joshua* is part western and part vigilante flick. With Isela Vega, Brenda Venus and Stacy Newton.

VHS: S18139. $19.95.

Larry Spangler, USA, 1976, 75 mins.

Mack

One of the most popular (and one of the most violent) blaxploitation films made, *Mack* is the story of a Black pimp in Oakland. With Max Julien, Don Gordon, Richard Pryor, Carol Speed, Roger E. Mosley.

Michael Campus, USA, 1973, 110 mins.

Monkey Hustle

The ghetto is facing the wrecking ball to make way for a super highway. The good folks of the neighborhood get together with the underworld to stop the destruction. Shot in Chicago, the film stars Yaphet Kotto (*Alien*, *Friday Foster*) and Rudy Ray Moore (*Dolemite*, *Rude*)

VHS: S13766. $59.98.

Arthur Marks, USA, 1977, 90 mins.

Penitentiary

The first and best of Jamaa Fanaka's *Penitentiary* films is the story of Too Sweet, a prisoner trying to gain early release by joining the prison boxing team. He is foiled by his nemesis, Jesse Amos (Donovan Womack), who wins the title and also kills Too Sweet's best friend. The film ends as Amos meets Too Sweet's challenge to a fight to the finish.

VHS: S07524. $59.95.

Jamaa Fanaka, USA, 1979, 99 mins.

Penitentiary II

A falsely accused man, Too Sweet (Leon Isaac Kennedy), is sent back to the penitentiary where he must once again use his boxing prowess to survive. The same facility unfortunately also houses the man who killed his girlfriend. Revenge is in the air. With Mr. T., Glynn Turman, Ernie Hudson and Malik Carter.

VHS: S18828. $14.95.

Jamaa Fanaka, USA, 1982, 103 mins.

Penitentiary III

While still exciting, this third part of the series begins to make the audience yearn for an early release for Too Sweet. Less a social commentary than a *Rocky* in prison, this film still offers a good deal of action. Leon Isaac Kennedy returns.

VHS: S21466. $14.98.

Jamaa Fanaka, USA, 1987, 91 mins.

Petey Wheatstraw

An African-American folktale is retold by Dolemite himself, Rudy Ray Moore. The story is about a man so useless that he cuts a deal with Satan himself— he has to marry the devil's ugly daughter. USA, 93 mins.

VHS: S21460. $29.95.

The Return of Superfly

Curtis Mayfield and Ice-T provide the music for this third sequel to *Superfly*. The plot revolves around Superfly and his Harlem exploits—hassling drug dealers and avoiding the cops. Features Margaret Avery, Nathan Purdee and Sam Jackson.

VHS: S21464. $14.95.

Sig Shore, USA, 1990, 94 mins.

Scream, Blacula, Scream

Pam Grier isn't a vigilante out for justice this time around. Here she plays Lisa, a voodoo princess out to convince Black vampire, Manuwalde, to stop bleeding dry the Black community in Los Angeles. Set in both California and Africa, the film is a sequel to the popular *Blacula*. Features Richard Lawson, Don Mitchell, Lynn Moody and Michael Conrad as the Sheriff.

VHS: S07450. $59.98.

Bob Kelljan, USA, 1973, 95 mins.

Shaft

Richard Roundtree stars as a Black private detective on the trail of kidnappers. The film portrays Roundtree as a self-assured tough guy hired by a Harlem organized crime figure (Moses Gunn) to find his abducted daughter. Shaft calls on Black revolutionaries to get the job done. Isaac Hayes won an Academy Award for the theme song.

VHS: S09159. $19.95.

Gordon Parks, USA, 1971, 98 mins.

Shaft's Big Score

Trouble is brewing over the numbers racket in Queens as various gangsters vie for control. Shaft, of course, is in the middle trying to solve the murder of a friend. The film is notable for a great New York City chase scene which involves just about every method of motorized transportation imaginable. With Richard Roundtree, Moses Gunn and Drew Bundini Brown.

VHS: S18480. $19.98.

Gordon Parks, USA, 1972, 104 mins.

Sheba, Baby

Pam Grier portrays Sheba, a woman determined to track down the men leaning on her father. Her detective work leads her to an underworld figure named Shark whom Sheba finds may be more than she can handle. Also starring Rudy Challenger, Austin Stoker, D'Urville Martin and Charles Kissinger.

VHS: S07448. $59.98.

William Girdler, USA, 1975, 90 mins.

Soul Vengeance

A Black man is arrested and brutalized for a crime he did not commit. Upon his release he is out for bloody vengeance. Plenty of platform shoes and dashikis.

VHS: S18833. $14.95.

Jamaa Fanaka, USA, 1975, 91 mins.

Space Is the Place

Sun Ra, avant-garde jazz keyboardist and arranger, returns from his interplanetary odyssey and both threatens and encourages young urban Blacks to believe he's the "alter destiny". He commands them to return to space with him. The film is part music, part blaxploitation. Ra's Intergalactic Arkestra perform their classics "Watusi", "Outer Spaceways Inc." and "The Satellites Are Spinning".

VHS: S19121. $24.95.

John Coney, USA, 1974, 63 mins.

Superfly

Ron O'Neal plays a rather curious hero in Gordon Parks, Jr.'s *Superfly*. He is a pimp and a drug dealer who defies the system and manages to leave his life of vice with a hefty retirement fund. Features Carl Lee, Julius Harris, Sheila Frazier and Charles McGregor. Curtis Mayfield provides the music.

VHS: S21465. $19.98.

Gordon Parks Jr., USA, 1972, 98 mins.

Superfly TNT

This sequel finds Superfly in Europe fighting for the independence of Africa. An arms dealer, the suave Roscoe Lee Browne, enlists the ex-hustler to overthrow a brutal dictatorship. This film is the very definition of blaxploitation. Features Sheila Frazier from *Superfly* and Robert Guillaume.

VHS: S21475. $14.95.

Ron O'Neal, USA, 1973, 87 mins.

Space is the Place
(Rhapsody Films, Inc.)

Super Soul Brother

A socially conscious comedy about a classic underachiever who ingests a strange potion that endows him with supernatural gifts. These gifts are put to use in a criminal enterprise with comic results. 1989, 80 mins.

VHS: S18834. $14.95.

Sweet Sweetback's Baadasssss Song

A ghetto orphan, raised in a whorehouse, is forced to flee for his freedom after he kills two white policemen whom he catches beating a young Black man. The film is extremely violent and filled with considerable sexual stereotypes but it is a first-rate action film which looks at an African-American coming to terms with both his rage and his community. Features Simon Chuckster, Hubert Scales, John Dullaghan and John Amos.

VHS: S06195. $59.95.

Melvin Van Peebles, USA, 1971, 90 mins.

Urban Jungle

Part of the new wave of films resembling 70s blaxploitation pictures, it tells the story of a ruthless Housing Commisssioner who forces the poor out into the streets in order to make a quick buck. Somehow this all relates to S & M and drug-dealing priests. The heroes of this picture are a couple of two-bit drug merchants who decide to help the community instead of poison it. Their help, however, is brutal violence.

VHS: S21467. $79.95.

Daniel Matmor, USA, 1994, 90 mins.

Foreign Feature Films

An African Dream

An English school teacher moves to South Africa in 1906 and befriends an African man. Naturally the local white community sees this as subversive and the rumors fly until things get out of hand. Set in the tense decade following the Second Boer War between England and the Afrikaaners, the paranoia and hostility left from the war rings true. With John Kani, Dominic Jephcott, John Carson, Richard Haines, Joy Stewart and Lyn Hooker.

VHS: S12539. $14.95.

John Smallcombe, Great Britain, 1990, 94 mins.

Black and White in Color

Colonial West Africa during World War I is the setting for this comedy by Jean-Jacques Annaud. In the absence of military advice local French residents plan an assault on a German outpost. The film shows World War I in microcosm as trenches are dug and little is done. The treatment of Africans in the film shows how they were used by Europeans. Thousands died in World War I defending colonial masters in a war which meant nothing to them. French with English subtitles.

VHS: S06211. $39.95.

Jean-Jacques Annaud, France, 1977, 88 mins.

Black Orpheus

In this adaptation of the Greek myth of *Orpheus and Eurydice*, Orpheus is a streetcar conductor while Eurydice is a young woman fleeing a murderer. Set during Carnival in Rio de Janeiro, the film mixes the love story with the celebration. American dancer Marpessa Dawn is Eurydice. The film was honored with an Oscar for Best Foreign Film and also won the Grand Prize at Cannes. In Portuguese with English subtitles.

VHS: S00138. $29.95.
Laser: LD70346. $79.95.

Marcel Camus, Brazil, 1958, 103 mins.

Chocolat

A young French woman recalls her youth in French Cameroon. Her mother and a Black servant are involved in a veiled sexual game of "cat and mouse" of which her father, a colonial officer, is unaware. The film depicts the isolation and boredom of the Europeans in the midst of a culture where they did not belong.

VHS: S11534. $79.98.
Laser: LD70916. $49.95.

Claire Denis, France, 1988, 105 mins.

City of Blood

An ancient myth about a murderous spirit which comes to modern South Africa. The weapon of choice is a spiked club. An investigating coroner tracks the vengeful spirit on its trail of destruction. The film is a mixture of traditional folk tale and modern detective drama.

VHS: Currently out of print. May be available for rental in some video stores.

Darrell Roodt, South Africa, 1987, 100 mins.

Coup De Torchon (Clean Slate)

Set in colonial West Africa and dealing primarily with the corruption and decadence of resident Europeans, this film revolves around a harrassed police chief. Phillipe Noiret is the commissar who moves from corrupt dunce to vicious killer as his wife cheats on him, his colleagues ridicule him and a pair of unfortunate pimps taunt him. French with English subtitles.

VHS: Currently out of print. May be available for rental in some video stores.

Bertrand Tavernier, France, 1981, 128 mins.

Cry, the Beloved Country

South African minister/author Alan Paton's book about the racism, poverty and inhumanity of apartheid tells the story of an aging country minister looking for his son in Johannesburg. He is shocked and depressed by the sordid and impoverished surroundings. Unable to find any help, a young priest (Sidney Poitier) befriends him and assists him in his search. Canada Lee, of Hitchcock's *Lifeboat* and Rossens' *Body and Soul* is the old minister in a tour-de-force performance.

VHS: S14783. $69.95.

Zoltan Korda, Great Britain, 1951, 111 mins.

Cry, The Beloved Country
(Monterey Movie Company)

The Crying Game

Forest Whitaker, a British soldier captured by the I.R.A., asks Stephen Rea, one of his captors, to check up on his "girlfriend", Jaye Davidson. A film about deception, terrorism and love from Irish director Neil Jordan (*Mona Lisa*). Winner of an Academy award for Best Original Screenplay.

VHS: S18749. $19.98.

Neil Jordan, Great Britain, 1992, 112 mins.

Dark City

A soldier fighting apartheid is captured and tortured. Yet even under threat of pain and death he will not compromise. Shot in Zimbabwe with a cast drawn primarily from Johannesburg's Market Theatre, this film takes the brutality and injustice of apartheid and places it on a one-to-one basis. There are no abstract "oppressed masses" but one single human being who is the victim of the system. This premise makes the racist system all the more repulsive.

VHS: S18062. $29.95.

Chris Curling, South Africa, 1990, 98 mins.

Dingaka

Filmed on location in South Africa, *Dingaka* deals with the differences between traditional African laws and the European laws imposed by the Afrikaaner/English rulers. A man, following tribal law, kills the murderer of his daughter and in turn is accused of murder under the laws of South Africa. A white lawyer must argue his case. An early, more serious film by James Uys, the director of *The Gods Must Be Crazy*.

VHS: S01779. $19.98.

Jamie Uys, Great Britain, 1965, 96 mins.

The French Way

Josephine Baker stars as a would-be matchmaker in one of her later film roles. Baker is a nightclub owner trying to reopen her club. In between her romantic meddling she performs a number of songs. French with English subtitles.

VHS: S01627. $34.95.

Jacques de Baroncelli, France, 1940, 72 mins.

The Gods Must Be Crazy

A light-hearted, if misleading, look at the !Kung people of Southern Africa. A bushman finds a Coke bottle which he believes has fallen from the gods and resolves to return it to them before the object tears his community apart. The simple bushman's encounters with modern men constitute most of the plot while a group of inept Communist revolutionaries provide the rest. The absolute isolation of the bushmen is exaggerated for comic effect.

VHS: S01704. $19.95.
Laser: LD71008. $34.98.

James Uys, South Africa, 1984, 109 mins.

The Gods Must Be Crazy II

In this sequel to the popular James Uys film, N!Xau the bushman discovers that his children have disappeared. Without his knowledge, they have been taken for a joy ride by a pair of poachers. In the search for his children he encounters a new troop of crazy white people and various not-too-understanding members of the animal kingdom. With Lena Farugia and Hans Strydom.

VHS: S14005. $19.95.

Jamie Uys, USA/Botswana, 1989, 90 mins.

*The Gods
Must Be Crazy*
(Twentieth Century-Fox)

Harder They Come

One of the best collections of reggae music ever put together makes this "rags to riches" film truly remarkable. A young man follows his dream of stardom to the city, winds up on the wrong side of the law and eventually comes out on top. The gritty realism of the film was played out in real life; one performer was killed by police and another was on death row by the time the film was released. The soundtrack features Toots and the Maytals, Desmond Decker and, of course, Jimmy Cliff. The first genuinely Jamaican film.

VHS: S00541. $19.95.
Laser: LD70753. $49.95.

Perry Henzell, Jamaica, 1973, 104 mins.

Kasarmu Ce: This Land Is Ours

A young man must avenge the murder of his grandfather and combat the attempts of a rich greedy interloper who wants to seize control of his village's land. A Nigerian film set in the area of the country inhabited by the Hausa, the film combines Hausa traditional storytelling with Western narrative. Cinematography by Peter Murphy. Screenplay by Saddik Balewa. Hausa with English subtitles.

VHS: S18889. $29.95.

Saddik Balewa, Nigeria, 1991, 84 mins.

Kitchen Toto

A film about the interracial friendship between a Kenyan houseboy, a "kitchen toto", and the son of the white policeman he serves. Their friendship begins during the mythical Mau Mau rebellion against the British. Written and directed by Kenyan resident Harry Hook. With Edwin Mahinda, Bob Peck, Phyllis Logan and Robert Urquhart.

VHS: S09800. $79.95.

Harry Hook, Kenya/Great Britain, 1987, 95 mins.

L'Etat Sauvage (The Savage State)

A white U.N. official returns to an African nation that has just become independent. The unstable nation is still suffering the ill effects of colonial rule. He finds that his wife is now living with a minister in the new government. All hints of equality vanish as a racial and sexual confrontation commences. With Jacques Dutronc, Marie-Christine Barrault and Michel Piccoli. French with English subtitles.

VHS: S14988. $59.95.
Laser: Widescreen. LD71610. $49.95.

Francis Girod, France, 1978, 111 mins.

Last Supper

A slave owner repents his past actions and seeks redemption. He "piously" instructs his slaves in the values of Christianity. Twelve of the slaves come together to re-enact the Last Supper as the immorality of their bondage is laid bare. Set in 18th century Cuba and directed by Tomas Gutierrez Alea. Spanish with English subtitles.

VHS: S12466. $69.95.

Tomas Gutierrez Alea, Cuba, 1976, 101 mins.

The Magic Garden
(The Pennywhistle Blues)

A South African musical with an all-Black cast, *The Magic Garden* follows the trail of stolen money which was intended for the church donation box. Everyone who comes in contact with the tainted money has a story to tell. Filmed in English, this film is even more bizarre when one considers the political climate and level of intolerance in South Africa in 1960.

VHS. S05482. $29.95.

Donald Swanson, South Africa, 1960, 63 mins.

Me Yu an' Mi Taxi

Jamaica's best comedians appear in this acclaimed comic production. Oliver Samuels, "the dean of Jamaican comedy", is featured. A truly riotous and hilarious effort. Jamaica, 1990, 106 mins.

VHS: S15331. $29.95.

Mona Lisa

Bob Hoskins is a working class, small time criminal who was apparently left holding the bag by his gangster boss (Michael Caine). Upon his release he expects to be taken care of and winds up chauffeuring a high priced prostitute (Kathy Tyson). Eventually he falls for her with disastrous results. With Robbie Coltrane and Clarke Peters.

VHS: Currently out of print. May be available for rental in some video stores.

Neil Jordan, Great Britain, 1986, 104 mins.

No Fear, No Die

An illegal cockfighting club is the center of this French film about two African immigrants. Both men supply fighting birds and train them for a club owner. Things become complicated when the boss' mistress becomes involved. From the director of *Chocolat*. French with English subtitles.

VHS: S20785. $79.95.

Claire Denis, France, 1993, 97 mins.

Notes for an African Orestes

Searching for non-actors to cast in Aeschylus' ancient play, *Orestes*, Pasolini analyzes East African culture. The Marxist filmmaker/poet was not preoccupied solely with historical accuracy but with artistic endeavor and its relationship to contemporary politics. Pasolini's interviews with African students and their opinions on where and when the film should be set are eye openers when contrasted with Pasolini's Eurocentrism. This film is a mix of history, personal search, documentary and fictional elements. Italian with English subtitles.

VHS: S09928. $39.95.

Pier Paolo Pasolini, Italy, 1970, 75 mins.

Obeah Wedding

An unlucky woman falls for a conniving Casanova whose only interests are either prurient or financial in this Jamaican drama. Starring Richard Mullings as Roy Sweetness and Leonie Samuels as Shirley. Jamaica, 1989, 100 mins.

VHS: S15333. $29.95.

Place of Weeping

A drama of one woman's personal fight for freedom. She must combat both the resentment of her own people and the system of apartheid. It's a film about individual action and responsibility in the face of oppression. Geini Mhlophe is the woman while James Whyle is the reporter who assists her.

VHS: S03037. $19.95.

Darrell Roodt, South Africa, 1986, 88 mins.

Playing Away

A team of primarily Black West Indians now living in the Brixton area is invited to play a cricket match in a small, very white village outside London. The occasion for the match is "Third World Week" and this satirical comedy-drama provides laughs and much food for thought about race relations in contemporary England. With Norman Beaton and Robert Urquhart.

VHS: S07171. $14.95.

Horace Ove, Great Britain, 1987, 100 mins.

Princess Tam Tam

Josephine Baker becomes the object of desire for a French author who has come to North Africa to write a novel. At first he is simply distracted from his work but he soon becomes fixated. Shot partially in Tunisia, this musical comedy allowed Baker to do more than simply "be erotic". She is a first-rate comedienne and actress. French with English subtitles.

VHS: S10867. $29.95.

Edmond Greville, France, 1935, 77 mins.

Quilombo

Exploited and abused slaves in northeastern Brazil leave their plantations and form Quilombo de Palmares—their own democratic nation in the jungle. The Portuguese authorities do not want a democratic refuge for slaves on their borders and they set out to crush the insurrection. Carlos Diegues

(*Xica*) directs this story of an early rebellion (set in the mid 1600s). Musical score by Gilberto Gil. With Antonio Pompeu, Toni Tornado, and the dazzling Zeze Motta as Dandara the temptress. Portuguese with English subtitles.

VHS: S14573. $79.95.

Carlos Diegues, Brazil, 1984, 114 mins.

Respectful Prostitute

A prostitute is coerced by a wealthy family to give false testimony at a murder trial. On trial is a senator's nephew accused of killing a Black man. The value of African-American life at the time in the South along with the corruption of the judicial process are both depicted. Screenplay by Jean-Paul Sartre.

VHS: S07458. $19.95.

Marcel Pagliero/Charles Brabant, France, 1952, 75 mins.

Round Midnight

A fading Black jazz musician travels to Paris in the late 1950s. His alcoholism and lethargy are counteracted by a French fan who prods him into musical action. Dexter Gordon, in an Academy Award-nominated performance, is the aging musician. Herbie Hancock won an Oscar for the score. English dialogue.

VHS: S03495. $19.98.
Laser: LD70669. $29.98.

Bertrand Tavernier, France, 1986, 132 mins.

Princess Tam Tam
(Kino International)

Shaka Zulu

Shaka was the Zulu leader who revolutionized warfare and political organization in Southern Africa. He introduced the stabbing spear which led to drastically increased battle casualties (usually among Shaka's foes). He introduced a strict Spartan style of military discipline and authoritarian rule. Unfortunately he was also responsible for causing what was referred to in the region as the "Mfecane" or "time of troubles". A largely historical, if partially mythological, telling of the life of this remarkable leader.

VHS: S03661. $14.99.

William C. Faure, Great Britain, 1983, 300 mins.

Quilombo
(New Yorker Films)

Sugar Cane Alley

A grandmother in Martinique sacrifices everything to bring happiness to her 11-year old grandchild. Both child and grandmother are difficult, shrewd and poverty stricken in the 1930s French colony. Euzhan Palcy (*A Dry White Season*) directs this breakthrough film. With Darling Legitimus, Garry Cadenat, Routa Seck and Joby Bernabe. French with English subtitles.

VHS: Currently out of print. May be available for rental in some video stores.

Euzhan Palcy, France/Martinique, 1984, 107 mins.

The Threepenny Opera

This film, adapted from the play by Bertolt Brecht, is perhaps a bit less grim than intended, but an entertaining musical nonetheless. The film is the story of petty criminal "Mackie" and his love affair with "Polly", another "street"

---

person. Their story is told against the backdrop of a world of thieves and swindlers. Sammy Davis, Jr. is the featured balladeer and makes the most of every second of screen time. The cast also includes Curt Jurgens (star of the interracial romance, *Tamango*). In English.

VHS: S14661. $29.95.

Wolfgang Staudte, Germany/France, 1962, 124 mins.

Uncle Tom's Cabin

Another adaptation of Harriet Beecher Stowe's controversial novel about social and racial conditions and Black enslavement in the pre-Civil War South. When Abraham Lincoln met Stowe, he reportedly told her, "So, you're the little lady who started this big war". With Herbert Lom as the nefarious Simon Legree.

VHS: S18836. $19.95.

Geza von Radvanyi, France/Germany/Yugoslavia/Italy, 1969, 113 mins.

A World of Strangers

Henning Carlsen's adaptation of Nobel prize winning writer Nadine Gordimer's novel demystifies official government reports and media representation to provide a frightening and kaleidoscopic portrait of the faces, events and personalities imprisoned under the iron-clad racial separation laws and fascist ideology of apartheid. It was shot surreptitiously on location in South Africa. The faces afflicted by apartheid become real and tangible. With Athol Fugard's frequent cinematic collaborator Zakes Mokae.

VHS: S17928. $59.95.

Henning Carlsen, South Africa, 1962, 89 mins.

Xica

Xica (Zeze Motta) is a beautiful Black slave who uses her sexual charm and intellect to reap the rewards of Brazil's economic boom in the 18th century. Diamonds, mined by slaves, made Brazil fantastically rich (and decadent). Xica ascends to the role of unofficial Empress, gleefully mocking her former masters while stockpiling newly found assets and power. A witty but thoughtful film from Carlos Diegues, Brazil's highly acclaimed director. Featuring Walmor Chagas, Jose Wilker, Marcus Vinicius and Altair Lima. Portuguese with English subtitles.

VHS: S19417. $79.95.

Carlos Diegues, Brazil, 1976, 109 mins.

The Young One

Spanish director Luis Buñuel deals with American racism in his only English language film. A jazz musician flees a bogus rape charge by boat and winds up on the islands off the Carolina coast. On the island are a racist gamekeeper and a beautiful, innocent girl. They are joined by a well meaning, if bigoted, minister and a violently racist boat captain. The men and girl grapple, literally and figuratively, over race and sex until at the end, various compromises—although not solutions—are found.

VHS: S19462. $59.95.

Luis Buñuel, USA/Mexico, 1960, 95 mins.

Zou Zou

A laundress steps in to take over for the leading player and saves the show. Josephine Baker is the laundress-turned-star and she makes the most of this vehicle built entirely around her. Jean Gabin, on the verge of international stardom, co-stars but like everyone else is overshadowed. Particularly unforgettable is Baker's rendition of "Haiti". French with English subtitles.

VHS: S10866. $29.95.

Marc Allegret, France, 1934, 92 mins.

Zulu Dawn

The battle of Islandwana was the single greatest defeat ever inflicted upon the British in Africa. Zulu leader, Cetswayo, tried to avoid battle at all costs knowing that even victory would bring ultimate defeat. Yet after continual provocation he was forced to act. British military formalities and incompetent command led to a massacre. The film follows historical fact closely and features an all-star cast including Peter O'Toole, Burt Lancaster, Bob Hoskins and Denholm Elliot.

VHS: S07363. $19.95.

Douglas Hickox, Great Britain, 1979, 121 mins.

Children's and Family Films

Aesop's Fables

Bill Cosby plays the master storyteller Aesop in this imaginative, freewheeling program that combines live action and animation. The program's featured story is the classic tale of *The Tortoise and the Hare*. USA, 1986, 30 mins.

VHS: S02514. $14.95.

African Story Magic

An urban child is exposed to the wonder and magic of traditional African folklore. Brock Peters narrates this tale of cultural awakening as legends and rituals are brought to life.

VHS: S17765. $12.98.

Peter Thurling, USA, 1992, 27 mins.

African Journey

A Canadian high school student's father takes a job with an African mining company. Initially angry with his father for leaving, the young man, Luke, finds himself in Africa on a visit. There he encounters Themba, the son of one of his father's colleagues. The two become friends despite the cultural differences that separate them. This is an adventure film about bridging ethnic differences. Two volume set. From the *Wonderworks* series originally aired on PBS.

VHS: S15785. $79.95.

George Bloomfield, USA, 1989, 174 mins.

Afro-Classic Folk Tales Vol. I

This collection of Afro-centered folk tales will promote positive self-affirming values among all children. Storyteller Sybil Destu narrates two traditional folk tales: an animated film about the spider, Anansi, and another about a tiger. USA, 1993, 30 mins.

VHS: S20620. $29.95.

Afro-Classic Folk Tales Vol. II

This second installment of Afro-Classic Folk Tales includes a "Brer Rabbit" and "Woodpecker" cartoon, as well as an old African tale told by puppets. 30 mins.

VHS: S20621. $29.95.

And the
Children Shall Lead
(Public Media, Inc.)

Afro-Classic Mother Goose

In this collection the favorite tales of Mother Goose find new expression with an Afro-centric twist. Playtime rhymes are updated in this fresh look at childhood stories. 30 mins.

VHS: S20622. $29.95.

Anansi

Reggae hit-makers UB40 and Oscar-winner Denzel Washington unite to recount the Jamaican tale of Anansi, the spider, who outwits a prideful snake and wins all stories for himself. In the end, Anansi gets caught in his own web of lies and loses his hair in the process. Illustrated by Steven Guarnaccia, written by Brian Gleeson. From the *Rabbit Ears: We All Have Tales* series. USA, 1991, 30 mins.

VHS: S14454. $9.95.

And the Children Shall Lead

A product of the Rainbow Television Workshop, this is the story of a young Black girl growing up during the Civil Rights movement. Set in Mississippi, the focus of the film is the role of children in the movement and its positive effect upon them. Featured actors include Danny Glover, LeVar Burton and Denise Nichols. From the *Wonderworks* series originally aired on PBS.

VHS: S12404. $29.95

Michael Pressman, USA, 1984, 58 mins.

Bebe's Kids

The late Robin Harris' (*Mo' Better Blues, House Party*) nightmare children are brought to life in this animated feature. The lead character is out for a day of romance but winds up stuck with *Bebe's Kids*. Features Faizon Love, Vanessa Bell Calloway, Wayne Collins, Jonell Green, Marques Houston, Tone-Loc and Nell Carter.

VHS: S21453. $92.95.

Bruce Smith, USA, 1992, 74 mins.

Bill Cosby's Picturepages: Numbers

Entertainer Bill Cosby uses his powers of authority and sublime skills as an educator and communicator to instruct children on numbers and number systems. The work features two activity books and a video in the package. USA, 1985, 30 mins.

VHS: S04517. $19.95.

Bill Cosby's Picturepages: Words and Letters

From Bill Cosby's award-winning *Picturepages*, this informative series from Rainbow Home Video uses imagination to teach children the fundamentals of words and letters. The materials include the video and two activity books. USA, 1985, 30 mins.

VHS: S04516. $19.95.

Brer Rabbit and the Wonderful Tar Baby

The comic adventures of that original American troublemaker, Brer Rabbit—Bugs Bunny's great grandfather—are bawdy, exuberant and inspired. They've become entwined in the fabric of children's storytelling. This animated adaptation is a classic, hilarious tale in which Brer outsmarts his wily nemesis, Brer Fox, with the aid of a clever invention he calls a "tar baby". Narrated by Danny Glover. USA, 1991, 30 mins.

VHS: S12475. $9.95.

Brer Rabbit and Boss Lion

Danny Glover narrates this animated installment in the *Rabbit Ears American Heroes & Legends* series. When the peaceful folk of Brer Village are threatened by mean old Boss Lion, it is up to Brer Rabbit to teach the troublemaker a powerful lesson in how to behave. Blues legend Dr. John supplies a down-home score full of gritty Bayou blues. For ages 5 and up. USA, 1992, 34 mins.

VHS: S16811. $9.95.

Brother Future

T.J. has some trouble with the law. While trying to escape from the Detroit Police he is knocked out and transported back to 1822 in the city of Charleston. There he is a slave and learns a valuable lesson about the responsibilities of freedom and what it takes to become truly free. From the *Wonderworks* series originally aired on PBS.

VHS: S15786. $29.95

Roy Campanella II, USA, 1991, 116 mins.

Dreadlocks and the Three Bears

The classic tale "Goldilocks and the Three Bears" is transformed into an essay about identity, heritage and roots. Director Alile Sharon Larkin draws on the works of collage artists Leo Lionni, Romare Bearden and Varnette Honeywood to re-imagine the story of Dreadlocks, who finds herself in the home of the Three Bears, in Teddy Bear Forest. Written and illustrated by Larkin.

VHS: S18327. $14.95.

Amandillo Cousin, USA, 1992, 13 mins.

Ed & Chester Bible Stories

Selected Bible stories come to life with these puppet plays by talented African-American puppeteer Ed Winters. USA, 30 mins.

VHS: S20624. $29.95.

Brother Future
(Public Media, Inc.)

Ed & Chester Show

Puppet plays and skits by Ed Winters illustrate delightful tales that instruct and teach African-American values. USA, 1992, 55 mins.

VHS: S20623. $29.95.

Follow the Drinking Gourd

Subtitled *A Story of the Underground Railroad*, Morgan Freeman narrates this absorbing and moving tale adapted from the folksong about one family's bid for freedom, achieved through the Underground Railroad. The gritty blues score is by Taj Mahal. Illustrated by Yvonne Buchanan and written by Bernardine Connelly. From the award-winning *Rabbit Ears* series. USA, 1992, 30 mins.

VHS: S17888. $9.95.

Free to Be...You and Me

Marlo Thomas, Alan Alda, Harry Belafonte, Dick Cavett, Mel Brooks, Dustin Hoffman, Roberta Flack, Kris Kristofferson are all part of this joyous spectacle, which uses song, stories and poetry to help children realize their goals and desires. Through this video they will learn to express themselves and be who they are.

VHS: S00464. $14.98.

Marlo Thomas, USA, 1974, 44 mins.

The Gift of Amazing Grace

Tempestt Bledsoe is the only member of a gospel singing family who can't sing. But the former Cosby Show star is able to bring her family back together when things go wrong. USA, 48 mins.

VHS: S16581. $9.98.

The House of Dies Drear

Howard Rollins (*A Soldier's Story*, *Ragtime*) stars as the head of a family that has just moved to a new house. Unfortunately the house is haunted by the ghost of an abolitionist who transports the family back to the days of slavery. Gloria Foster and Moses Gunn also star in this African-American ghost story. From the *Wonderworks* series originally aired on PBS.

VHS: S14484. $29.95.

Allan Goldstein, USA, 1988, 116 mins.

How the Leopard Got His Spots

This program tells the tale from Kipling's *Just So Stories* about how a yellowish brown leopard learned to adapt to new surroundings. Danny Glover narrates this animated folk tale. From the *Rabbit Ears: We All Have Tales* series. USA, 1984, 30 mins.

VHS: S09506. $14.95.

Human Race Club: A Story About Making Friends/A Story About Prejudice and Discrimination

From Joy Berry's animated series. Children are instructed on the cruel lessons and blatant unfairness of discrimination and prejudice, as well as the joys of friendship in the animated stories *The Fair Weather Friend* and *The Unforgettable Pen Pal*.

VHS: S10989. $29.95.

Joy Berry, USA, 1989, 60 mins.

Jazz Time Tale

A young girl undergoes a social and personal transformation following her encounter with the legendary piano player Fats Waller. Narrated by Ruby Dee. Illustrated by Barry Jackson and written by Brad Kessler.

VHS: S17764. $9.98.

Michael Sporn, USA, 1992, 29 mins.

John Henry

Denzel Washington narrates this poetic tale about the physically imposing, tireless nation builder who single-handedly defeated the steam drill in a steel driving competition. Legendary blues performer B.B. King provides the score for this animated story. From the *Rabbit Ears: American Heroes and Legends* series. USA, 1993, 30 mins.

VHS: S17887. $9.95.

Koi and the Kola Nuts

Oscar-winner Whoopi Goldberg humorously retells this African folktale about the proud son of a chief who sets out to find his rightful place in the world. Grammy and Oscar-winning composer Herbie Hancock provides the score. Illustrated by Reynold Ruffins and written by Brian Gleeson. In Hi-Fi Stereo. From the *Rabbit Ears: We All Have Tales* series. USA, 1992, 30 mins.

VHS: S16549. $9.95.

The Mighty Pawns

A teacher tries to help the youth of the inner city in an unusual fashion. Generally the idealistic offer advancement through physical sport. In this case the means to the end is more cerebral; it is chess. A look at the excitement of the game and its positive influence. Winner of the Silver Plaque at the 1987 Chicago International Film Festival. From the *Wonderworks* series.

VHS: S13238. $29.95.

Eric Laneuville, USA, 1987, 60 mins.

Mr. Rogers: Music and Feelings

Aided by Ella Jenkins, Mr. Rogers explores the multiple moods, feelings and attitudes associated with music, with input from cellist Yo Yo Ma and the gang from the Neighborhood of Make-Believe. USA, 1986, 65 mins.

VHS: S05012. $19.98.

Puss 'n Boots

Gregory Hines portrays "The Master", a man with a magical cat (Ben Vereen). He courts and wins the favor of a beautiful woman. Features Alfre Woodard and Brock Peters. Part of the *Faerie Tale Theatre* series.

VHS: S02892. $14.98.

Robert Iscove, USA, 1984, 60 mins.

Roll of Thunder

Original watercolor and pastel illustrations highlight this award-winning adaptation of Mildred Taylor's Newberry Award-winning book based on her experiences growing up in a tightly knit Black family in Depression-era Mississippi. USA, 46 mins.

VHS: S07703. $119.00.

Runaway

Overwhelmed with guilt after the accidental death of a friend, a young man flees society. Blaming himself, he seeks a hiding place in the New York subway tunnels where he is helped by a disabled veteran (Charles Dutton). He is also assisted by a young waitress played by Jasmine Guy. Based on Felice Holman's novel *Slake's Limbo*. From the *Wonderworks* series aired on PBS.

VHS: S13237. $29.95.

Gilbert Moses, USA, 1989, 59 mins.

The Savior Is Born

Morgan Freeman gives a reading of the first Christmas, from the gospels of Matthew and Luke. It is beautifully illustrated by Robert Van Nuit, with music by the Christ Church Cathedral Choir of Oxford, England. From the *Rabbit Ears: Greatest Stories Ever Told Collection*. 1992, 30 mins.

VHS: S18002. $12.98.

Taking Care of Terrific

Melvin Van Peebles is cast as a street musician in this installment of the Wonderworks series. An imaginative teenager, her boyfriend, and a sheltered little boy team up to plan a joyous evening for several bag ladies. Their efforts do not work out as planned. With Joanne Vannicola and Jackie Burroughs. USA, 1988, 58 mins.

VHS: S15788. $29.95.

Tales From Africa (Central)

The works include *Old Man and Deer*, *The Origin of the Animals*, *The Law of Mapaki*, *Musar and His Parents*. From the series *Fairy Tales from Exotic Lands*. USA, 1981, 60 mins.

VHS: S06732. $29.95.

Runaway
(Public Media, Inc.)

Words by Heart

In the early 1900s, Lena Sills and her parents are the only Black people living in Bethel Springs, Missouri. The family exists as barely tolerated outcasts. Lena wins a Bible recitation contest at school and begins to question the treatment her family receives. Charlotte Rae and Robert Hooks star in this installment in the *Wonderworks* series.

VHS: S14482. $29.95.

Robert Thompson, USA, 1984, 116 mins.

Why the Sun and the Moon Live in the Sky

Adapted from the book by Elphinstone Dayrell, this animated video tells the Nigerian legend about the time when the Sun and Moon existed on land. When Water emerges—accompanied by people and animals—the Sun and Moon seek refuge in the sky. 1971, 11 mins.

VHS: S20003. $49.95.

You Must Remember This

Robert Guillaume is Uncle Buddy, a former independent filmmaker, who doubts the worth of his past work. But his niece will not let him forget his past so easily. She researches Black cinema and discovers that Uncle Buddy was a big part of history. She then tries to convince him to be proud of his past. Also starring Tim Reid (*WKRP in Cincinnati*), Vonetta McGee, Tyra Ferrell and Vonte Sweet. From the *Wonderworks* series originally aired on PBS.

VHS: S16011. $29.95.

Helaine Head, USA, 1992, 110 mins.

Non-Fiction Films

African-American Art: Past and Present

A comprehensive survey of African-American art, with more than 65 artists represented, this program is divided into three parts: *African Art, 18th and 19th Century Fine Art Survey* and *20th Century Fine Art Survey: In the Artist's Words*. Three volume set. USA, 1992, 90 mins.

VHS: S20319. $199.00.

Always for Pleasure

New Orleans is the background for this high-spirited documentary. A "jazz funeral", Mardi Gras celebrations, St. Patrick's Day parades and revivals of Black/Indian traditions are all explored by innovative filmmaker Les Blank in this look at the traditions of a great Southern city and its African-American heritage.

VHS: S00040. $49.95.

Les Blank, USA, 1978, 58 mins.

Amos 'n' Andy: Anatomy of a Controversy

Reviled as racist and rarely seen today, *Amos 'n' Andy* was a popular radio and television program. This is the first authorized look at the show and its cast. Clips from the television show, some never before seen, are combined with interviews with Redd Foxx, Marla Gibbs and others. USA, 1983, 60 mins.

VHS: Currently out of print. May be available for rental in some video stores.

Anatomy of a Riot

This video looks at the roots of the Los Angeles riots in the aftermath of the first Rodney King trial. The program offers video accounts and interviews with people who witnessed the violence. USA, 1992, 47 mins.

VHS: S20422. $19.98.

Anderson Platoon

Joseph B. Anderson, a Black West Point educated lieutenant, leads a combat unit during the Vietnam War. Young men from different backgrounds are thrown together and made dependent upon one another for survival. Their anger and fear show the strain of combat on both the individual soldier and the group. Scenes depicting something as simple as a meal have great significance when considered in light of the possibility of sudden death which could occur at literally any moment. Director Pierre Schoendoerffer won an Academy Award for Best Documentary of 1967.

VHS: S02404. $39.95.

Pierre Schoendorffer, France, 1967, 65 mins.

Benjamin E. Mays: Mentor of Martin Luther King, Jr.

This famous author, scholar and philosopher was president of Morehouse College for 27 years. His important influence as an educator and community member was felt by many including Martin Luther King, Jr. and former President Jimmy Carter. In this documentary the lasting legacy of this great role model is revealed.

VHS: S20746. $19.95.

Rex Barnett, USA, 20 mins.

Benjamin O. Davis, Jr.: American

The Tuskegee airmen were a group of African-American aviators who distinguished themselves in combat during World War II and after the war as well. General Benjamin O. Davis founded the unit and is the subject of this documentary. He was also the first African-American to graduate from West Point in this century.

VHS: S18445. $19.95.

Felix C. Lowe, USA, 1991, 60 mins.

Bento

A young African-Brazilian leaves his country home to start over in a poor neighborhood in the big city of Sao Paolo. Disadvantages outweigh the opportunities for a young, poor, Black Brazilian to be successful. Bento is determined to make life better for himself and his neighbors in an environment where life is a daily struggle to survive. Produced by Maryknoll Media. 14 mins.

VHS: S10838. $24.95.

Benjamin E. Mays: Mentor of Martin Luther King Jr.
(History on Video)

Betye and Alison Saar

African-American mother and daughter artists, Betye and Alison Saar, are the focus of this tape. Betye is a mixed media artist frequently using "found" objects in her art. Alison is a sculptor whose work is done largely in wood. USA, 30 mins.

VHS: S21456. $49.95.

Beyond Hate Trilogy: Beyond Hate

Beyond Hate examines both the hated and the haters. Guests include Nobel Prize winners Elie Wiesel and Nelson Mandela as well as former U.S. President Jimmy Carter and Czech President and playwright, Vaclav Havel. Also interviewed are perpetrators and victims of what have come to be called "hate crimes". The program tries to analyze the need to hate and the effect it has upon those at whom it is directed. Bill Moyers conducts the interviews.

VHS: S14285. $39.95.

Catherine Tatgel/Dominique Lasseur, USA, 1992, 90 mins.

Beyond Hate Trilogy: Hate on Trial

Bill Moyers reports on the 1990 trial of hatemongers Tom and John Metzger, who were charged with inciting the murder of an Ethiopian student in Portland, Oregon. These two talk-show-circuit racists denied that they could be held responsible for the murder despite the influence they exerted on the killers through their racist instruction, propaganda and preaching. Commentary by lawyers, activists and journalists, and direct testimony from the defendants drive at an extremely sensitive question: when do First Amendment rights stop and hate crimes begin?

VHS: S15869. $49.95.

Catherine Tatgel/Dominique Lasseur, USA, 1992, 146 mins.

Biography: Jackie Robinson

A program first broadcast on the Arts and Entertainment channel which uses interviews, archival footage and photographs to trace the life of this legendary figure, Jackie Robinson.

VHS: S20442. $19.95.

Black American Literature

Professor Valerie Smith focuses on the development of African-American literature during a time of resurgent racism (1890s-1930s). Included in the discussion are authors from the turn-of-the-century up to and including the poets and novelists of the Harlem Renaissance. 45 mins.

VHS: S08201. $145.00.

The Black Americans of Achievement

From Sojourner Truth to General Colin Powell this video collection chronicles the achievements of a diverse group of African-Americans. Athletes, scientists, politicians and writers share the stage in a series of half hour segments. Archival footage and photographs are used to describe the lives and achievements of these men and women. 30 minutes each.

Booker T. Washington
VHS: S17383. $39.95.

Colin Powell
VHS: S17384. $39.95.

Dr. Martin Luther King, Jr.
VHS: S17385. $39.95.

Frederick Douglass
VHS: S17386. $39.95

George Washington Carver
VHS: S17387. $39.95.

Harriet Tubman
VHS: S17388. $39.95.

Jackie Robinson
VHS: S17389. $39.95.

Jesse Jackson
VHS: S17390. $39.95.

Madame C.J. Walker
VHS: S17391. $39.95.

Malcolm X
VHS: S17392. $39.95.

Sojourner Truth
VHS: S17393. $39.95.

Thurgood Marshall
VHS: S17394. $39.95.

The Black Americans of Achievement Box Set. 360 mins.
VHS: S17395. $479.40.

Black Artists Short Subjects

Volume 1: *The Negro in Sports* (Jesse Owens, Mary McNabb, Jackie Robinson, Willie Mays, Larry Dolby, Luke Easter, The Harlem Globetrotters and others), *Brown Bomber* (Joe Louis), *Joe Louis vs. Max Schmelling*, *The Negro in Entertainment* (Louis Armstrong, Duke Ellington, Bill Robinson and Fats Waller), *The Negro in Industry* (narrated by Claude A. Barnett, director of the Associated Negro Press).
VHS: S21425. $29.95.

Volume 2: *Slow Poke* (Stepin Fetchit), *Symphony in Black* (Duke Ellington and His Orchestra, Billie Holiday), *Hi-De-Ho* (Cab Calloway), *Black and Tan* (Duke Ellington and His Cotton Club Orchestra), *Jammin' the Blues* (Lester Young, Red Callender, Harry Edison and Marlowe Morris).
VHS: S21426. $29.95.

Volume 3: *Music Hath Harm* (Valerie Graham, Spencer Williams, Roberta Hyson, Harry Tracy and Nathan Curry), *Boogie Woogie Dream* (Albert Ammons, Pete Johnson and Teddy Wilson and His Band), *Rufus Jones For President* (Ethel Waters, Sammy Davis, Jr. and Hamtree Harrington).
VHS: S21427. $29.95.

The Black Athlete

This examination of Black athletes includes those who literally defined greatness in their respective sports. The careers of such notables as Jesse Owens, Muhammad Ali, O.J. Simpson, Kareem Abdul Jabbar, Arthur Ashe, Edwin Moses and many others are explored. Commentary by novelist James A. Michener. USA, 1979, 58 mins.
VHS: S16564. $19.95.

Black History: Lost, Stolen or Strayed

Bill Cosby hosts this examination of the accuracy of the ways in which American historians have traditionally documented significant historical achievements by Black Americans. USA, 1968, 54 mins.
VHS: S14604. $19.95.

The Black Military Experience

This interesting collection of shorts about Black military life includes films made during WWII: *The Negro Soldier*, *The Navy Steward*, and *The Negro Sailor*.
VHS: S15480. $29.95.

Black Panthers: Huey Newton/Black Panther Newsreel

A film documentary of the "Free Huey Newton" rally in California, with the speakers including Eldridge Cleaver, James Foreman, Bobby Seale, H. Rap Brown, Stokely Carmichael, and Bob Avakian. Includes the short *Black Panther Newsreel*, featuring interviews with Huey Newton in the Alameda County Jail. 1968, 53 mins.

VHS: S03358. $49.95.

Black Power in America: Myth or Reality?

This is a survey of some of the changes found in American society since the beginning of the Civil Rights movement of the 60s. *Black Power in America* focuses on Black Americans like Mayor Tom Bradley of Los Angeles and Franklin Thomas of the Ford Foundation, men who have achieved power and influence difficult to attain in the past. This tape looks at contemporary education, and at a wide range of events with provocative insights into Black America.

VHS: S10089. $129.95.

William Greaves, USA, 1988, 59 mins.

Black Profiles

The lives of famous African-Americans serve as the inspiration for this documentary. Paul Lawrence Dunbar, Booker T. Washington, Dr. George Carver, and Dr. Martin Luther King are all covered in this inspirational and educational work. USA, 1993, 50 mins.

VHS: S20625. $29.95.

Black Studies: Then and Now

This examination of African-American culture traces the struggles and accomplishments through a vast historical prism, from the end of slavery to the political and social movements led by Dr. Martin Luther King, Jr. to the celebrations of Kwanzaa, Juneteenth and other holidays. Designed for children in grades 4-6.

Black Studies: Then and Now: Slavery and Plantation Life. This video presents a subjective view of the experiences of being a slave, what it means and feels to be captured, traded and treated as property. The program also studies the origins of slavery. 14 mins.

VHS: S19985. $65.95.

Black Studies: Then and Now: Rebels and Abolitionists. A historical examination of the cruel legacy of slavery and its impact on African-American freedom, from its pre-Civil War roots to the Emancipation Proclamation to the surrender of Confederate troops at Appomattox. 14 mins.

VHS: S19986. $65.95.

Black Studies: Then and Now: Dr. Martin Luther King, Jr. The life and legacy of Dr. King are examined. The topics explored include the Supreme Court decision outlawing school desegregation, the Montgomery Bus Boycott and the march to Selma. USA, 1988, 15 mins.

VHS: S19987. $65.95.

Blacks Britannica
(David Koff)

Black Studies: Then and Now: Black Heritage Holidays. An African-American family honors its cultural heritage by observing Kwanzaa, a holiday involving elaborate table decorations and the dispensing of gifts to award the children's accomplishments, as well as teaching values from Africa. 20 mins.

VHS: S19988. $65.95.

Black Studies: Then and Now: Complete Set. The complete four-volume set.

VHS: S19989. $229.00.

Blacks Britannica

Blacks Britannica chronicles the institutionalized racism of the British government and the extra-governmental attacks of neo-fascist groups upon Anglo-Africans. The resistance of the Anglo-African population to both of these adversaries is detailed. Labelled a "danger", the film was banned in the United Kingdom and its viewing was restricted in the United States by order of the Federal Courts. Eventually these restrictions were lifted. The program deals more than with the "every day" hate mongering of a few fanatics: it looks at the roots of the problem including its economic and cultural aspects.

VHS: S10841. $39.95.

David Koff, Great Britain, 1978, 58 mins.

Booker T. Washington: The Life and the Legacy

This docudrama is about the controversial leader of Black America at the turn of the century. His policies of Black economic self-reliance and political accommodation were debated nationwide. With Maurice Woods as Booker T. Washington.

VHS: S03419. $79.95.

William Greaves, USA, 1986, 30 mins.

Circle of Recovery

Seven African-American alcoholics and drug addicts are the focus of this PBS special. The men are shown battling their addictions with the aim of becoming beacons of hope to their community. An inspiring documentary hosted by Bill Moyers. Tom Casciato, USA.

VHS: S15268. $29.95.

Colin Powell: A General's General

Produced by CNN, this is the life story of Colin Powell, the first African-American to become Chairman of the Joint Chiefs of Staff. 60 mins.

VHS: S20512. $14.98.

The Color of Love

A documentary about the attraction of taboo sexual attractions, *The Color of Love* examines interracial relationships. An effort is made to deal with the confusion and loss of identity such relationships sometimes bring. The very nature of attraction is also approached. Ray Marsh, USA, 90 mins.

VHS: S18816. $19.95.

Consuming Hunger

A provocative three-video program that explores and challenges the treatment by the media of hunger issues, particularly the Ethiopian famine. The videos invite viewers to examine the crucial impact that media images exert on the public and to analyze the intent and outcome of those images. Produced by Maryknoll Media. USA, 1988, 29 mins each.

Prog. 1: Getting the Story. News events from the Third World face a tough fight for Western television air time. Yet images determine the Western World's view of the Third World: the dramatic pictures from Ethiopia launched a major relief effort, but those pictures almost didn't get aired. *Getting the Story* shows how the tragedy in Ethiopia went from just another famine to become the most moving news story of the decade, exploring the "rules" of television news and our own attitudes toward the Third World.

VHS: S05844. $24.95.

Prog. 2: Shaping the Image. *Shaping the Image* raises questions about the impression of Africa created by television coverage of the Ethiopian famine. What was our response to the famine? Was "Live Aid" an outpouring of generosity or a celebration of rock and roll? Are we ready to listen to Africans and to our own poor tell their own story?

VHS: S05846. $24.95.

Prog. 3: Selling the Feeling. *Selling the Feeling* explores the Madison Avenue treatment of problems such as domestic hunger and homelessness. The death of thousands in Ethiopia made us aware of the plight of our own poor, hungry and homeless. Yet when the events are over, are we any different as a nation in our treatment of the poor?

VHS: S05845. $24.95.

A Conversation with Gwendolyn Brooks

A poet of the city, Gwendolyn Brooks, discusses her influences, her family and her work. Brooks's work, which often deals with the impact of poverty and neglect in the ghetto, is put in context of her life. Produced by the Library of Congress, this tape is a fascinating look into the mind and background of the Pulitzer Prize-winning writer. 28 mins.

VHS: S08130. $29.95.

A Conversation with Magic

Former L.A. Laker and AIDS activist Earvin "Magic" Johnson discusses the disease frankly with students. The tape deals with how people can and cannot contract the disease, and also includes a discussion on condoms. USA, 1994, 26 mins.

VHS: S21257. $29.95.

Deep North

Media attempts to deal with racism in the United States tend to focus on the South. Documentary filmmaker William Greaves turns North to discuss racism there. Groups of New Yorkers are brought together to confront other races, their own hostility and their misperceptions. The film uses group therapy and psychodrama to bring out hidden emotions.

VHS: Currently out of print. May be available for rental in some video stores.

William Greaves, USA, 1988, 48 mins.

The Dream Awake

This seven-part series, told in verse, is a portrait of the social, cultural and historical forces that shaped the African-American community. The series looks at Africa, pre-Revolutionary and pre-Civil War life, the rise of the Black cowboy and the emergence of Black intellectuals.

Part 1: Africa
VHS: S20004. $39.95.

Part 2: The Amistad, Crispus Attucks, Harriet Tubman and the Emancipation Proclamation
VHS: S20005. $39.95.

Part 3: The Black Cowboy
VHS: S20006. $39.95

Part 4: The Black Quartet
VHS: S20007. $39.95

Part 5: The Martyrs
VHS: S20008. $39.95

Part 6: Resurrection City and the Children
VHS: S20009. $39.95

Part 7: The Black Arts
VHS: S20010. $39.95

The Dream Awake Complete Set
VHS: S20011. $179.95

Divine Horsemen: The Living Gods of Haiti

Maya Deren, the pioneering experimental filmmaker, filmed various Haitian religious groups and their dances, ceremonies and invocations. The primacy of music and dance in these practices are evident. The piece is a non-judgmental examination of what is often referred to in the United States as voodoo. Teiji and Cherel Ito edited the film after Maya Deren's death.

VHS: S00349. $29.95.

Maya Deren, USA, 1947-51, 52 mins.

Ebony/Jet Guide to Black Excellence

This three-volume series introduces youth to the charismatic African-American individuals who have achieved success in a range of fields, including business, politics, education and the arts. USA, 1991. 35 minutes each.

Prog. 1: The Entrepreneurs: In this charismatic, revealing series about African-American achievement and empowerment, this program profiles the will and determination of three successful entrepreneurs: publisher John H. Johnson, Maxima Corporation CEO Joshua I. Smith, and actress and television commentator Oprah Winfrey.

VHS: S17100. $24.95.

Prog. 2: The Leaders: Trailblazers L. Douglas Wilder, Governor of Virginia, Marian Wright Edelman, Founder and President of the Children's Defense Fund and Dr. James P. Corner, Director of Yale University's Child Study Center, explain how they persevered and assumed positions of leadership to open doors for others.

VHS: S16595. $24.95.

Prog. 3: The Entertainers: TV's No. 1 dad, Bill Cosby, Maya Angelou, author, actress, singer, talk-show host and professor and Charles Dutton, Broadway, film and TV star, entertain and inspire with their tales of persistence and endurance.

VHS: S16596. $24.95.

Faith Ringgold: The Last Story Quilt

This film, winner of the 1992 Cine Gold Eagle Award, created and produced by Linda Freeman, is an insider's look at how one woman has fulfilled her dream of becoming an artist through patience, perseverance and education. Ringgold is credited with developing the "Black Light" color palette, spending years painting before working with soft sculptures, masks, murals, and finally quilts. Ringgold's mastery of all these media is used to build a positive view of a persistent, gifted artist.

VHS: S18392. $24.95.

David Irving, USA, 1991, 28 mins.

Famous Black Americans

This important series on African-Americans examines their contributions to the country's social, artistic, cultural and political framework. The series covers role models like militant freedom fighters, Civil War heroes and contemporary artists and politicians. Designed for students in grades 4-6.

Black Heroes: Freedom Fighters, Cowboys & More. This program offers a panoramic study of African-American heroes, from Crispus Attucks, the first patriot to die in the Boston Massacre of 1770 to the seminal contributions of Dr. Martin Luther King, Jr., winner of the Nobel Peace Prize. 22 mins.
VHS: S19994. $65.95.

Black Heroes: Builders, Dreamers and More. The historical accomplishments of Dr. Carter Goodwin Wodson, Phyllis Wheatley, Mary McLeod Bethune and Dr. George Washington Carver are highlighted in this special tribute to teachers, preachers and researchers. 23 mins.
VHS: S19995. $65.95.

Black Americans: Artists, Entertainers and More. In recounting the significant artistic accomplishments of painter Henry Tanner, poet Gwendolyn Brooks, opera diva Leontyne Price and actor Sidney Poitier, this program showcases the vast cultural diversity of African-Americans. 20 mins.
VHS: S19996. $65.95.

Black Americans: Political Leaders, Educators, Scientists. The historical legacy of the social, political and Civil Rights protests is examined through the lives of four figures: Blanche K. Bruce, Thurgood Marshall, Ralph J. Bunche and Shirley Chisholm. 20 mins.
VHS: S19997. $65.95.

Famous Black Americans Set
VHS: S19998. $229.00.

FBI's War on Black America

J. Edgar Hoover and the FBI were concerned over the threat to internal security from Black Americans and organized a campaign to discredit organizations and individuals. This video is a truly frightening spectacle of conspiracy and abuse of power.
VHS: S13167. $29.98.
Denis Mueller/Deb Ellis, USA, 1990, 50 mins.

Fields of Endless Day

Using both dramatizations and documentary footage this film traces the origins and history of Blacks in Canada, from the 17th century and the arrival of the first explorers to activist groups of this century. Produced by the National Film Board of Canada.

VHS: S07664. $49.95.

Terence Macartney-Filgate, Canada, 1978, 59 mins.

Franck Goldberg: Sampler

French video artist Franck Goldberg offers an outsider's view into inner city life of New York City. Included here are *Red Souvenir*, a documentary-style look at kids in New York, *No Sellout*, a rap music video based on Malcolm X's speeches, *Lynch*, the story of the police killing of a young graffiti artist in the New York subway and *Promised Land*, an examination of the aimless violence of the U.S.

VHS: S07126. $39.95.

Franck Goldberg, France, 1985-86, 60 mins.

Frederick Douglass: An American Life

A fast-paced, yet intimate portrait of the famous 19th century abolitionist and human rights advocate, Frederick Douglass. The film portrays the people and events which influenced his long and remarkable life, including meetings with such notable figures as Harriet Tubman, John Brown and Abraham Lincoln as well as his appointment as U.S. Ambassador to Haiti.

VHS: S03420. $79.95.

William Greaves, USA, 1986, 30 mins.

From These Roots

Using authentic autographs, the film, narrated by Brock Peters and featuring music by Eubie Blake, recreates a vivid portrait of the Harlem Renaissance during the Roaring Twenties. It documents the artistic, social and political re-birth of Afro-America, and includes such well-known indivi-duals as Cab Calloway, Marcus Garvey, Langston Hughes, James Weldon Johnson, Alain Locke, Claude MacKay, Paul Robeson and Ethel Waters.

VHS: S03421. $79.95.

William Greaves, USA, 1986, 28 mins.

Gordon Parks' Visions

Gordon Parks' career has included bestselling novels and popular films (*Shaft, The Learning Tree*). In addition, he is a world-class photo journalist. In these various occupations he has developed a keen insight and wit. This video is a look at the world through his eyes. 1991, 60 mins.

VHS: S14608. $19.95.

Great Black Baseball Players

From the first Black player to today's superstars, this compilation of baseball greats is hosted by Ernie "Mr. Cub" Banks and includes everyone from Jackie Robinson to Hank Aaron and Ozzie Smith. Once excluded from the Major Leagues, this is a look at some of baseball's most dominant Black players.

VHS: S12664. $19.95.

Haiti: Killing the Dream

Haitian history is traced from the time of the great Haitian patriot Toussaint L'Ouvrature to the current crisis. The years of dictatorship and U.S. invasions are discussed along with interviews with exiled president Jean-Bertrand Aristide, military officers and resistance leaders. USA, 58 mins.

VHS: S21191. $24.95.

Hale House: Alive With Love

Dr. Lorraine Hale begins by telling the story of one child, born addicted to heroin. From there the story blossoms into the founding of Hale House, a home for children who are born addicted to drugs. 28 mins.

VHS: S21457. $49.95.

Home Feeling

This film focuses on the history of Blacks in Toronto, Canada and their attempts to consolidate their community and make the country really their home. They meet with resistance from the police but persevere despite less-than-ideal conditions. The film focuses mainly on the lives of several of the residents, and their relationship with police, social service agencies and other institutions. Produced by the National Film Board of Canada.

VHS: S07668. $49.95.

Jennifer Hodge, Canada, 58 mins.

Ida B. Wells

This famous African-American woman fought for human rights at a time in American history when these concerns were largely ignored. Her work as a journalist shed important light on the injustices faced by African-Americans in the South after the Civil War. This documentary tells the story of her heroic life.

VHS: S20745. $19.95.

Rex Barnett, USA, 1993, 27 mins.

Ida B. Wells
(History on Video)

Images: Tribute to Harold Washington

A tribute to the late Harold Washington, the first Black mayor of Chicago. Combining photography with an exclusive interview, this portrait provides an intimate glimpse into the private world of Harold Washington—his childhood, his values, and his dreams.

VHS: S06019. $49.95.

Lois White, USA, 1987, 24 mins.

In Motion: Amiri Baraka

A fascinating exploration of the writer and political activist formerly known as Leroi Jones. Following Baraka from his early days as a poet in New York City's Greenwich Village to his present literary and political activities, *In Motion: Amiri Baraka* is a portrait of a man of singular commitment to social change. Interspersed throughout the film are excerpts from Baraka's powerful play *The Dutchman*, one of the archetypal literary works of the 1960s, as well as scenes from other Baraka plays. Allen Ginsberg, A.B. Spellman and Joel Oppenheimer provide insight into Baraka as a poet while activists Ted Wilson and Askia M. Toure talk about his political activism in Harlem.

VHS: S10909. $59.95.

St. Clair Bourne, USA, 1985, 60 mins.

In Plain English

Ethnic activists from many cultures gather to discuss issues ranging from assimilation and racism to ethnic identity and ways of attacking discrimination. Julia Lesage's documentary takes place at the University of Oregon and also tries to deal with the experiences of all the activists in the context of a wider college curriculum. African-Americans, Asian-Americans, Hispanics, Pacific Islanders, and Native Americans all participate in the forum.

VHS: S17437. $50.00.

Julia Lesage, USA, 1992, 42 mins.

Introduction to Richard Wright's Fiction

Prof. Valerie Smith approaches the work of Richard Wright with special emphasis on his most celebrated work, *Native Son*. The poverty and oppression suffered by Wright and his family are shown in the context of his writing. USA, 1988, 45 mins.

VHS: S08183. $145.00.

Jacob Lawrence: The Glory of Expression

This documentary is about the life of African-American painter Jacob Lawrence. His work has consisted primarily of epic depictions of the struggles of African-Americans. Considered one of America's greatest modern painters, he was the first African-American to have his work exhibited in a major New York gallery. 28 mins.

VHS: S21454. $49.95.

Jesse Owens Returns to Berlin

Using actual film highlights of the fateful 1936 Olympics and Owens's on-camera recollections, Bud Greenspan, the host, retells the story of one of sports' greatest triumphs—in which the 22-year old Owens defeated Hitler's showcase for the "master race". Emmy Award-winner. USA, 1976, 46 mins.

VHS: S06635. $14.95.

Just Doin' It

A fascinating look at the Black barbershop—which is a lot more than a place to get groomed. It also functions as a community center, a place where gossip and camaraderie mix with philosophy, religion and politics. An engaging view of life in urban Black America.

VHS: S03424. $79.95.

William Greaves, USA, 1984, 36 mins.

Kartemquin Films, Vol. 3: Trick Bag

Three films capture the history and apocalyptic social and personal changes of the Vietnam era. *Trick Bag* (1975, 21 mins.) allows gang members, Vietnam vets and young factory workers to relate their personal experiences of racism. *What the Fuck Are These Red Squares* (1970, 15 mins.) looks at striking students at the School of the Art Institute in the wake of the killing of student protestors at Kent State and Jackson State. *Hum 255* (1969, 28 mins.) traces the activities of two students and their return to the University of Chicago following their expulsion for illegally occupying the Administration building. They confront current students about their attitudes, moral and social values and the meaning of education. USA, 1969-75, 64 mins.

VHS: S18200. $29.95.

Looking for Langston

British filmmaker Isaac Julien's controversial biography of the brilliant, moody and fascinating Black American author Langston Hughes, interweaves the poetry of Essex Hemphill and Bruce Nugent with archival footage, period music and the texture and rhythms of the Harlem Renaissance. A stylized, expressive piece of work about identity, sexuality, racism, repression, role playing and art, it's a cool, multifaceted perspective of a distinctive writer.

VHS: S16641. $39.95.

Isaac Julien, Great Britain, 1989, 65 mins.

Mama Florence and Papa Cock

Alan Leder's personal account of an elderly Jamaican couple living amidst the growing tourist trade of Negril. The film is a warm and often humorous glimpse of the changing tenor of rural Jamaica reflected in the lives of an old village family.

VHS: S01955. $45.00.

Alan Leder, USA, 1983, 17 mins.

Mandela in America

An authorized, commemorative video account of Nelson Mandela's triumphant visit to the United States. This inside look includes an exclusive interview with Mandela and follows him as he meets such leading Americans as President Bush, Jesse Jackson, Eddie Murphy, Ted Kennedy and Jane Fonda. Music performed by Tracy Chapman, Aretha Franklin and Stevie Wonder, who wrote "Keep Our Love Alive" for this historic fundraising tour. USA, 1990, 90 mins.

VHS: S13265. $19.98.

Mean to Be Free: John Brown's Black Nation Campaign

A historical documentary about John Brown, a white preacher, who fought to end slavery and gain the rights of citizenship for all Black people. Brown used any means he could to bring about the demise of the institution of slavery and was hanged for his raid on the Federal arsenal at Harpers Ferry. He had planned to use the captured weapons to arm slaves for an uprising. The tape uses historical photos and the words of Frederick Douglass and Harriet Tubman. Performed and produced by the Department of Afro-American Studies, University of California, Berkeley. USA, 53 mins.

VHS: S10106. $39.99.

Millennium: Tribal Wisdom and the Modern World

The PBS series that interweaves documentary and dramatization to study divergent cultures and societies. Hosted by Harvard anthropoligist David Maybury-Lewis and scored by composer Hans Zimmer.

Adrian Malone, USA, 1992, 120 minutes each.

Prog. 1: Shock of the Other/Strange Relations. This vibrant PBS series provides a penetrating look into radically different and enclosed cul-

---

tures from around the world. In *Strange Relations*, this program studies sex, romance and marriage within traditional cultures.

VHS: S17058. $29.95.

Prog. 2: Mistaken Identity/An Ecology of Mind. This segment reveals how individual identities and expressions are shaped by larger concerns of culture and community, as a group of former headhunters show their unusual view of death. The second program studies how three divergent cultures explore intellectual, psychological and emotional connections.

VHS: S17059. $29.95.

Prog. 3: The Art of Living/Touching the Timeless. This program concerns creativity, self-preservation and expression in relation to tribal and modern people, and how art is used to expand and deepen maturity and understanding. The second part relates two magical stories of faith and spiritual adventure.

VHS: S17060. $29.95.

Prog. 4: A Poor Man Shames Us All/Inventing Reality. This program shows how spirituality, love, family, responsibility and enlightenment are a necessary corrective to worries over money and material possessions. In the second program, three different cultures weigh questions of science and nature, magic and reality, and how the are distinctions drawn between them.

VHS: S17061. $29.95.

Prog. 5: The Tightrope of Power/At the Threshold. Leaders within the same state grapple over issues of power and conciliation in an effort to merge common goals. In *At the Threshold*, the values of compassion, wisdom, identity and family are discussed for their future relevance and power.

VHS: S17062. $29.95.

Complete Set. A specially-priced, five-tape, boxed set of the PBS series. 600 mins.

VHS: S17063. $149.95.

Muhammad Ali vs. Zora Folley

From Madison Square Garden, a World Heavyweight bout fought on March 22, 1967. Don Duphy reports the blow-by-blow. Win Elliot supplies the colorful commentary. Pre-fight training films and interviews are shown, as is a post-fight interview with Ali and his father. USA, 1967, 68 mins.

VHS: S05455. $29.95.

The Nat "King" Cole Story

Nat "King" Cole stars in this short documentary about his life from saloon pianist to recording artist. Songs include "Sweet Lorraine", "Pretend" and "Straighten Up and Fly Right".

Will Cowan, USA, 1955, 30 mins.

Nationtime, Gary

Sidney Poitier and Harry Belafonte narrate the official documentary film record of the First National Black Political Convention held in Gary, Indiana in 1972, which brought together virtually the entire hierarchy of Black political power in America. Featured are Reverend Jesse Jackson, Mayor Richard Hatcher, Coretta Scott King, Dick Gregory, Amiri Baraka, Isaac Hayes, Bobby Seale and others. Newly re-edited version. USA, 1973, 90 mins.

VHS: S03423. $99.95.

Native Land

Paul Robeson, in his last film, narrates this documentary which explores the threats to American values in the forces unleashed by economic depression. Many of the artists who worked on this project through the collective called Frontier Films were themselves the victims of the House UnAmerican Activities Committee in the 1950's. In the debate on American values this film stands as a powerful testament to the enduring traditions of democratic ideals. This collector's version is mastered from the finest print available.

VHS: S20743. $59.95.

Paul Strand, USA, 1942, 88 mins.

Negro Soldier

Frank Capra supervised this documentary which focuses on Black participation in World War II. Langston Hughes hailed it as the most remarkable Negro film ever flashed on the American screen.

VHS: S03347. $19.98.

Frank Capra, USA, 1944, 40 mins.

A Newsreel Library of America in Sports

Except for the World War II reports, sports highlights were the most popular moments of the theatrical newsreel. Among the 79 stories featured in this collection is a piece on Jesse Owens's triumph in Hitler's Berlin. 90 mins.
VHS: S15947. $29.95.

Nightline: Louis Farrakhan

The controversial Nation of Islam leader, Louis Farrakhan, counters criticisms and clarifies statements he has made. Produced by ABC. Hosted by Ted Koppel. 50 mins.
VHS: S14029. $14.98.

Nightline: Nelson Mandela

Nelson Mandela appears in this debate on the future of South Africa. His remarks now seem prophetic. Hosted by Ted Koppel. 90 mins.
VHS: S14063. $14.98.

Only the Ball Was White

A television documentary on the formation and rise of the baseball Negro Leagues, and the great ballplayers who were denied a chance to play in the then racially segregated Major Leagues. The program features interviews with "Satchel" Paige, Roy Campanella, Buck Leonard, Jimmy Crutchfield, David Malarcher, Effa Manley and Quincy Trouppe. Narrated by Paul Winfield. USA, 1992, 30 mins.
VHS: S20421. $19.98.

Paris Is Burning

Filmmaker Jennie Livingston's film deals primarily with the African-American and Hispanic drag queens of New York City. She uses both personal interviews and footage from "Balls"—the extravagant social functions/contests. The Balls are not simply drag shows but have been divided into different categories. The level of seriousness among the contestants varies widely. The film is more than fun and games, since some of those included are truly tragic figures. Participating are such legends as Dorian Corey, Pepper Lebeija, Venus Xtravaganza, Octavia St. Laurent and Willi Ninja.
VHS: S16701. $19.95.
Laser: LD72195. $34.95.
Jennie Livingston, USA, 1990, 71 mins.

Passin' It On

Passin' It On deals with the false arrest and imprisonment of Dhoruba, the leader of the New York City chapter of the Black Panthers. Harassed by local and Federal authorities, he was framed and sent to prison for the murder of two police officers. Nineteen years later, in 1991, he was proven innocent and freed. This video tells his story through archival footage, interviews and actual testimony.

VHS: S21246. $29.95.

John Valadez/Peter Miller, USA, 1993, 57 mins.

Paul Robeson

Known as both a singer and an actor, Paul Robeson was foremost a humanitarian. He stood up for the rights of the poor and the victims of racism many years before it became "chic". This, along with his Communist leanings, earned him harassment from the U.S. government which lasted practically until the day he died. His life in the U.S. and abroad is examined by a Morehouse College historian.

VHS: S20946. $19.95.

Rex Barnett, USA, 36 mins.

Paul Robeson
(History on Video)

The People vs. Paul Crump

A powerful documentary—the debut film by William Friedkin (*French Connection, To Live and Die in L.A.*)—*The People vs. Paul Crump* is an impassioned plea for mercy and justice, based on the true story of Paul Crump—a man who is still in Illinois prison. In 1953, five young Black men robbed a food plant in the Chicago stockyards. Their getaway went awry, one security guard was shot to death, and five employees were severely beaten. Within a week, all five were arrested. The fifth man, Paul Crump, then 22, was sentenced to die in the electric chair. He is sentenced to life in prison, and was at the brink of execution some 15 times between 1953 and 1962. William Friedkin interviewed Paul Crump in jail. Because Friedkin believed in Crump's innocence, in his record of rehabilitation as a model prisoner and his worth as a human being, he made this artistic tour-de-force which is an impassioned plea for Crump's return to society.

VHS: S06320. $39.95.

William Friedkin, USA, 1962, 52 mins.

Portrait of the Caribbean

A production of the British Broadcasting Corp. and Turner Broadcasting System, this seven-hour series looks at the political, cultural and social formation of the region, an historically interlocking piece that considers the past, present and future. The program studies the profound legacy contributed to the area by Spain, France, England and parts of Africa. Narrated by Stuart Hall.

Iron in the Soul/Out of Africa. The first part examines the brutal history and contemporary legacy of slavery in the British Caribbean, draws on excerpts from a Jamaican plantation overseer's diary. The second part considers the energy, diversity and harshness of Haiti. Its history and culture is contrasted with Jamaica. Great Britain, 1992, 110 mins.

VHS: S18330. $29.95.

Paradise Lost/La Grande Illusion. The Spanish legacy in the Caribbean and living conditions in the Dominican Republic are explored through the shared perspective of several witnesses—a wealthy woman, a veterinarian, a baseball scout, and a male peasant. The second program considers the cultural divide and confusion of Martinique, and the question of its identity and cultural heritage, as part of the Caribbean or France. Great Britain, 1992, 110 mins.

VHS: S18331. $29.95.

Worlds Apart/Following Fidel/Shades of Freedom. The fractured identities and difficult conditions experienced by East Indians in the West

Indies is the subject of the first program. The second installment looks at the tormented and conflicted state of Cuba, the legacy of Fidel Castro's political revolution and the great demand for freedom. *Shades of Freedom* attempts to answer final questions, posed about the future and direction of the Caribbean, and the lasting repercussions of slavery and colonialism, as Stuart Hall travels through Jamaica and Antigua. Great Britain, 1992, 150 mins.

VHS: S18332. $29.95.

Portrait of the Caribbean Complete Set.
VHS: S19391. $79.95.

The People vs. Paul Crump
(Facets Multimedia, Inc.)

Portrait of Jason

A male prostitute, Jason, agreed to talk to filmmaker Shirley Clarke about his life and "craft". He is articulate, witty and self-aware in this film that started with 12 hours of footage. Being Black and being gay are shown as the double edged sword that Jason has had to dodge throughout his life.

VHS: Currently out of print. May be available for rental in some video stores.

Shirley Clarke, USA, 1967, 105 mins.

Portraits in Black

This program includes three award-winning films highlighting the Black American experience: *Paul Laurence Dunbar*, an early Black poet, *Two*

Centuries of Black American Art and *Gift of the Black Folk*, which depicts the lives of Frederick Douglass, Harriet Tubman and Denmark Vesey. VHS: S01050. $39.95.

Carlton Moss, USA, 1990, 60 mins.

The Race for Mayor

Chicago's 1983 mayoral campaign sparked nationwide interest in the growth of Black political awareness. The stunning victory of Harold Washington, a Black U.S. Congressman, over Chicago's Democratic "machine" heightened the expectations of Blacks all over the country. This independent documentary with Mayor Washington, Jesse Jackson, former mayor Jane Byrne, Richard Daley, and Democratic political boss Edward Vrdolyak—shot in churches, city streets, empty lots, Polish restaurants, political offices and Operation PUSH offices—paints a complex picture of the fusing of a new political coalition, and places it in the context of the historic evolution of successive waves of ethnic groups who seek to wrest control from earlier entrenched minorities.
VHS: S02312. $79.95.

Howard Gladstone/James Ylisela, USA, 1983, 29 mins.

Rare Black Short Subjects

A collection of rare short-films featuring African-Americans. It includes *The Negro in Sports*, *Entertainment and Industry*, *The All American Newsreel* and *Kilroy Was Here*.
VHS: S15479. $29.95.

Robert Colescott: The One-Two Punch

This motivational and educational video is a study of an award-winning artist who with humor, irony, and sarcasm satirizes racial and gender stereotypes. 28 mins.
VHS: S21455. $49.95.

Robert Coles: Teacher

Robert Coles, the Pulitzer Prize-winning child psychologist, is the focus of this documentary. The film interviews children and documents their responses to questions about racial, social, political and economic issues. The film also considers Coles's groundbreaking work as a Harvard professor of literature; Coles discusses his views on the connection between intellectual growth and spiritual maturity and grace. USA, 1991, 57 mins.
VHS: S17103. $39.95.

The "Rodney King" Case:
What the Jury Saw in *California v. Powell*

This two-hour video is taken from the 150-hour gavel-to-gavel coverage recorded by Court TV in the controversial police brutality trial of several Los Angeles police officers in 1992. Court TV chief anchor and managing editor Fred Graham hosts and interprets the proceedings in an effort to make the legal process understandable to the viewer. Nearly everyone in America saw the shocking amateur video of Rodney King being beaten by members of the LAPD; don't miss this opportunity to see what else the jury saw in Simi Valley.

VHS: S16708. $24.98.

Dominic Palumbo, USA, 1992, 116 mins

Running with Jesse

Running with Jesse tells the political, social and personal story behind Jesse Jackson's 1984 bid for the U.S. presidency. Organizers from across the U.S. share experiences; the issues of the Rainbow Coalition are illustrated through music, public demonstrations, speeches and interviews and people from all sides assess the campaign's impact and the future for the Coalition.

VHS: S03724. $55.00.

Leanna Wolfe, USA, 1986, 57 mins.

Sitting in Limbo

Two Black teenagers confront the poverty and problems they face. Their relationship helps them to get through in this bittersweet story of inner city life.

VHS: S18832. $29.95.

John N. Smith, Canada, 1986, 95 mins.

Something New Out of Africa

Priests are crossing the Atlantic to work among foreign people. These missionaries, however, are from Nigeria and are coming to work among Black Catholics in Louisiana and Texas. The priests and their new parishoners discuss the impact of cultural differences. USA/Nigeria, 29 mins.

VHS: S15691. $19.95.

The Tallest Tree in the Forest

This tape is a look at Paul Robeson, his performances and his political views. From his early days as a performer Robeson refused to be quiet on the issue of race and earned the enmity of many. This along with his views on the Soviet Union (which he regarded in a positive light) led to his blacklisting. USA, 1977, 85 mins.

VHS: S21469. $24.95.

This House of Power

A documentary about the history of the African-American church, from its origins as a separate "invisible institution" among slaves to its present-day role as a major force for social change. Hosted by CBS anchor Hosea Sanders. 60 mins.

VHS: S20545. $29.95.

Toni Morrison: Profile of a Writer

Toni Morrison has established herself as the leading chronicler of the Black experience in America and as one of America's finest novelists. This program focuses on Morrison on the eve of publication of her new novel, *Beloved*, which won the Pulitzer Prize for fiction. Morrison talks about the problems of dealing with painful material, and of writing about ordinary people whose experiences seem monumentally larger than life.

VHS: S07599. $39.95.

Alan Benson, Great Britain, 1987, 52 mins.

Torture of Mothers: The Case of the Harlem Six

A docudrama based on Truman Nelson's book of the same title, *The Torture of Mothers* is the story of police overreaction to youthful hijinx. The overturning of a fruit stand leads to the unwarranted arrest of bystanders who are savagely beaten while in custody. The film depicts police relations with African-Americans in a bleak light as it chronicles community resistance to organized, sanctioned police brutality. Re-enactments feature Ruby Dee and narration by *A Soldier Story*'s Adolph Caesar.

VHS: S14535. $39.95.

Woodie King, Jr., USA, 1991

The Untold West: The Black West

African-Americans made a significant contribution to the Western expansion of the United States. Often choosing to move West rather than deal with the racial situation in the East, Black farmers, cowboys, businessmen and even the occasional outlaw left their mark. This video focuses on some of these pioneers and those they influenced.

VHS: S20957. $14.98.

Where Did You Get that Woman?

This multiple-award-winning film weaves the urban Black experience, Chicago blues music and the plight of the poor and aging into an extraordinary portrait. Joan Williams, a spunky 77-year old, is a restroom attendant in a Chicago nightclub. Filmmaker Loretta Smith weaves Williams' personal recollections, many telling of hardship, with archival stills and classic blues and folk music, into a visual and aural record of Black rural history during the early part of the century.

VHS: S12926. $44.95.

Loretta Smith, USA, 1987, 30 mins.

The Civil Rights Movement

The Assassination of Martin Luther King, Jr.

Martin Luther King, Jr. was the frequent subject of government surveillance and this documentary shows the extent to which the government went to discredit Dr. King and his movement. The private communications of Lyndon Johnson and previously unreleased FBI records are used as evidence. USA, 1993, 90 mins.

VHS: S18512. $59.98.

Dr. Martin Luther King, Jr.: A Historical Perspective

A new examination of Dr. King's extraordinary life using rare and largely never-before-seen footage and photographs, this program looks at the ideas, thoughts and causes of Dr. King's life. 90 mins.

VHS: S20542. $59.95.

Eyes on the Prize I

The seminal, award-winning PBS series on the Civil Rights Movement, covering the years 1954-65, brilliantly interweaves archival footage, news materials, and contemporary interviews with prominent figures who played roles in the incidents, moments and battles for equality and justice.

Prog. 1: Awakenings. This part considers the years 1954-56, and the early formation of the protest movement orchestrated by Civil Rights organizations, the churches, and local leaders to protest "Jim Crow Laws", the "separate but equal" doctrines, and rampant segregation that existed in the South. The program studies the lynching of Emmett Till and the 1955-56 Montgomery, Alabama Bus Boycott, triggered when Rosa Parks refused to give up her seat.

VHS: S16920. $19.95.

Judith Vecchione, USA, 1987, 60 mins.

Prog. 2: Fighting Back. This program focuses on the struggle for equal education, studying the historic 1954 Supreme Court ruling, *Brown vs. the Board of Education*, as nine Black teenagers attempted to integrate Central High School in Little Rock, Arkansas in 1957, and James Meredith's daring, life-threatening decision to enter the University of Mississippi in 1962.

VHS: S16921. $19.95.

Judith Vecchione, USA, 1987, 60 mins.

Prog. 3: Ain't Scared of Your Jails. The Freedom Summer movement is explored in this program, looking at the massive number of college students and young activists who poured into the South to test the legal challenges of inequality.

VHS: S16922. $19.95.

Orlando Bagwell, USA, 1987, 60 mins.

Prog. 4: No Easy Walk. This episode looks at the charismatic, grass roots origins of Martin Luther King's nonviolent campaign to attack institutional racism in Albany, Georgia, and Birmingham, Alabama, where the city's police chief, Bull Connor, turned attack dogs and fire hoses on demonstrators, capturing international attention.

VHS: S16923. $19.95.

Prog. 5: Mississippi: Is This America? In 1961 Mississippi was the staging ground for the first constitutional struggle and argument: how the Civil Rights Movement would galvanize their energy and forces to empower Blacks with the right to vote.

VHS: S16924. $19.95.

Orlando Bagwell, USA, 1987, 60 mins.

Prog. 6: Bridge to Freedom. Ten years after the movement began, following the private joys, frustration, landmark victories and eternal struggle,

Black and white participants converge for history, marching fifty miles for freedom to Selma, Alabama.

VHS: S16925. $19.95.

Callie Crossley/James DeVinney, USA, 1987, 60 mins.

Complete Set. All six programs available in a one-volume, boxed set, encased in a beautiful, slipcase edition.

VHS: S16926. $119.95.
Laser: LD71780. $129.95.

Eyes on the Prize II

Eight additional volumes of the award-winning documentary about the Civil Rights Movement covering the years 1964 to 1985.

The Time Has Come/Two Societies. *The Time Has Come*: The second generation of the Civil Rights Movement includes such charismatic leaders as Malcolm X and Stokely Carmichael. *Two Societies:* The battle lines are drawn in Watts, Cicero and Detroit as civil unrest shakes the very foundation of the movement.

VHS: S17211. $24.95.

Power!/The Promised Land. *Power!*: Three stories that capture the essence of the movement in the late 60s: The election of Carl Stokes as the first Black mayor of a major city, the rise of the Black Panther Party and the uprising in the Ocean Hill-Brownsville section of Brooklyn. *The Promised Land:* The issues of war, poverty and economic justice are intertwined as Vietnam becomes a flashpoint, Martin Luther King, Jr. is assassinated in Memphis and the Poor People's Campaign comes to Washington, D.C.

VHS: S17213. $24.95.

Ain't Gonna Shuffle No More/A Nation of Law? *Ain't Gonna Shuffle No More*: Black pride comes to the forefront of the movement with the emergence of Muhammad Ali, the student takeover of Howard University and the first National Black Political Convention in Gary, Indiana. *A Nation of Law?*: As the Black Panther Party rises in prominence, the FBI launches hundreds of covert actions against them, resulting in the death of Panther leader Fred Hampton.

VHS: S17215. $24.95.

Sam Pollard/Sheila Bernard, USA, 1990, 60 mins.

The Keys to the Kingdom/Back to the Movement. *The Keys to the Kingdom*: Court-ordered busing leaves deep scars in Boston as white parents react violently to the enforced change. In Atlanta, affirmative action takes center stage with the election of Black mayor Maynard Jackson. The Supreme Court sends out mixed signals in the Bakke Decision. *Back to the Movement:* Miami explodes in the worst racial riot in a decade as an all-white

---

jury acquits the white officers accused of murdering a Black man during a traffic stop. Harold Washington is elected mayor of Chicago through the grassroots efforts of the Black community.

VHS: S17217. $24.95.

Jacqueline Shearer/Judith Vecchione, USA, 1990, 120 mins.

The Complete Set. All eight volumes in either a four-tape boxed set or a four-disk set.

VHS: S19883. $99.95.
Laser: LD71964. $149.95.

Eyes on the Prize I and II: The Commemorative Edition. This collector's edition brings together the two separate editions, *Eyes on the Prize I: 1954-64*, and *Eyes on the Prize II: 1964-1985*. The 14-hour collection is presented in a handsome, velvet-lined leather case. The package also includes the companion book, *Eyes on the Prize: Voices of Freedom*, by producer Henry Hampton.

VHS: S16927. $349.95.

King: Montgomery to Memphis

This documentary tells the story of Rev. Martin Luther King, Jr. beginning with the successful Montgomery Bus Boycott and ending with his tragic death on April 4, 1968. The film examines Dr. King's achievements and setbacks along with his steadfast belief in nonviolence. One of the earliest black and white documentaries made about Dr. King. USA, 1988, 103 mins.

VHS: S06088. $19.95.
Laser: LD71079. $49.95.

Malcolm X: Death of a Prophet

Also titled *El Hajj Malik El Shabazz*, a docu-drama about the last 24 hours in the life of Malcolm X. Director Woodie King, Jr. uses archival footage and reenactments to depict the frightening last hours of the African-American leader. Morgan Freeman (*Glory*, *Driving Miss Daisy*) stars while Yolanda King, daughter of Martin Luther King, Jr., plays Malcolm X's wife Betty. Freeman's Malcolm X, despite his awareness of peril, is focused on his work and concerned with his family. The music is composed and performed by jazz legend Max Roach; Ossie Davis narrates.

VHS: S14536. $39.95.

Woodie King, Jr., USA, 1991, 60 mins.

Martin Luther King Commemorative Collection

Two documentaries on one tape commemorating the late Dr. Martin Luther King: *In Remembrance of Martin* interweaves past and present to take the viewer from the days of the Civil Rights Movement to America's first recognition of Martin Luther King, Jr. Day as a National Holiday; *The Speeches of Martin Luther King* includes some of Dr. King's most famous speeches, including "I Have a Dream" and "I Have Been to the Mountaintop". USA, 115 mins.

VHS: S06540. $29.95.

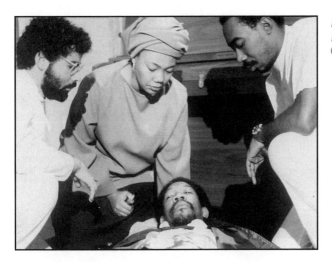

Malcolm X:
Death of a Prophet
(Essenay Entertainment)

Martin Luther King: I Have a Dream

Dr. King's speech given August 28, 1963, on the steps of the Lincoln Memorial before over 200,000 Civil Rights marchers is one of the most often quoted speeches of our times. The speech is captured here in its entirety. USA, 1986, 25 mins.

VHS: S02361. $14.95.

Martin Luther King, Jr.: Legacy of a Dream

Martin Luther King, Jr. inspired a nation in troubled times. This concise survey, narrated by James Earl Jones, examines the life and times of the Civil Rights leader, revealing his enduring legacy. USA, 1974, 29 mins.

VHS: S15678. $14.98.

The Real Malcolm X: An Intimate Portrait of the Man

Dan Rather hosts this documentary on the life of the slain African-American leader. The material features archival footage, excerpts from some of his

---

most interesting speeches and interviews with his contemporaries. An even-handed look at Malcolm X produced after the resurgence of interest in his life and career. USA, 1992, 60 mins.

VHS: S17683. $19.98.

The Speeches of Martin Luther King

The words of the great leader in a collection of his famous speeches. USA, 1992, 60 mins.

VHS: S07027. $19.95.

Documentaries about Africa

7-Up in South Africa

The establishment of apartheid in South Africa in 1948 led to many tragedies. Here 19 children afflicted by the political and social barriers of minority rule are contrasted. The children's hopes and aspirations are at odds with their fears and the grim reality of everyday life. A film which is especially interesting because of the dismantling of apartheid in recent years.

VHS: S19244. $19.95

Angus Gibson, South Africa, 1993, 83 mins.

Africa

Hosted by Basil Davidson, author of more than 30 books about Africa, this series reveals the history and present-day life of the continent.

John Percival/Christopher Ralling/Andrew Harries/Mick Csaky, USA, 1984, 120 mins each.

Part I: Different But Equal/Mastering A Continent: *Africa, Part I* begins with a brief look at the European racist attitude toward Africans and quickly turns to an examination of the prehistory and great civilizations of North Eastern Africa. Egypt and Nubia are examined in historical and modern context. Special attention is paid to Meroe with its still undeciphered alphabet, iron production and architecture. Also of note is the mention of medieval African St. Maurice. *Mastering A Continent* continues with an examination of three communities and their strategies for survival in the local environments. Each village offers a different view of African existence. The emphasis of the second segment is more anthropological while the first is historical.

VHS: S02400. $69.95.

Part II: Caravans of Gold/Kings and Cities: The first of two episodes on this video deals with trade in medieval Africa and the rise of empires that monopolized the trade routes (Ghana, Mali, Songhai). The discussion shifts to the gold-producing region ruled by the Asante. Asante Royal traditions are examined. The rise of Islam, the situation of coastal East Africa and the Tuareg peoples of the desert are also examined. The second segment focuses on the ancient cities of Africa: the Hausa rulers, the Emirs of Ife, the Yoruba city of Oyo and Benin are all included. European descriptions and drawings from the period show a positive view of Africa which would soon change to negative.

VHS: S02401. $69.95.

Part III: The Bible and the Gun/This Magnificent African Cake: These two installments of the series shift the focus from African history and culture to the pernicious influence of Europeans. The programs look at the role of explorers (including Stanley and Livingstone), missionaries, and businessmen such as Cecil Rhodes. The second installment looks at the grab for land by the Europeans and the origins of this late 1800's development.

VHS: S02402. $69.95.

Africa, Part IV: The Rise of Nationalism/The Legacy: Following World War II, the European grip on Africa began to weaken. By the late 50s and early 60s the continent was to achieve its independence. These struggles for independence are the subject of the first episode. The program covers independence movements in Ghana, Kenya, Algeria and the Belgian Congo (Zaire). The European determination to hold onto their colonies and the violence involved is shown to vary from nation to nation. *The Legacy* looks at the aftermath of colonial rule: unnatural borders, poor infrastructure and other problems are explored as are the measures African nations are taking to deal with the reality of colonialism and the necessity of reconciling this with African tradition.

VHS: S02403. $69.95.

Africa Speaks to the World

At the U.N., a new spotlight has been turned on Africa, but this time by Africans themselves. Acknowledging their mistakes, yet affirming their strengths, they now ask the world's governments and churches to work with them in a new spirit to further develop the many nations on the continent. African leaders from government and church engage in this new dialogue, and discuss progress being made, with video input from Tanzania and Zimbabwe. Produced by Maryknoll Media. 28 mins.

VHS: S06269. $24.95.

Art of the Dogon

Dogon art, like much of the art of Western Africa, is utilitarian. The desert nation of Mali is the home of most Dogon and it is the setting in which this artistic tradition began. Rare film footage of Dogon ceremonies and dances help to frame this look at the art and life of a centuries-old African culture. USA, 1988, 24 mins.

VHS: S08476. $29.97.

Black Man's Land Trilogy

The three-part series focusing on the effects of British colonialism in the continent of Africa.

David Koff/Anthony Kowarth, Great Britain, 1986, 52 mins.

Vol. 1, White Man's Country: The birth of British colonialism in Kenya is the starting point of this series, devoted to the history of the East African nation. The heavy casualties inflicted upon Africans resisting European domination show the lie in the popular excuse of the "white man's burden" to "civilize" non-Europeans. Following the initial bloodletting, the British moved to make all the best land in Kenya available to whites only. There was continued—if sometimes muted—resistance from Africans. The program is from an African standpoint and examines how Africans past and present viewed the British occupation. Contemporary footage and period photos along with eyewitness interviews are employed.

Home Video. VHS: S10843. $39.95.

Vol. 2, Mau Mau: Did the famed "Mau Mau" rebellion in Kenya actually ever happen or was it simply an attempt by British colonials to insure Britain would remain in control of Kenya? This is the focus of this volume and the point is made force-fully. Every death of a white in Kenya was attributed to the "Mau Mau" (a word that means nothing in any African language of the region) and used as an excuse for greater repression. Fewer than forty British died while thousands of Kenyans perished or were held prisoner. The Land Freedom Army, Kenya's revolutionary army, was formed during this time and archival and newsreel footage is used to examine the real situation. Both sides are interviewed to get past the mythology surrounding the war.

Home Video. VHS: S10844. $39.95.

Vol. 3, Kenyatta: The father of Kenya, Jomo Kenyatta, was involved in the politics of his nation from the 1920s until his death in 1978. Exiled and later imprisoned by the British, Kenyatta became the first Prime Minister of Kenya in 1961, and an important voice for the entire continent. Once in power, he had to walk a line between recovering land taken by Europeans and avoiding a complete flight of white capital. Again archival footage along with current images are used as well as interviews with Kenyatta's supporters and detractors. The program is an even-handed portrait of one of modern Africa's most important, complicated and contradictory figures.

Home Video. VHS: S10845. $39.95.

David Koff/Anthony Kowarth, Great Britain, 1986, 52 mins.

Come Back, Africa

In the 1960s, South Africa was at its most repressive. Voices of dissent, particularly those from Blacks, were ruthlessly silenced. Seemingly minor infractions resulted in imprisonment, or worse. This was the environment in which this film was produced. Under the guise of making a musical, the filmakers produced this docu-drama which chronicles the desperate conditions in the slums encircling Johannesburg and the effort of the racist government to destroy the family unit through pass laws and sex segregation of workers. Miriam Makeba appears in a small role. Winner of the Italian Film Critics Award at the Venice Film Festival.

VHS: S02860. $29.95.

Lionel Rogosin, South Africa, 1960, 83 mins.

Falashas

Falashas are the legendary "Black Jews" of Ethiopia. Isolated and independent, they have often been targets for their Christian and Muslim countrymen. This documentary, filmed in 1973, prior to the 1984 famine airlift of many Falashas to Israel, is the story of their rituals and lifestyle, unknown to the outside world. Although Meyer Levin's documentary does not directly compare how closely these practices resemble those of other Jewish communities, the similarities and differences in many cases are obvious.

VHS: S06578. $34.95.

Meyer Levin, USA, 1973, 27 mins.

Black Man's Land Trilogy, Vol. 3: Kenyatta
(David Koff)

Folks Like Us

The Catholic diocese of Bismarck, North Dakota, sent four people—a priest, a deacon, a nurse and a speech pathologist—to Bura, Kenya. Filmed in Kenya and North Dakota, this documentary studies the team at work and the impact of their project on families and friends back home. Kenya/USA, 1992, 29 mins.

VHS: S15858. $19.95.

Four Days of the Masai

So fierce was the reputation of the Masai as warriors that the British colonialists were more interested in co-opting them rather than confronting them. This documentary details the daily life of the Masai. Much of their life revolves around protecting and caring for their livestock. They retained their nomadic lifestyle despite the British encroachment by using their cattle as a means of satisfying their tax "obligations" to the British Crown. The Masai live today relatively untouched by Western influence. Narrated in English.

VHS: S10731. $325.00

Jean-Caude Luyat, France/Kenya, 1980, 98 mins.

From Sun-Up

Flora M'mbugu produced this story of the daily lives of the women of Tanzania. The women carry water, chop wood, cook and manage money-making ventures. Filmed in Tanzania with an all-African crew, the film points to the women's reliance on one another as their hope for the future. Tanzania, 28 mins.

VHS: S04927. $24.95.

General Idi Amin Dada

A dark spot in Africa's history is illustrated as dictator Idi Amin unwittingly lampoons himself in front of the camera of Barbet Schroeder. Amin's flight ahead of invading Tanzanian troops must have been slightly less galling to him than his performance here. Amin threatened Schroeder's life over the film.

VHS: S13908. $59.99.

Barbet Schroeder, France, 1975, 113 mins.

Glimpses of West Africa

An educational film about three African nations, their cultures, climate and geography. Explored are the French-speaking nations of Cote d'Ivoire,

---

Mali and Senegal. An ethnographic study of cultures not often seen in American classrooms. The program contains a transcript and lesson plan. 32 mins.

English Narration. VHS: S19800. $49.95.

Herdsmen of the Sun

The Wodaabe people of the Northern Sahel are the focus of German director Werner Herzog's film. The hardships suffered by these people during the drought of the mid-1980s as well as their culture and rituals are dispassionately displayed without comment. The nomadic Wodaabe, living in marginal lands, were in dire straights during the drought but had somewhat recovered by the time this film was shot. Once a year, the Wodaabe men decorate themselves with beads and blue lipstick and festive hats to participate in a sort of beauty pageant. The women must decide who is the most beautiful, and choose a mate. French, English, and Peul with English subtitles.

VHS: S16054. $59.95.

Werner Herzog, Germany, 1988, 52 mins.

*Herdsmen
of the Sun*
(Interama, Inc.)

Jaguar

Three young men leave their homes in Niger, a landlocked nation that is quite poor, to travel to the richer nation of Ghana to seek their fortune. A herdsman, a fisherman and their companion do indeed "make it" in the big city but they become homesick for their own country and return. They have become "jaguars" with a knowledge of the modern world. The film is a key work of ethnographic filmmaking by the great and innovative Jean Rouch. English narration.

VHS: S10730. $350.00.

Jean Rouch, France/Niger, 1955, 96 mins.

The Journey, Volume 4.

This volume of the 16-hour documentary epic on the issues of peace around the globe by a world-wide filmmaking collective, led by the great documentarian Peter Watkins, deals with Africa. It includes parts 10, 11 and 12 in which women of a Mozambique farming collective discuss the civil war in their country and its effects on their ability to produce food. Watkins also details the amount the U.S. Government pays American colleges and universities for their part in nuclear weapons design and production.

VHS: S14299. $29.95.

Peter Watkins, Sweden, 1987, 870 mins.

Karibu

Although the family is probably the most important social unit in East Africa, urbanization draws young people away from their villages to the big cities. These newcomers often face difficulties they had not anticipated and thus wind up in trouble. Meaning "welcome" in Swahili, *Karibu* examines parishes in Nairobi which are trying to become "welcoming families" for newcomers. 29 mins.

VHS: S15864. $19.95.

Les Maitres Fous

The Hauku were a small religious group which flourished in parts of West Africa in the first part of the twentieth century. French documentary filmmaker Jean Rouch was asked to film a Hauku ceremony. In one part of the rite participants fall into a trance and become possessed. Oddly enough the "possessors" were associated with the Western colonial powers. Rouch shot the film in 1954 and it remains an impressive ethnographic work. English narration.

VHS: S10728. $200.00.

Jean Rouch, France/Ghana, 1957, 35 mins.

The Journey
(Facets Multimedia, Inc.)

Lion Hunters

The Gao hunters, part of the Songhai ethnic group, are the focus of this documentary. Fulani herders in West Africa frequently ran afoul of lions and animals and were sometimes killed. The Fulani leaders would then request the assistance of the Gao through the Songhai hierarchy. The film is a look at a symbiotic relationship between two ethnic groups as well as a look at the skills of the hunters themselves. The Gao's skills apparently include the ability to differentiate between lions based upon their habits in the kill. The movie was shot when the area (Mali/Niger) was still ruled by France. English narration.

VHS: S10729. $300.00.

Jean Rouch, France/Mali, 1965, 68 mins.

Mandela: The Man and His Country

Filmed shortly after Nelson Mandela's release from the notorious Robin Island prison, this tape looks at his role in the anti-apartheid movement. Includes interviews with Jesse Jackson and James Michener and moving footage shot as Mandela was freed from prison. USA, 1990, 50 mins.

VHS: S12291. $19.98.

Masks from Many Cultures

The use of ceremonial masks in both serious and festive events is examined on a multicultural level. The program includes masks from Mardi Gras in New Orleans, Dominican Republic, New Guinea, Bali, China, Tibet, Japan, Korea, Mexico, Guatemala, Bolivia, Native Americans and several African nations. 1993, 21 mins.

VHS: S18514. $39.95.

Nightline: South African Debate

A video of ABC's Nightline town hall meeting on South Africa. 55 mins.
VHS: S14037. $14.98.

Once Upon a Time

The Kenyan tradition of oral history has fallen on hard times. The ability to pass on both legends and practical advice has been hurt by the encroachment of the modern world. This tape uncovers why the legacy of diviners, healers, poets, storytellers and singers is finding a home with the Catholic Church in Africa. 29 mins.
VHS: S15862. $19.95.

Sons of Bwiregi

Maryknoll Father Ed Hayes is filmed giving aid to the Tanzanian people, torn between old customs and the modern world. When one member of the tribe wants to remarry after the death of his wife, Father Hayes is given the opportunity to show the people that some traditions must change. An effort to show how a future can be built upon traditions of the past. Produced by Maryknoll Media. 25 mins.
VHS: S04935. $24.95.

Streetmother

Mary Mutahi was once a beauty queen. Crowned "Miss Nairobi," she eventually turned in her mantle and now cares for 80 children that call her house home. She is a new mother to these children, once sadly abandoned to the streets of Nairobi. Produced by Maryknoll Media. 25 mins.
VHS: S10839. $24.95.

Lion Hunters
(Interama, Inc.)

Music, Dance and Comedy

Music from Africa

Brother With Perfect Timing

South Africa's great pianist, Abdullah Ibrahim, performs with his band. 90 mins.

VHS: S07741. $29.95.

Juju Music: King Sunny Ade

King Sunny Ade, the most widely known performer of Juju music, performs here with Ebenezer Obey. Juju is a mix of the traditional music of Nigeria and popular Western music. An energetic performance. 1988, 51 mins.

VHS: S14741. $19.95.

Lions of Dakar

This video is a musical documentary about Afro-Pop, a West African amalgam of traditional and Western musical styles. Dakar, Senegal is the center of the genre which includes many of Africa's best known performers. Youssou N'Dour, famous in the United States for his work with Peter Gabriel, performs. Also appearing are Ismael Lo and Super Diamono. French narration with English subtitles. 50 mins.

VHS: S19797. $49.95.

The Master Musicians of Jahjouka

Performances at weddings, in a saint's tomb, in homes and in the village square document and preserve the rich musical history of a remote Moroccan village. Paul Bowles, Timothy Leary, Brion Gysin and others describe with unusual clarity how the Jahjouka musicians and their music have been affected by Western culture. Most striking is the performance of an ancient pagan ritual in which BuJlud, "The Father of Skins", appears in Jahjouka for the annual feast of sacrifice.

VHS: S16514. $45.00.

Michael Mendizza, USA, 1983, 60 mins.

Repercussions

A seven-part celebration of the roots of African-American music, shot over a three-year period, documenting the journey that traditional music made across the Atlantic. (For *Parts 1-4* see *Popular Music*).

Parts 5 & 6: The Drums of Dagbon/Caribbean Crucible. The first part focuses on the Dagbamba drummers in northern Ghana, and their complex social role. *Caribbean Crucible* traces the complex and fascinating ties that bind the music of coastal West Africa to the music of Europe. The film explores the sounds of reggae and deejay. 120 mins.

VHS: S03175. $39.95.

Part 7: Africa Comeback: The Popular Music of West Africa. Africa's own popular music industry has grown rapidly over the past two decades, and this final program explores the Highlife of Ghana, the Afro-Beat and Juju of Nigeria. The popular music scene in Ghana is explored through its most famous musicians, including Nana Ampadu and the African Brothers, Koo Nimo, Smart Nkansah and the Sunsum Band and Segun Adewale. 60 mins.

VHS: S03176. $39.95.

Rhythms of Resistance

The music of Black South Africa is explored. Included are Ladysmith Black Mambazo, Malombo, Johnny Clegg, The Mahotella Queens and others. 63 mins.

VHS: S12605. $19.95.

Salif Keita: Destiny of a Noble Outcast

Originating from Mali in West Africa, Salif is a unique voice in African music. A direct descendant of Emperor Sundiata Keita, the warrior king who founded the Mandinka Empire in the 13th century, Salif triumphed over the handicaps of being an albino in Black Africa, and the tradition of the now politically powerless aristocracy which did not permit the vocation of professional musician. Live performance, interviews, and dramatized sequences over two continents draw a detailed portrait of this remarkable artist. Recorded in Hi-Fi stereo. 90 mins.

VHS: S16257. $14.95.

Gospel

Al Green...Everything's Gonna Be Alright

Al Green Live at the Celebrity Theater in Anaheim, California. 60 mins.
VHS: S21611. $29.95.

Al Green on Fire in Tokyo.

Al Green performs in Tokyo. 60 mins.
VHS: S14547. $29.95.

Allen T.D. Wiggin

The gospel performer and Epic recording artist performs live in New York City. 60 mins.

VHS: S21612. $29.95.

America's Music Gospel

Levar Burton hosts a two-part look at American gospel. *Part 1* features Andre Crouch and Mahalia Jackson while *Part 2* features Linda Hopkins and Sandra Crouch.

Part 1: 60 mins.
VHS: S05042. $19.95.
Part 2: 60 mins.
VHS: S05043. $19.95.

Angelic Gospel Singers

"Sweet Home", "Touch Me Jesus" and "Somebody's Praying For Me" are the featured songs.

VHS: S21613. $29.95.

Arvis Strickling Jones: From the Inside Out

A live performance featuring Dorothy Norwood and the First Union Choir. 60 mins.

VHS: S21614. $29.95.

Repercussions
(Public Media, Inc.)

Bishop Jeff Banks/Revival Mass Choir

Recorded live at A.M.E. Church in Newark, New Jersey. "Didn't I Tell You", "Let Me Talk in the Spirit" and " You Can Make It If You Try" are featured. 60 mins.

VHS: S21615. $29.95.

Breathe On Me: Rev. James Cleveland

A live performance with the Northern and Southern Community choirs of the G.M.W.A. 60 mins.

VHS: S21616. $29.95.

Clark Sisters

A live concert by the Clark sisters recorded at the World of Faith Christian Center in Detroit. 60 mins.

VHS: S21617. $29.95.

Clouds of Joy

A live concert by the Mighty Clouds of Joy. 60 mins.

VHS: S21618. $24.95.

Commissioned in Concert

A concert at the State Theatre in Detroit. With a special appeerence by Derrick Brinkley. 90 mins.

VHS: S21619. $29.95.

D.F.W. Mass " I Will Let Nothing Separate Me"

Includes "I Will Say Yes To The Lord," "Don't Give Up" and other songs.

VHS: S21620. $29.95.

Down Memory Lane: Rev. James Cleveland

Recorded live at the Mount Pigsah Baptist Church in Chicago. Also features Inez Andrews, Albertina Walker and the Barnet Sisters. 60 mins.

VHS: S21621. $29.95.

Dr. Charles G. Hayes and the Cosmopolitan Church of Prayer

Includes "I'll Never Forget", "My Soul Cries Out" and "Step Back Let God Do It".
VHS: S21622. $29.95.

Florida Mass Choir: "Higher Hope"

Recorded live in Lakeland, Florida. Features the songs "Higher Hope", "Waymaker" and "I Found the Answer". USA, 1990.
VHS: S21623. $29.95.

Florida Mass Choir: "Now I Can See"

Recorded live in Lakeland, Florida with Rev. Arthur T. Jones. 60 mins.
VHS: S21624. $29.95.

Georgia Mass Choir: "I Sing Because I'm Happy"

Recorded live at the Greater Rising Star Baptist Church. USA, 1993.
VHS: S21625. $29.95.

Glory of Gospel

Vol. 1. Talented young gospel performers from choirs and colleges across the U.S. perform. 60 mins.
VHS: S21626. $29.95.

Vol. 2. Revival themes and the rhythm of African song are explored. 60 mins.
VHS: S21627. $29.95.

Vol. 3. Part 3 continues with performances by a new generation of gospel singers. 60 mins.
VHS: S21628. $29.95.

Vol. 4. The U.S. Airforce Choir, Rutgers University Choir and others perform. 60 mins.
VHS: S21629. $29.95.

Gospel Keynotes Live

Filmed at Mississippi's Jackson State University.
VHS: S21630. $29.95.

Gospel's Best From Saturday Night Sing

This tape features the gospel talents of The Williams Brothers, Ricky Dillard, Danniebelle Hall, Daryl Coley, The Fairfield Four, Albertina Walker and The Barrett Sisters. USA, 1994, 45 mins.
VHS: S21327. $14.95.

Greatest Week In Gospel

Marvin and Rickie Johns, Soul Stirrers, Nicholas, The Five Blind Boys, Commissioned, Pop Staples, Higher Dimensions and Deleon all appear.

Part 1: 80 mins.
VHS: S21631. $29.95.

Part 2: 80 mins.
VHS: S21632. $29.95.

Part 3: 80 mins.
VHS: S21633. $29.95.

Part 4: 80 mins.
VHS: S21634. $29.95.

Hallelujah: A Gospel Celebration

The original Five Blind Boys, Inez Andrews and Bishop Kelsey are featured.
60 mins
VHS: S14610. $19.95.

Hezekiah Walker and the Love Fellowship Crusade Choir

This tape is a live concert recorded at Atlanta's Morehouse College and features "Christ Did It All", "I Will Go in Jesus Name" and "Calling My Name". 58 mins, 1994, USA.
VHS: S21326. $14.95.

Homecoming

Willie Neal Johnson, the Gospel Keynotes, Robert Blair and the Fantastic Violinaires, the Jackson Southernaires and the Williams Brothers all appear. 55 mins.

VHS: S21635. $29.95.

Jackson Southernaires

Recorded live at Jackson State University in Jackson, Mississippi. Features the songs "What Shall I Render" and "What A Friend We Have in Jesus". USA, 1987.

VHS: S21637. $29.95.

Jesus Paid It All

Recorded live in Atlanta, Georgia, this tape features Rev. Donald Vails and Rev. R.L. White. USA, 120 mins.

VHS: S21638. $29.95.

L. Barnes & Red Budd Choir: So Satisfied

Recorded at the Center Stage Theater in Atlanta. 55 mins.

VHS: S21639. $24.95.

L.A. Mass Choir

The L.A. Mass Choir is captured live in Anaheim with a guest appearance by Higher Dimension. USA, 60 mins.

VHS: S21640. $29.95.

Mahalia Jackson "Give God The Glory"

Mahalia Jackson's final tour of Europe is the setting for this documentary which studies the singer's life and music. 88 mins.

VHS: S21636. $29.95.

McDonald's Gospelfest

Marilyn McCoo and Glynn Turman host this gospel celebration. Featuring Edwin Hawkins, Daryl Coley, and The Conquerors.

Part 1: 60 mins.
VHS: S21641. $24.95.

Part 2: 60 mins.
VHS: S21642. $24.95.

Mississippi Mass Choir

Recorded live at the Mississippi State Coliseum. USA, 120 mins.
VHS: S21643. $29.95.

Mississippi Mass Choir: God Gets The Glory

A new gospel collection from the Mississippi Mass Choir.
VHS: S21644. $29.95.

New Jersey Mass Choir

The New Jersey Mass Choir is filmed live at the Aaron Davis Hall in New York City. With Donnie Harper and the New Jersey Mass Choir. USA, 1992, 60 mins.
VHS: S21645. $29.95.

New York Restoration Choir: Thank You Jesus

Includes "We Worship You", "Lamb Of God" and "Ain't That Love".
VHS: S21646. $29.95.

Oh Happy Day

Shirley Caesar, The Mighty Clouds of Joy, Rev. James Cleveland and the Clark Sisters all perform. 60 mins.
VHS: S21647. $29.95.

Parade of Stars

A four part series featuring the work of gospel's greatest.

Vol. 1: 60 mins.
VHS: S21648. $29.95.

Vol. 2: 1989, 60 mins.
VHS: S21649. $29.95.

Vol. 3: 1990, 60 mins.
VHS: S21650. $29.95.

Vol. 4: Live Gospel: 1990, 60 mins.
VHS: S21651. $29.95.

Pentecostal Community Choir with Minister Keith Pringle

Includes " No Greater Love ", "Help Him Lift Me Up" and others.
VHS: S21652. $29.95.

Pilgrim Jubilees

Recorded live in Jackson, Mississippi. Includes "We're The People" and "Feel the World".
VHS: S21653. $29.95.

Rev. Clay Evans: I'm Going Through

Recorded live at the Fellowship Baptist Church in Chicago.
VHS: S21658. $29.95.

Rev. Ernest Davis, Jr. and the Wilmington Chester Mass Choir: "He's Preparing Me"

Recorded live at the Church of Atlanta Lighthouse. 80 mins.
VHS: S21656. $29.95.

Rev. F.C. Barnes and Co.

A live performance in Atlanta.
VHS: S21654. $24.95.

Rev. James Cleveland and the L.A. Gospel Messengers

Includes "We're On Business For The King", "Great Things" and others.
VHS: S21655. $29.95.

Rev. James Moore: Live With The Mississippi Mass Choir

Includes "We Worship Christ The Lord", "God Don't Need No Matches" and "God Will Take Care Of You". 80 mins.
VHS: S21657. $29.95.

Rick Grundy Chorale

Video performances by gospel's recent stars include "I'm Standin' Here" and "Just Say the Word". 60 mins.
VHS: S21659. $24.95.

Roots of Gospel

The New World Gospel Choir performs in Biblical settings.
Part 1: 60 mins.
VHS: S21660. $24.95.
Part 2: 45 mins.
VHS: S21661. $24.95.

Say Amen, Somebody

A celebration of gospel music featuring Willie Mae Ford Smith, Thomas A. Dorsey, The Barrett Sisters and the O'Neal Twins. *People Magazine* referred to this film as one of the ten best of 1983. A cheerful and uplifting musical.
VHS: S01162. $24.95.
Laser: LD71322. $39.95.
George Nierenberg, USA, 1983, 100 mins.

The Sensational Nightingales: Ministry In Song

Includes "Nichodemus", "It's Gonna Rain" and " Ain't That Love".
VHS: S21662. $29.95.

T'ain't Nothin Changed

A musical look back at the history of gospel. Features Dr. Mattie Moss Clark. 60 mins.

VHS: S21663. $29.95.

Tramaine Hawkins

Feature "I'll Give It To You", "Praise The Name Of Jesus" and other songs. 90 mins.

VHS: S21664. $24.95.

Walter Hawkins and Love Alive IV

Includes "Solid Rock", "I Can't Bear It", "He Knows" and other songs. 1990, 60 mins.

VHS: S21665. $29.95.

Wanda Nero Butler: New Born Soul

The award-winning gospel singer is captured live in San Francisco. Special guest appearence by Arvis Strickling Jones. 60 mins.

VHS: S21666. $29.95.

Williams Brothers: "I'm Just A Nobody"

Recorded live at Jackson State University, Mississippi. Includes "I'm Just A Nobody", "He'll Understand" and "Jesus Made A Way".

VHS: S21667. $29.95.

Willie Banks and the Messengers

"For The Wrong I've Done", "Hear Me When I Call" and "God Is Still In Charge" are performed along with other songs. 60 mins.

VHS: S21668. $29.95.

Willie Neal Johnson and the New Keynotes: "The Country Boy Goes Home"

Recorded with the Tyler Chapter Choir in Tyler, Texas. Includes "With God I'm Satisfied" and "Hold On".

VHS: S21669. $29.95.

The Winans: Live in Concert

A live performance featuring Vanessa Bell Armstrong. 120 mins.
VHS: S21670. $29.95.

The Winans: Return

Grammy winners The Winans sing selections from their gospel hit album *Return*. Includes "It's Time" and "Friend of Mine". 81 mins.
VHS: S21671. $24.95.

Popular Music

Buried Treasures: Volume 3—Rap Source

This addition to the performance series captures the unique beginnings of the rap movement in music and music video. The street style and edge that continues to influence rap today and more recent developments in the genre are included. Highlights of the program include the earliest works by Eric B. & Rakim, the rare 1992 live version of "Bring the Noise", a collaboration between speed metal band Anthrax and rap artists Public Enemy. With Def Jeff, Isis and Professor X. 35 mins.
VHS: S16684. $14.95.

Chuck Berry: Rock and Roll Music

Rock and roll legend Chuck Berry is featured live in this 1969 performance. D.A. Pennebaker, director of *Don't Look Back*, captures such classics as "Johnny B. Goode", "Maybelline", and "Sweet Little Sixteen". 45 mins.
VHS: S16089. $14.98.
D.A. Pennebaker, USA, 1969, 45 mins.

Chuck Berry at the Roxy

Chuck Berry plays his best-known hits, "Roll Over Beethoven", "Johnny B. Goode", "Hail, Hail Rock and Roll" and "Nadine". Recorded live in Los Angeles, Berry is joined on stage by Tina Turner.
VHS: S19895. $14.95.
Scott Sternberg, USA, 1982, 60 mins.

Diana Ross Live

Diana Ross performs jazz classics in this December 1992 show at the Ritz Theatre in New York. Along with trumpeter Gil Askey and director Steve Binder, she reinterprets the works of Billie Holiday, Rodgers and Hart, George Gershwin and Count Basie. The numbers include "God Bless the Child", "My Man", "Good Morning Heartache" and "The Man I Love". A look at Diana Ross as she continues to broaden her range. Also included is backstage documentary footage.
VHS: S18319. $24.95.
Laser: LD71856. $34.95.
Steve Binder, USA, 1992, 90 mins.

Grover Washington, Jr. in Concert

Leading jazz and pop performer Grover Washington, Jr. is captured at the height of his craft, performing "Just the Two of Us", "Winelight" and other numbers with band members Richard Tee, Steve Gadd and Eric Gale. "Perhaps the finest audio of any home video to date" (*Billboard*). 60 mins.
VHS: S19228. $19.98.

Guitar Legends

Among the artists included here are B.B. King who performs "Heartbreaker" and Jimi Hendrix who performs "Hey Joe". 33 mins.
VHS: S19315. $14.98.

Jimi Plays Berkeley

Hendrix is captured live in the famous Memorial Day concert. Mitch Mitchell is on bass while Billy Cox is on drums.
VHS: S00655. $19.98.
Billy Pilafian, USA, 1971, 55 mins.

Jimi Hendrix: Experience

Possibly the greatest guitarist of rock `n' roll, Jimi Hendrix is profiled here on and off the stage. Narrated by British blues master Alexis Korner, the film features "Purple Haze", "Foxy Lady" and a special acoustic performance of "Hear My Train A Comin'". Directed by Peter Neal. 33 mins.
VHS: S16091. $14.98.

Let the Good Times Roll

In its 25 year history, the New Orleans Jazz and Heritage Festival has captured a wide variety of American music, representing roots/rock, gospel, zydeco, cajun, blues, world beat and jazz. *Let the Good Times Roll* embraces over 40 performances demonstrating the history, heritage and influence of the New Orleans scene on American music. Featured musicians include the Dirty Dozen Brass Band, John Lee Hooker, Wynton Marsalis and Band, Robert Cray, Queen Ida, and the Neville Brothers. 86 mins.

VHS: S16038. $19.95.

Listen Up: The Lives of Quincy Jones

A feature-film portrait of composer and musician Quincy Jones. The film traces his career from a chart-busting pioneer of pop music to composing scores for over 40 movies and producing/arranging the top selling album of all time—Michael Jackson's *Thriller*. Features appearances by Ray Charles, Frank Sinatra, Rev. Jesse Jackson, Ice-T, and dozens more.

VHS: S14105. $19.98.
Laser: LD70614. $29.98.

Ellen Weissbrod, USA, 1990, 114 mins.

Little Richard: Keep on Rockin'

Truly one of the pioneers of rock `n' roll, Little Richard is captured live by documentary director D.A. Pennebaker. "Tutti Frutti", "Lucille" and six more favorites are featured. 30 mins.

VHS: S16092. $14.98.

Marvin Gaye

This video is a a look at the life and music of the late Marvin Gaye. Hosted by Smokey Robinson, the tape also features Ashford and Simpson and Motown founder Berry Gordy Jr.. 60 mins.

VHS: S21675. $19.95.

Quincy Jones: A Celebration

Ray Charles and James Ingram are among the stars performing in this musical tribute to the great Quincy Jones. 60 mins.

VHS: S21672. $14.95.

Repercussions

A seven-part celebration of the roots of African-American music, shot over a three-year period, documenting the journey that traditional music made across the Atlantic (for *Parts 5-7* see *Music from Africa*).

Parts 1 & 2: Born Musicians/On the Battlefield. The first film focuses on the professional musicians of West Africa, and particularly the Mandinka Music of the Gambia; the second, on how African musical sensibility came to be integrated into American gospel music, particularly in Alabama, in the form of traditional unaccompanied male gospel quartets. 120 mins.
VHS: S03173. $39.95.

Parts 3 & 4: Legends of Rhythm and Blues/Sit Down and Listen: The Story of Max Roach. *Legends* tells the story and records the music of some of the greatest living blues performers who migrated from Mississippi to the West, generating the way for rock `n' roll. Legendary performers like Big Mama Thornton, "Hound Dog" creator Lowell Fulson and Lloyd Glen are featured. *Sit Down and Listen* concentrates on the Afro-American tradition at its most sophisticated and daring—the art jazz of the postwar East Coast, and on its great leader, drummer Max Roach. 120 mins.
VHS: S03174. $39.95.

Right On!: Poetry on Film

The original Last Poets, the forerunners of rap music, appeared in 1968 to perform their mixture of guerilla poetry, blues, gospel and jazz. Their music was born of the social protest and turmoil of the time. Gylan Kain, Felipe Luciano and David Nelson were the Last Poets and here is the only film to have captured the revolutionary essence of their work.
VHS: S16689. $19.95.
Herbert Danska, USA, 1971, 80 mins.

Sentimental Journey

The late singer/actress Pearl Bailey hosts *Sentimental Journey*, a trio of special programs dedicated to some of the greatest moments in musical television. Discover the roots of today's contemporary sound with appearances by Sammy Davis, Jr., Duke Ellington, Lionel Hampton, Eartha Kitt, Stevie Wonder, Sarah Vaughan and many more. 147 mins.

VHS: S16587. $29.95.

Shindig!: Legends of Rock `n' Roll

A collection of classic rock and roll performances taken from the 60s music series, featuring Aretha Franklin, Tina Turner, Bo Diddley, Little Anthony and the Imperials, Chuck Berry, "The Godfather of Soul" James Brown, and others. 30 mins.

VHS: S17402. $14.95.

Sign O' The Times

Prince directs this concert film featuring himself and percussionist Sheila E. Recorded live in Holland and in Prince's home state of Minnesota. The film covers material from the *Sign O' The Times* album and from earlier recordings. Also features the Sheena Easton video "U Got The Look" that was written by Prince.

VHS: S06618. $19.95.

Prince, USA, 1987, 85 mins.

The Temptations

The group that put Motown records into the big time is captured live in concert. Songs range from their own hits such as "The Way You Do the Things You Do" and "Just My Imagination" to interpretations of "Jesus Christ, Superstar". Recorded live at Harrah's in Atlantic City.

VHS: Currently out of print. May be available for rental in some video stores.

Gary Legon, USA, 1983, 60 mins.

The Temptations and The Four Tops

Stevie Wonder hosts this tribute to the two great Motown groups, The Temptations and The Four Tops. Guests include Aretha Franklin and Eddie Kendricks. 60 mins.

VHS: S21674. $12.95.

Tina Turner: The Girl from Nutbush

This documentary on the life and music of Tina Turner examines her poverty-stricken youth in rural Tennessee, her move to St. Louis and her troubled relationship with Ike Turner. The story documents her destructive collaborations with Ike and her hard-fought liberation when she reinvents herself as a solo performer. The work includes interviews with Cher, Ann-Margret, Mark Knopfler, Keith Richards and Elton John and a candid interview with Ike Turner. Tina performs "What's Love Got to Do with It",

"Private Dancer", "River Deep, Mountain High", "Proud Mary" and "We Don't Need Another Hero". Includes duets with Mick Jagger, David Bowie and Bryan Adams. 105 mins.

VHS: S19303. $19.99.

Reggae

Aswad "Live"

A live effort by one of England's most prolific and popular reggae bands. Their work has ranged from Pop to Dub and has always had a political edge. Here they perform their biggest hit, "Don't Turn Around" and titles from "Too Wicked" including a cover of "Give a Little Love". From a concert filmed at Hammersmith Odeon in December 1988. Recorded in Hi-Fi stereo, 70 mins.

VHS: S16159. $19.95.

Roots, Rock, Reggae

The Maytals, Lee "Scratch" Perry and other reggae notables are joined in this musical documentary. The film looks back at one of reggae's greatest moments: Kingston, Jamaica in 1977. 63 mins.

VHS: S08893. $19.95.

Time Will Tell: Bob Marley

Bob Marley was, before his death in 1981, not only the king of reggae music but an international phenomenon. The first words following the lowering of the colonial flag in Zimbabwe were "Ladies and Gentlemen Bob Marley and the Wailers". His collaboration with Peter Tosh (who also died tragically young), and the origins of his music, based upon the poverty and also the spirituality of his homeland, are explored here. Includes "No Woman, No Cry", "I Shot the Sheriff" and the ballad, "Redemption Song".

VHS: S17433. $19.95.

Declan Lowney, Great Britain, 1991, 85 mins.

Soul

James Brown & Guest B.B. King

James Brown, the "Godfather of Soul", performs with abandon in this taped concert at the Beverly Theater in Beverly Hills, California. He performs all his best known works, including "It's a Man's World", "Papa's Got a Brand New Bag", "Hot Pants" and "Sex Machine". Also appearing are blues legend B.B. King, (who performs "The Thrill Is Gone"), and pop superstar Michael Jackson. 66 mins.

VHS: S19581. $14.95.

James Brown: The Lost James Brown Tapes

In 1979, a semi-retired James Brown was lured back to the stage. The "Godfather of Soul" delivered a triumphant return performance. Unfortunately, the tapes of this comeback languished in legal limbo for 12 years and were only made available in the early 90s. Included here are "Papa's Got A Brand New Bag", "Please Please Please", "Georgia On My Mind" and an extra funky, twenty minute-long version of "Sex Machine". 60 mins.

VHS: S16090. $14.98.

Shindig! Presents Soul

Aretha Franklin, Booker T. and the MGs and James Brown are featured in this recording.

VHS: S14687. $12.95.

Artie Ripp, USA, 1990, 30 mins.

Blues

Albert King

Albert King, a true blues giant, first appeared in 1953 as a recording artist. He eventually signed with Stax where during the 1960s he produced a number of classic blues recordings. Included here are some of his best-known songs: "Blues Riff", "The Grass Ain't No Greener", "Born Under a Bad Sign", "They Call It Stormy Monday" and "Let the Good Times Roll".

VHS: S19681. $24.95.

An American Songster

A musical portrait of John Jackson, singer/guitarist and banjo player from Virginia. Jackson's career is traced from his discovery in a gas station by folklorist Chuck Perdue to international recognition. Filmed over several years at Jackson's home and at concerts. 30 mins.

VHS: S04167. $19.95.

Renato Tonelli, USA, 1985, 30 mins.

B.B. King Live at Nick's

B.B. King performs some of his classics live at Nick's in Dallas, Texas. Included are "The Thrill is Gone", "Everyday I Have the Blues" and "Nightlife".

VHS: S21063. $14.95.

Miles Kidder, USA, 1983, 50 mins.

Beale Street

W.C. Handy wrote the blues, Boss Crump abused his power, and Martin Luther King, Jr. marched days before his death on Beale Street, a street which is now the target of "urban renewal". This film is an oral history of the place. Among the Beale Streeters featured are B.B. King, the Hooks Brothers, Bobby Blue Bland, Prince Gabe, Maurice "Fess" Hulbert, and Rufus Thomas.

VHS: S07770. $39.95.

Krasilovsky/Rickey/Baldwin, USA, 1981, 28 mins.

Big City Blues

Jim Brewer talks about the links between traditional blues and the new urban sound in this Chicago-filmed musical documentary. Performers include Son Seals and harpist Billy Branch. St. Clair Bourne, USA, 28 mins.

VHS: S03194. $24.95.

Blues Accordin' to Lightnin' Hopkins

Lightnin' Hopkins, as captured by Les Blank, reveals more than the inspiration for his music. He returns to his hometown where he explores country blues, Hopkins' genre, as a vanishing art form.

VHS: S00160. $49.95.

Les Blank, USA, 1975, 31 mins.

Blues Like Showers of Rain

Features Lightnin' Hopkins and Otis Spann. 30 mins.
VHS: S03185. $24.95.

*The Blues Accordin'
to Lightnin' Hopkins*
(Flower Films)

Blues Masters

Vol. 1. *Blues Masters* is a collection of the royalty of the blues. *Vol. 1* features Bessie Smith and Leadbelly doing "St. Louis Blues" among many other performances. Also included are Son House, Mamie Smith, Roy Milton and his Orchestra, Jimmy Rushing, Ethel Waters and Big Bill Broonzy. The documentary merges archival recording footage and photographs. 51 mins.
VHS: S19163. $19.98.

Vol. 2. The second part of this series includes Billie Holiday singing "Fine and Mellow" and Muddy Waters with "Hoochie Coochie Man." Other featured performers include Ida Cox, Big Mama Thornton, Joe Turner, Joe Williams, Buddy Guy, Jimmy Witherspoon and B.B. King. 51 mins.
VHS: S19164. $19.98.

Blues Summit in Chicago

Muddy Waters and many of his former collaborators, who are in themselves the stuff of legend, perform in this tribute to Waters. Aside from Waters, those appearing include Willie Dixon, Junior Wells, Koko Taylor, Mike Bloomfield and Buddy Miles. Songs include "Blow Wind Blow", "Long Distance Call", Messin' With The Kid", "Mannish Boy", "Got My Mojo Working" and "Hoochie Coochie Man". 60 mins.
VHS: S18716. $19.98.

Bo Diddley and the All Star Jam Show

Celebrate with Bo Diddley and friends during this all-star jam. Filmed live at Irvine Meadows in 1985. With Ron Wood, Carl Wilson, Mick Fleetwood, John Mayall and others. USA, 1985, 55 mins.

VHS: S15741. $19.95.

Boogie in Blue

A lively documentary biography of Harry "The Hipster" Gibson, also known as "The Mad Boogie Woogie Genius". Performance material, archival photography and interviews with Gibson and his family are used to put together a picture of the man and his music. Directed by Gibson's daughter Arlena Gibson and granddaughter Flavyn Feller. 40 mins.

VHS: S17914. $24.95.

Good Mornin' Blues

B.B. King narrates this documentary/performance video about country blues, its origins and its current artists. Bukka White, Big Joe Williams, Furry Lewis, Johnny Shines, Sam Chatmon and Gus Cannon all appear while the recordings of Son House, Charlie Patton and Willie Brown are used. A good introduction to the genre and a piece of blues history.

VHS: S17998. $24.95.

Johnny Taylor Live in Dallas

Rhythm and blues great Johnny Taylor performs live in Dallas, Texas. Includes "Who's Makin' Love To Your Old Lady", "Just Because" and "I Don't Want To Lose Your Love". 60 mins.

VHS: S21680. $24.95.

Koko Taylor: Queen of the Blues

Buddy Guy and Willie Dixon back up Koko Taylor in this performance and documentary. Songs include "I'm A Woman", "Let the Good Times Roll", "Beer Bottle Boogie", "I'd Rather Go Blind" and others. Interspersed footage reveals Taylor's roots and climb from Tennessee farm girl to blues legend. 60 mins.

VHS: S15877. $19.98.

Ladies Sing the Blues

Bessie Smith, Lena Horne, Billie Holiday, Dinah Washington, Ethel Waters, Sister Rosetta Tharp, Ida Cox, and Sarah Vaughan head the list of women performing blues classics. Horne performs "The Man I Love" and "Unlucky Woman" while Bessie Smith pitches in with "St. Louis Blues". 60 mins.

VHS: S19223. $19.98.
Laser: LD71905. $29.98.

Mark Naftalin's Blue Monday

Blue Monday party with John Lee Hooker & Charlie Musselwhite. Boogie and blues from the great John Lee Hooker. Features Charlie Musselwhite on harmonica. 30 mins.

VHS: S12337. $24.95.

Masters of Comic Blues

This two-part series captures blues artists Mance Lipscomb, Lightnin' Hopkins, Rev. Gary Davis and Sonny Terry. 60 minutes each.

Mance Lipscomb and Lightnin' Hopkins. Rare footage from the 60s captures these blues greats at their peak. Taj Mahal hosts this performance/tribute to two blues legends.

VHS: S15702. $24.95.

Rev. Gary Davis and Sonny Terry. Also shot in the 60s, this video again captures two great blues artists at their best, communicating the power and brilliance of the American blues. Hosted by Taj Mahal.

VHS: S15704. $24.95.

Muddy Waters

A program about Chicago blues artist Muddy Waters. Born on a plantation near Clarksdale, Mississippi, Waters moved to Chicago and developed music which combined the idiom of the Mississippi Delta with the harsh poetry of the Chicago streets. Numbers include "Hoochie Coochie Man", "My Home Is in the Delta", "Baby You Don't Have to Go" and "I'm a King Bee".

VHS: S19679. $24.95.

Ornette: Made in America

Ornette Coleman, a musical trailblazer, is captured by the camera of Shirley Clarke. He discusses his views of America and his own music as he returns to his hometown in Texas.

VHS: S04477. $39.95.

Shirley Clarke, USA, 1985, 95 mins.

Out of the Blacks Into the Blues

A two-part work, this video uses both interviews and performances to tell the story of the blues.

Out of the Blacks Into the Blues, Part 1: Along the Old Man River. Features such performers as Bukka White, Furry Lewis, Roosevelt Sykes, Robert Peter Williams, Brownie McGhee and Sonny Terry.

VHS: S17999. $24.95.

Out of the Blacks Into the Blues, Part 2: A Way to Escape the Ghetto. This program includes the works of B.B. King, Willie Dixon, Mance Lipscomb, Brownie McGhee, Junior Wells, Buddy Guy, Sonny Terry and Arthur "Big Boy" Crudup.

VHS: S18000. $24.95.

The Search for Robert Johnson

The victim of a fatal shooting in his 20s, Robert Johnson left behind a very small body of recorded work. His influence on blues and popular music is, however, incalculable. Interviews with those who knew him and some of those influenced by him paint a tragic picture of an artist who died before his time.

VHS: S16882. $19.98.

Willie Dixon

Chicago blues artist Willie Dixon interweaves traditional elements of Black folklore and storytelling with the pessimism and soulful intensity of country blues. The numbers include "29 Ways", "I Think I Got the Blues", "It Don't Make Sense", "Gonna Rock This House Tonight" and "T'ain't Nobody's Business".

VHS: S19680. $24.95.

Zydeco Gumbo

Clifton Chenier the "King of Zydeco" performs with Terence Simien, Boozoo Chavis and John Delafose.
VHS: S12344. $19.95.

Jazz

Abbey Lincoln: You Gotta Pay the Band

The video edition features live and studio versions of songs on the album "You Gotta Pay the Band", as well as clips of the 1950s and 1960s movies in which Abbey starred. Stan Getz appears in his last recording session with guest Spike Lee. Also appearing are Tony Bennett and Ruth Brown. 58 mins.
VHS: S15713. $24.95.
Laser: LD70283. $19.95.

After Hours

Coleman Hawkins and Roy Eldridge are captured live in an early morning jam session.
VHS: S03192. $24.95.

Alberta Hunter: My Castle's Rockin'

Legendary singer/songwriter Alberta Hunter opened her personal archives to the director of this film. Included are renditons of "Handy Man", "Black Shadows" and "My Castle's Rockin'". Footage also includes pieces with various friends and colleagues of Hunter's including Louis Armstrong, Eubie Blake, Bessie Smith, King Oliver, Paul Robeson and Fats Waller. The final interview with Alberta Hunter, at age 89, is also included. 1984, 59 mins.
VHS: S17611. $19.98.

Anything For Jazz

Jaki Byard appears on piano with his Big Band the "Apollo Stompers".
VHS: S03184. $19.95.

Archie Shepp: I Am Jazz...It's My Life

Saxophonist Archie Shepp plays and discusses what his career as a jazz musician has meant to him. 52 mins.
VHS: S12332. $19.95.

Ben Webster: The Brute and the Beautiful

Saxophonist Ben Webster wrote and played with the likes of Duke Ellington, Benny Carter, Teddy Wilson, Gerry Mulligan and Jimmy Witherspoon. A fascinating look at the legendary jazz saxophonist Ben Webster. This film traces his origins in Kansas City in the 1920s and his European exile and final performance in Holland, in September, 1973. 60 mins.
VHS: S17964. $24.95.

The Best of Blank

Documentary director Les Blank chronicles the music from 15 of his films. Among the artists included here are Dizzy Gillespie and Lightnin' Hopkins.
VHS: S16986. $49.95.

Big Ben: Ben Webster in Europe

A portrait of tenor saxophonist Ben Webster. Songs include "My Romance" and "Perdido". Recorded in 1967.
VHS: S12334. $19.95.

Celebrating Bird:
The Triumph of
Charlie Parker
(Kultur Video)

Built By Hand: String Trio of New York

Progressive music from Charles Burham, James Emery and John Lindberg. Recorded in 1988. 30 mins.

VHS: S12335. $24.95.

Carmen McRae Live

Vocalist/pianist Carmen McRae is captured live in Tokyo. She performs such classics as "That Old Black Magic", "Thou Swell" and closing with the poignant "With One More Look at You". The backup band includes Pat Coil, Bob Bowman and Mark Pulice.

VHS: S12011. $39.95.
Laser: LD70332. $39.95.

Hiroshi Fukumoto, Japan, 1986, 82 mins.

Carnegie Hall Salutes The Jazz Masters

This tape is a celebration of Verve Records' jazz artists. Included are Herbie Hancock, Abbey Lincoln, Omar Hakim and Vanessa Williams. 1994, USA, 120 mins.

VHS: S21298. $24.95.
Laser: LD72423. $34.94.

Celebrating Bird: The Triumph of Charlie Parker

This video is an authorized documentary on the great Charlie Parker. The great saxophonist's career is chronicled from his beginings in Kansas City to his final days in New York. Interviews with family and friends are interspersed with live performances. 58 mins.

VHS: S05401. $29.95.

Chester Zardis: The Spirit of New Orleans

A documentary on the life and art of the revolutionary African-American bassist Chester Zardis. Director Preston McClanahan shows Zardis in his neighborhood, discussing his music and involved in simple acts of cooking, playing or just talking. A host of musical talents also perform and discuss jazz. These include Danny Barker, Louis Nelson, Jeanette Kimball, Wendell Brunious and Dr. Michael White. Leading jazz authorities Alan Lomax and William Russell contribute their insights and assessments of Zardis' work.

VHS: S19124. $29.95.

Preston McClanahan, USA, 1989, 88 mins.

Different Drummer: Elvin Jones

Elvin Jones' career is examined including rare footage of his work with John Coltrane. 30 mins.

VHS: S03189. $24.95.

Dizzy Gillespie

Dizzy Gillespie was the subject of Les Blank's first musical documentary. Included are interviews about his origins and music theory. There is of course plenty of music from Gillespie's oddly shaped horn.

VHS: S09298. $34.95.

Les Blank, USA, 1965, 20 mins.

Chester Zardis:
The Spirit of
New Orleans
(Rhapsody Films, Inc.)

Dizzy Gillespie: A Night in Chicago

Turning from "Tunisia" to Chicago this video records a performance by the late Dizzy Gillespie in the Windy City. In this concert Dizzy plays his standards including "Swing Low, Sweet Cadillac", "Embraceable You", " Round Midnight" and "A Night in Tunisia". 53 mins.

VHS: S19173. $19.98.

Dizzy Gillespie: Live in London

Recorded at London's Royal Festival Hall, this tape captures an excellent performance by Dizzy Gillespie. Also appearing are James Moody, Slide Hampton, Arturo Sandoval, Claudio Roditti, Paquito D'Rivera, Mario Rivera and Flora Purim, The soundtrack won a Grammy for Best Big Band Jazz Ensemble. 91 mins.

VHS: S19002. $29.95.

Dizzy Gillespie: A Night in Tunisia

The late Dizzy Gillespie relates the musical story of his life and work. The program begins with a rehearsal and ends with live performance. The great trumpeter also discusses his writing of the famed tune "A Night in Tunisia" as well as the influence of Afro-Cuban rhythms on his work and on jazz in general. 28 mins.

VHS: S19224. $19.98.
Laser: LD71908. $29.98.

Eddie Jefferson

The great vocalist is captured in his final performance. Two days following this concert he passed away. 50 mins.

VHS: S12336. $19.98.

Ernie Andrews: Blues For Central Avenue

Ernie Andrews sings, backed by Buddy Collette and Harry "Sweets" Edison. 50 mins

VHS: S07744. $39.95.

Harlem Hotshots

A compilation of the best rhythm and blues and jazz stars of music's golden age. Featured are Lionel Hampton in *Airmail Special, Love You Like Mad*; Dizzy Gillespie in *Dizzy Atmosphere, Boogie in C*; Ruth Brown in *Have a Good Time*; Big Joe Turner, Bill Bailey and others. USA, 1953, 50 mins.

VHS: S04852. $29.95.

Harlem Swings

This series captures many of the great jazz and comic artists of the thirties, forties and fifties performing their best known acts. USA, 1950.

Harlem Swings, Volume 1. *Pie Pie Blackbird* (features Eubie Blake, Nina Mae McKinney); *Don Redman and His Orchestra with Red and Struggle*; *Adolph Zukor Presents Cab Calloway's "Hi-De-Ho", A Rhapsody in Black and Blue* (Louis Armstrong); *Adolph Zukor Presents Duke Ellington and His Orchestra in "Symphony in Black"*, and *Murder in Swingtime* (Les Hite and His Orchestra).
VHS: S21420. $29.95.

Harlem Swings, Volume 2. *The Nat "King" Cole Musical Story* narrated by Jeff Chandler; *Studio Films Inc. Presents Lionel Hampton, Sarah Vaughan, Martha Davis, Mantan Moreland and Nipsey Russell, The Larks, Little Buck and Count Basie, Amos Milburn, The Three Businessmen of Rhythm, Dinah Washington, Freddy and Flo, Nat "King" Cole and The Clovers.*
VHS: S21421. $29.95.

Harlem Swings, Volume 3. *Open the Door Richard* (Dusty Fletcher), *Slow Poke* (Stepin Fetchit), *Rufus Jones for President* (Ethel Waters, Sammy Davis, Jr. and Hamtree Harrington), *Caldonia* (Louis Jordan and His Tympany Five, Nicki O'Daniel, Richard Huey and Joan Clark).
VHS: S21422. $29.95.

Harlem Swings, Volume 4. *Harlem Hot Shots* (Leon Gross and His Orchestra, Cora Harris, "String Beans" Jackson, The Red Lily Chorus), *Virginia, Georgia and Caroline* (Cab Calloway); *R.C.M. Productions, Inc. Presents Louis Armstrong and His Band, Big Bang Boogie* (Lena Horne, The Ebony Trio and Private Alexander Brown); *Studio Films Inc. Presents Lionel Hampton, Joe Turner, Bill Bailey, Ruth Brown, Cab Calloway and Sarah Vaughan, Jittering Jitterbugs* (Hamtree Harrington and Lee Norman's Orchestra), *The Bronze Buckaroo* (Herbert Jeffrey).
VHS: S21423. $29.95.

Harlem Swings, Volume 5. *Rock 'n Roll Revue with Duke Ellington* (at the Apollo with Larry Darnell, Coles and Atkins, The Clovers, Dinah Washington, Nat "King" Cole, Lionel Hampton, Delta Rhythm Boys, Mantan Moreland, Nipsy Russell, Ruth Brown, Little Buck and Martha Davis).
VHS: S21424. $29.95.

Herbie Hancock Trio: Hurricane!

From his traditional jazz origins to his electric-funk hit single "Rocket", Herbie Hancock has performed and recorded a wide spectrum of styles. Here, along with his trio, Hancock is featured in an energetic electric performance.
VHS: S16727. $19.98.

Hi-De-Ho

Cab Calloway performs his trademark "Hi-De-Ho" and other musical numbers accompanied by Ida James and Jeni Le Gon. He also performs with dancers. Josh Binney, USA, 1947.

VHS: S07058. $34.95

Jazz: Earle Hines and Coleman Hawkins

Hines sings and plays piano while Hawkins adds saxophone. Includes "Crazy Rhythm" and "But Not For Me". 28 mins.

VHS: S21676. $24.95.

Jazz at the Smithsonian

The six-part series of jazz performances at The Smithsonian Institution.

Alberta Hunter. Her career began in Chicago singing in the speakeasies. She continued performing for the rest of her life with the likes of Louis Armstrong and King Oliver. Here, in a concert recorded in her 87th year, she performs "My Castle's Rockin'", "When You're Smiling", "Downhearted Blues", "Blackman" and others.

VHS: S05421. $29.95.

Clark Santee/Delia Gravel Santee, USA, 1982, 60 mins.

Art Blakey and the Jazz Messengers. Drummer Art Blakey and the Jazz Messengers are joined by Wynton and Branford Marsalis in this 1982 Smithsonian concert. Songs included are "Little Man", "My Ship", "New York" and "Webb City".

VHS: S07742. $29.95.

Clark Santee/Delia Gravel Santee, USA, 1982, 60 mins.

Art Farmer. Trumpeter Art Farmer performs live at the Smithsonian. His quartet includes Fred Hersch (piano), Dennis Irwin (bass) and Billy Hart (drums). Songs include "You Know I Care", "Red Cross", "Cherokee Sketches" and "Blue Monk".

VHS: S05429. $29.95.

Clark Santee/Delia Gravel Santee, USA, 1982, 60 mins.

Benny Carter. Alto saxophonist and trumpeter Benny Carter is featured in this Smithsonian concert. Carter, clearly one of jazz's greats, performs "Honeysuckle Rose", "Misty", "Take the A Train", "Cottontail" and "Autumn Leaves".

VHS: S05426. $29.95.

Clark Santee/Delia Gravel Santee, USA, 1982, 60 mins.

Joe Williams. The great Joe Williams performs at the Smithsonian Institution in 1982. Included are "Every Day I Have the Blues", "Who She Do", "Save That Time For Me" and others. Williams is backed by Kirk Stuart, Keeter Betts and Steve Williams.

VHS: S03828. $29.95.

Clark Santee/Delia Gravel Santee, USA, 1982, 60 mins.

Stanley Turrentine in Concert. Stanley Turrentine's saxophone is heard here in his first video release. He has played with the likes of Ray Charles, Shirley Scott, Max Roach and Jimmy Smith. Here he performs "Sugar", "Oop Bob Sh'bam", "Indian Summer", "Gibralter" and others.

VHS: S13930. $29.95.

Andy Cotten, USA, 1990, 60 mins.

Jazz in Exile

Many of the great American jazz musicians gravitated toward Europe. Included here are Richard Davis, Phil Woods, Dexter Gordon, Randy Weston, Johnny Griffin and others. USA, 1978, 58 mins.

VHS: S00653. $29.95.

Joe Williams: A Song Is Born

Joe Williams teams up with George Shearing in this live performance from the Paul Mason Winery. Williams, whose long career began with the Count Basie Orchestra, was voted best male vocalist in the 1992 Down Beat Critics' poll. Songs include "Just Friends", "Nobody's Heart Belongs to Me" and "Sometimes I'm Happy". 1991, 58 mins.

VHS: S17609. $19.98.

Keith Jarrett Last Solo

This tape features Jarrett in his legenday Tokyo Performances from 1984. Includes Harold Arlen's "Over the Rainbow". Kaname Kawachi, Japan, 1984.

VHS: S05422. $29.95.

Kenny Drew Live

Drew is captured live at the Brewhouse Theatre in Taunton performing such tunes as "Saint Thomas" by Sonny Rollins and "It Might As Well Be Spring" by Oscar Hammerstein. The backup band includes Alvin Queen on the drums and Niels-Henning Orsted Pedersen on bass. Stanley Dorfman, USA, 55 mins.

VHS: S18380. $19.95.

L.A. All-Stars

Hampton Hawes (piano), Leroy Vinnegar (bass), Harry "Sweets" Edison (trumpet) and Teddy Edwards (sax) perform a set. The tape also includes footage of vocalist Big Joe Turner and Sonny Criss playing saxophone. 28 mins.

VHS: S05634. $24.95.

Lady Day: The Many Faces of Billie Holiday

The life of Billie Holiday is examined in this documentary through rare archival footage and interviews with associates and performers she influenced. Those interviewed include Buck Clayton, Harry "Sweets" Edison (a Count Basie alumnus like Holiday) and her last accompanist, Mal Waldron. Ruby Dee reads passages from Lady Day's autobiography.

VHS: S13929. $29.95.

Matthew Seig, USA, 1991, 60 mins.

The Leaders: Jazz in Paris 1988

Arthur Blythe (alto-sax), Cecil McBee (bass) and Chico Freeman (tenor sax) are captured live in Paris. 54 mins

VHS: S12340. $19.95.

Les McCann Trio

Recorded live at Shelly's Manne Hole in Los Angles. Features a cover of Gene McDaniel's "Compared To What." 28 mins.

VHS: S04170. $19.95.

Lou Rawls Show with Duke Ellington

Rawls sings "Oh Happy Day" and other gospel and blues standards while Ellington adds his classics including "Satin Doll" and "Sophisticated Ladies". 48 mins.

VHS: S21677. $19.95.

The Mills Brothers Story

This nostalgic documentary about one of the most beloved vocal groups spans more than 50 years of their show business history. Through film clips dating back to 1932, you'll hear many timeless Mills Brothers songs, including "Paper Doll", "You Always Hurt (The One You Love)", "Till Then" and "Yellow Bird". 56 mins.

VHS: S15856. $29.95.

Mingus

A documentary about the life and music of the great bassist/composer. The hard times he faced, his poetry and his triumph in live music are all part of this tribute. The live section comes from a performance with his big band. Most of the film is shot in his New York apartment as he awaits eviction. USA, 1968, 58 mins.

VHS: S07743. $19.95.
Laser: LD71229. $29.95.

Modern Jazz Quartet

The Modern Jazz Quartet celebrate their 35th Anniversary at the Arts Festival in Freiberg, Germany. John Lewis (piano), Percy Heath (bass), Milt Jackson (vibraphone) and Connie Kay (drums) all appear. Songs include "Rockin' in Rhythm", "Echoes", "Django" and "A Day in Dubrovnik".

VHS: S20568. $19.95.

Hans-Klaus Petsch, USA, 1987, 60 mins.

Monk in Oslo

A documentary about the art and music of jazz pianist Thelonious Monk. His quartet of tenor saxophonist Charles Rouse, bassist Larry Gales and drummer Ben Riley were among the best jazz groups of the 60s. Filmed here in Norway, the quartet performs "Lulu's Back in Town", "Blue Monk" and "'Round Midnight". Produced for the Norwegian Broadcasting Corporation.

VHS: S19120. $19.95.

Harald Heide Steen, Jr., Norway, 1966, 33 mins.

Reed Royalty

This documentary traces the uses and development of jazz reed playing in relation to jazz's general evolution. The film is narrated in a loose style by Branford Marsalis, who performs two soprano saxophone numbers. The work also uses footage of Omer Simeon, Artie Shaw, Woody Herman, Benny Goodman, John Coltrane, Ornette Coleman and many others. 60 mins.

VHS: S17425. $29.95.

Ron Carter Live Double Bass

A "live" studio recording of innovative bassist Ron Carter. Features the title track, "Double Bass" and a medley of "Eight" and the spiritual, "Sometimes I

Feel Like a Motherless Child". The band includes Roland Hanna on piano, Lewis Nash on drums, Leon Maleson on bass and Kenyatte Abdur-Rahman performing the percussion duties. 55 mins.

VHS: S16002. $19.95.

Roots: Salute to the Saxophone

Four great saxophonists, Arthur Blythe, Chico Freeman, Sam Rivers and Nathan Davis team up in this celebration of the instrument. Features performances of "Never, Always", "Parker's Mood" and the seminal "Body and Soul". 55 mins.

VHS: S18378. $19.95.

Roy Ayers Live

Roy Ayers' vocal stylings are backed here by a first-rate band including Rex Rideout, Dennis Davis, Donald Nicks and Zachary Breaux. Featured songs include Ayers' own "Mystic Voyage" and Dizzy Gillespie's "Night in Tunisia". Stanley Dorfman, USA, 52 mins.

VHS: S18381. $19.95.

Shirley Horn: Here's to Life

Here's to Life records the production of Shirley Horn's album of the same title. In addition to the recording sessions, there is footage of other performances with her trio and interviews with those who knew and helped in her career, including Quincy Jones and Carmen McCrae.

VHS: S16524. $19.95.

Monk in Oslo
(Rhapsody Films, Inc.)

Sippie: Sippie Wallace

Singer Sippie Wallace recorded with Louis Armstrong, Sidney Bechet and King Oliver. This tape chronicles his life and music. 23 mins.
VHS: S03195. $24.95.

Standards II

Keith Jarrett, Gary Peacock and Jack DeJohnette team up in this "live" recording of jazz classics. Features "You Don't Know What Love Is", "Georgia On My Mind" and "On Green Dolphin Street".
VHS: S12010. $34.95.
Laser: LD70334. $39.95.
Kaname Kawachi, Japan, 91 mins.

Stations of the Elevated

A look at the bizarre beauty of grafitti-covered trains set to the music of jazz great Charles Mingus. The tape is an urban musical-documentary. 45 mins.
VHS: S12342. $19.95.

Tenor Titans

This documentary explores the development of the tenor saxophone as a solo instrument in jazz. Branford Marsalis traces this movement from Coleman Hawkins' recording "Body and Soul" through modern performers. Among the legends included are Bud Freeman, Lester Young, Stan Getz, Sal Nistico, Eric Dion, Frank Foster and Eddie "Lockjaw" Davis, Dexter Gordon, Charlie Rouse, Sam Taylor, Illinois Jacquet, Sonny Rollins and David Murray. These artists brought various "outside" influences and each made a separate contribution to the most American of musical styles, jazz. 60 mins.
VHS: S17426. $29.95.

Texas Tenor: The Illinois Jacquet Story

A documentary that deals with the life and music of Illinois Jacquet, the performer who developed a highly improvised sound that established the tenets of rhythm and blues while performing with Lionel Hampton's band. The director is fashion photographer Arthur Elgort, who elicits revealing insights into Jacquet's life and art through his contemporaries Hampton, Dizzy Gillespie, Clark Terry and Sonny Rollins.
VHS: S19119. $29.95.
Arthur Elgort, USA, 1991, 81 mins.

A Tribute to Bill Evans

Shot at the famed Brewhouse Theater, five legendary musicians gather to pay homage to Bill Evans. Trumpet and flugel horn player Kenny Wheeler, saxophonist Stan Sulzmann, bassist Dieter Ilg and drummer Tony Oxley interpret four of Evans' compositions, including "Blue in Green" and "Waltz for Debbie". 53 mins.

VHS: S18379. $19.95.

Texas Tenor:
The Illinois
Jacquet Story
(Rhapsody Films, Inc.)

Tribute to John Coltrane

"Mr. P.C.", "After the Rain/Naima" and "India/Impressions" make up the Coltrane tunes featured on this tape. Performing are Wayne Shorter (soprano sax), Dave Liebman (soprano sax), Richie Bierach (piano), Eddie Gomez (bass) and Jack DeJohnette (drums).

VHS: S12006. $29.95.

Kaname Kawachi, Japan, 1987, 57 mins.

Trumpet Course with Clark Terry

Band leader and trumpeter Clark Terry provides instruction for the trumpet beginner and tips for the intermediate musician. The tape begins with an introduction to the instrument and its accessories, then moves on to basic demonstration of how to play. There is also a thumbnail sketch of music theory.

VHS: S12155. $29.95.

John Clarke, USA, 1981, 52 mins.

Classical and Opera

Ariadne auf Naxos (Strauss)

Jessye Norman and Kathleen Battle, two African-American opera stars, are the featured performers in this Metropolitan Opera rendition of the Strauss Opera. Norman appears in the title role of Ariadne while Battle portrays Zerbinetta. James Levine conducts the Metropolitan Opera Orchestra with soloists Tatiana Troyanos and James King. In Hi-Fi stereo, 148 mins.

VHS: S16401. $34.95.

Shirley Verrett in "Cavalleria Rusticana"
(Video Artists International)

Cavalleria Rusticana

African-American diva Shirley Verrett gives a tour-de-force performance in this rendition of Mascagni's opera. A fitting tribute to the opera's 100th anniversary which was recorded at Sienna in 1990. 85 mins.

VHS: S13999. $39.95.

Faure/Poulenc Concert

Soprano Barbara Hendricks is featured in this performance of Faure's *Requiem* and Poulenc's *Gloria*. Filmed live at the St. Denis Basilica in France. USA, 1988, 70 mins.

VHS: S17316. $19.95.

Jessye Norman: A Christmas Concert

The famed diva sings pieces from Handel's *Messiah* and from Gounod, Bach, Brahms and Schubert. Also included are a wide range of spirituals including "Go Tell It on the Mountain", "He Shall Feed His Flock" and others. Conducted by Lawrence Foster and the Orchestre de L'Opera de Lyon. 68 mins.

VHS: S17667. $24.95.
Laser: LD71783. $34.95.

Jessye Norman: Live

Jessye Norman appears at Austria's prestigious Hohenems Festival in 1987. This recital features works by Handel, Schubert, Schumann, Brahms and Strauss, and Norman's signature encore "He's Got the Whole World in His Hand". In Hi-Fi Stereo, 1987, 60 mins.

VHS: S16274. $24.95.

Kathleen Battle at the Metropolitan Museum

The best known soprano of her generation, Kathleen Battle performs a solo recital for Deutsche Grammophon. The program matches material recorded for a live album at the Temple of Dendur in New York's Metropolitan Museum of Art. Battle performs works from Gershwin, Handel, Mozart, Strauss, Liszt and Puccini, among others.

VHS: S17240. $24.95.
Laser: LD71631. $29.95.

L'Africaine

The San Francisco Opera performs Giacomo Meyerbeer's piece about the so-called "Age of Exploration". Set on an African island this opera is a tale of greed, love and the lure of exploration. Features Shirley Verrett, and Placido Domingo as explorer Vasco da Gama. Conducted by Maurizio Arena, Directed by Lotfi Mansouri, 105 mins.

VHS: S10261. $49.95.

Shirley Verrett

The African-American diva's upbringing in the South and her rise to the top of the opera world are covered in this musical documentary. Featured musical performances include arias from *Samson and Delilah*, *Iphigenie en Tauride* and *Carmen*. USA, 1985, 60 mins.

VHS: S04684. $39.95.

Sound: Rahsaan Roland Kirk and John Cage

Two experimental musicians of the first rank here team up in a mesmerizing work. Recorded in 1967, 27 mins.

VHS: S21678. $24.95.

Treemonisha

The legendary Scott Joplin wrote one opera and this is it. It is a story of slaves on the plantation and their troubles. 92 mins.

VHS: S03835. $29.95.

Dance

Ailey Dances

Ailey's American Dance Theater performs five dance works. These include "Night Creatures", "Concerto for Symphony Orchestra and Ellington Band", "Cry", "The Lark Ascending" and "Revelations". Especially moving is "Cry," a piece composed as a birthday present for Ailey's mother in the days when he'd had no money for a "real" present. All pieces are introduced by Judith Jamison. USA, 1982, 90 mins.

VHS: S03638. $39.95.

Creole Giselle: Dance Theatre of Harlem

The acclaimed Dance Theatre of Harlem appears here in their trademark work, "Creole Giselle". The work is set in 1840s Louisiana and revolves around the lives of free Blacks away from their enslaved families. Virginia Johnson dances the part of Giselle in a critically applauded performance. Recorded live in Denmark. 88 mins, 1988.

VHS: S13931. $29.95.

Dance Theater of Harlem

The energy, creativity and classical perfection of the Dance Theater of Harlem are captured in dazzling performances of four signature pieces. The American classic, *Fall River Legend*, choreographed by Agnes de Mille, tells the story of the notorious Lizzie Borden. *Troy Game*, by Robert North, is a dynamic satire of the machismo attitudes inherent in sports. *The Beloved*, a ballet for two dancers by Lester Horton, confronts the themes of violence and fanaticism. *John Henry*, choreographed by Arthur Mitchell, is a celebration of the strength of the human will. 117 mins.

VHS: S12215. $39.95.

An Evening with Alvin Ailey and the American Dance Theater
(Public Media, Inc.)

Dance Black America

Narrated by Geoffrey Holder, this four-day festival held at the Brooklyn Academy of Music features the evolution of Black dance. Includes performances by the Alvin Ailey American Dance Theater and the Charles Moore Dance Theater. 1983, 87 mins.

VHS: S15335. $49.95.

Dancing

This 8-part series probes the traditions of dance in communities around the world—from the often-misunderstood waltz to the eloquent gestures of an Asante court dance in Ghana, and from the latest hip-hop in Morocco to a ballet class in Russia and a modern dance rehearsal in New York. Filmed on location on five continents, it explores the oldest and most compelling of languages: the art of communication called dance.

Dancing, Vol. 2: The Lord of the Dance. Dancers and dances have been worshipped as divine and feared as manifestations of the devil. Here we trace the cultural belief that shaped the great traditions of sacred and secular dance. Christianity has had an ambivalent view of dance in worship; Hinduism throughout India and the Yoruban religion of Nigeria combined worship and dance to create great dance/theater traditions. 58 min.
VHS: S18395. $29.95.

Dancing, Vol. 3: Dance at Court. In royal courts of the world, dance not only reached a pinnacle of elegance but played a role in the preservation of power and the maintenance of order and control. This function lives on in European ballet, the imposing dance of Asante kings in Africa, the refinement of Japan's Bugaku and the otherworldliness of the Javanese Bedoyo. 58 min.
VHS: S18396. $29.95.

Dancing, Vol. 7: The Individual and Tradition. This segment features extraordinary individuals who revolutionized dance: Isadora Duncan, Martha Graham, Katherine Dunham, George Balanchine, Twyla Tharp, Eiko and Koma, Sardono Kusumo and Garth Fagan. 58 min.
VHS: S18400. $29.95.

An Evening with Alvin Ailey and the American Dance Theater

Four rhythmic pieces from Alvin Ailey, whose work combines athleticism and balletic grace.
VHS: S19332. $39.95.

Jazz Hoofer Baby Lawrence

Lawrence dances and rare clips with Charlie Parker and Art Tatum are shown in this look at jazz dance. 28 mins.
VHS: S03179. $19.95.

Masters of Tap

This documentary introduces viewers to the lively history of tap dance with three acknowledged masters, Charles ""Honi" Coles, Chuck Green and Will Gaines, serving as guides and teachers. Coles, often called the greatest living exponent of tap dancing, entertains the audience with his experiences in show business during the 20's and 30's, and demonstrates his mastery with the audience.

VHS: S08483. $39.95.

Jolyon Wimhurst, USA, 1988, 61 mins.

A Tribute to Alvin Ailey

The late Alvin Ailey's work is celebrated in this dance tribute. Performances of four works: "For Bird with Love", "Witness", "Memoria" and "Episodes". Each dance is introduced by Judith Jamison, the dancer and choreographer whose career was nurtured to stardom by Ailey and who has succeeded him as director of the Alvin Ailey Dance Theater. The first three works were choreographed by Ailey himself while the last was a tribute by Ulysses Dove. 120 mins.

VHS: S15992. $39.95.

Twist

Canadian independent filmmaker Ron Mann made this entertaining work about the history of the 50s dance craze. Mann interweaves archival footage and interviews with Chubby Checker, Hank Ballard, Joey Dee and various dancers to comment on the racial, social and artistic implications of the Twist. Mann argues the movement was the catalyst for American rock and roll. Cinematography by Bob Fresco.

VHS: S19732. $89.95.
Laser: LD72280. $49.95.

Ron Mann, Canada, 1992, 78 mins.

Comedy

Best of Eddie Murphy—Saturday Night Live

19-year-old Eddie Murphy's career began with his stint on *Saturday Night Live*. When his popularity proved to be greater than the show, his role was expanded. Included here are some of his finest moments: "Mr. Robinson's Neighborhood", Buckwheat, James Brown and Little Richard Simmons ("Good Golly Miss Molly, you look like a hog"). USA, 1986, 78 mins. VHS: S08717. $19.95.

Eddie Murphy "Delirious"

Eddie Murphy raps about life, sex, childhood and more in this scathing, scatalogical, stand-up performance.

VHS: S21679. $14.95.

Bruce Gowers, USA, 1983, 69 mins.

Eddie Murphy: Raw

Eddie Murphy's second stand-up performance film, featuring many of his woman-bashing observations on life.

VHS: S21673. $14.95.

Robert Townsend, USA, 1987, 90 mins.

Richard Pryor: Live in Concert

The most popular Black performer of the 70s, Richard Pryor, performs some of his best known bits. Not a tape for the puritanical.

VHS: S04506. $19.98.

Jeff Margolis, USA, 1979, 78 mins.

Rude

Rudy Ray Moore, star of such films as *Disco Godfather* and *Dolemite*, performs as a stand-up comic. He employs characters from his films in his act—especially *Dolemite*.

VHS: S18831. $19.95.

Rudy Ray Moore, USA, 86 mins.

Uptown Comedy Express

Arsenio Hall, Chris Rock, Robert Townsend, Barry Sobel and Marcia Warfield are featured in this presentation of a wild and funny showcase from Los Angeles' Ebony Theatre. No one is safe from comic attack. Jesse Jackson, preachers in general, alcohol, sexual relationships all get their due.

VHS: S11252. $59.99.

Russ Petranto, USA, 1987, 56 mins.

Whoopi Goldberg: Fontaine...Why Am I Straight?

Again no one is safe from comic attack. Jim and Tammy Bakker, Jerry Falwell, Jesse Jackson and the Reverend Al Sharpton, are all lampooned by Whoopi Goldberg's stage persona, Fontaine. She's out of the Betty Ford clinic, and taking on the real world. 51 mins.

VHS: S11004. $59.99.

Director Index

Adlon, Percy
  Bagdad Cafe

Ahearn, Charlie
  Wild Style

Allegret, Marc
  Zou Zou

Anderson, Steve
  South Central

Annaud, Jean-Jacques
  Black and White in Color

Ardolino, Emile
  Sister Act

Armstrong, Robin
  Pastime

Attenborough, Sir Richard
  Cry Freedom

Audley, Michael
  Mark of the Hawk

Avildsen, John G.
  Lean on Me

Badham, John
  The Bingo Long Traveling All-Stars and Motor Kings

Bagwell, Orlando
  Eyes on the Prize Prog. 3: Ain't Scared of Your Jails
  Eyes on the Prize Prog. 5: Mississippi: Is This America?

Bail, Chuck
  Cleopatra Jones and the Casino of Gold

Balewa, Saddik
  Kasarmu Ce: This Land Is Ours

Barnett, Rex
  Benjamin E. Mays: Mentor of Martin Luther King, Jr.
  Ida B. Wells
  Paul Robeson

Benjamin, Richard
  Made in America

Benson, Alan
  Toni Morrison: Profile of a Writer

Beresford, Bruce
  Driving Miss Daisy
  Mister Johnson

Bernard, Sheila (with Sam Pollard)
  Ain't Gonna Shuffle No More / A Nation of Law?

Berry, Joy
  Human Race Club: A Story About Making Friends

Berry, John
  Tamango

Binder, Steve
  Diana Ross Live

Binney, Josh
  Boardinghouse Blues
  Hi-De-Ho
  Killer Diller

Blank, Les
  Always for Pleasure
  Best of Blank
  Blues Accordin' to Lightnin' Hopkins
  Dizzy

Bloomfield, George
  African Journey (Wonderworks)

Bourne, St. Clair
  Big City Blues
  In Motion: Amiri Baraka

Brabant, Charles (with Marcel Pagliero)
  Respectful Prostitute

Brambilla, Marco
  Demolition Man

Brest, Martin
  Beverly Hills Cop

Brooks, Richard
  Blackboard Jungle

Brown, Clarence
  Intruder in the Dust

Brown, Georg Stanford (with John Erman, Charles S. Dubin and Lloyd Richards)
  Roots: The Next Generations

Brown, Melville
  Check and Double Check

Buchanan, Larry
  Free, White, and 21

Buell, Jed
  Lucky Ghost

Bunuel, Luis
  The Young One

Burnett, Charles
  To Sleep with Anger

Campanella II, Roy
  Brother Future (Wonderworks)

Campus, Michael
  Mack

Camus, Marcel
  Black Orpheus

Capra, Frank
  Negro Soldier

Carew, Topper
  Talkin' Dirty After Dark

Carlsen, Henning
  A World of Strangers

Carpenter, John
  They Live

Casciato, Tom
  Circle of Recovery

Castle, Jr., Nick
  Tap

Chenal, Pierre
  Native Son (1951)

Clarke, John
  Trumpet Course with Clark Terry

Clarke, Shirley
  The Connection

Ornette: Made in America
  Portrait of Jason

Clavell, James
  To Sir, With Love

Clein, John
  Keep Punching

Clouse, Robert
  Black Belt Jones

Cohen, Larry
  Black Caesar

Colla, Richard A.
  Don't Look Back: The Story of Leroy "Satchel" Paige

Coney, John
  Space Is the Place

Connelly, Marc (with William Keighley)
  The Green Pastures

Cook, Fielder
  I Know Why the Caged Bird Sings

Coonley, Don
  Purdy's Station

Corman, Roger
  Shame (The Intruder)

Costa-Gavras
  Betrayed

Cotten, Andy
  Stanley Turrentine in Concert: Jazz at the Smithsonian

Cousin, Amandillo
  Dreadlocks and the Three Bears

Cowan, Will
  The Nat "King" Cole Story

Crane, Barry
  Half Slave, Half Free, Part 2: Charlotte Forten's Mission

Craven, Wes
  The People Under the Stairs

Crossley, Callie (with James DeVinney)
Eyes on the Prize Prog. 6: Bridge to Freedom

Csaky, Mike (with John Percival, Andrew Harries, Christopher Ralling)
Africa, Part I: Different But Equal / Mastering A Continent
Africa, Part II: Caravans of Gold / Kings and Cities
Africa, Part III: The Bible and the Gun / This Magnificent African
Africa, Part IV: The Rise of Nationalism / The Legacy

Curling, Chris
Dark City

Danska, Herbert
Right On! Poetry on Film
Sweet Love, Bitter

Dash, Julie
Daughters of the Dust
Illusions

Davis, Ossie
Cotton Comes to Harlem

de Baroncelli, Jacques
The French Way

Deitch, Donna
The Women of Brewster Place

Del Ruth, Roy
Broadway Rhythm

Demme, Jonathan
Philadelphia

Denis, Claire
Chocolat
No Fear, No Die

Deren, Maya
Divine Horsemen: The Living Gods of Haiti

DeVinney, James (with Callie Crossley)
Eyes on the Prize Prog. 6: Bridge to Freedom

Dickerson, Ernest R.
Juice

Diegues, Carlos
Quilombo
Xica

Donner, Richard
Lethal Weapon
Lethal Weapon II
Lethal Weapon III
The Toy

Dorfman, Stanley
Kenny Drew Live
Roy Ayers Live

Downey, Robert
Putney Swope

Drazen, Anthony
Zebrahead

Dreifus, Arthur
Double Deal
Murder on Lennox Ave
Sunday Sinners

Dubin, Charles S. (with John Erman, Georg Stanford Brown and Lloyd Richards)
Roots: The Next Generations

Duke, Bill
Deep Cover
Rage in Harlem
Raisin in the Sun (1989)

Duke, William
The Killing Floor

Eastwood, Clint
Bird

Elgort, Arthur
Texas Tenor: The Illinois Jacquet Story

Ellis, Deb (with Denis Mueller)
FBI's War on Black America

Eriksen, Gordon (with John O'Brien)
The Big Dis

Erman, John (with Charles S. Dubin, Georg Stanford Brown and Lloyd Richards)
Roots: The Next Generations

Evans, John
The Black Godfather

Falk, Harry
The Sophisticated Gents

Fanaka, Jamaa
Black Sister's Revenge
Penitentiary

Penitentiary II
Penitentiary III
Soul Vengeance
Street Wars

Faure, William C.
Shaka Zulu

Feller, Flavyn (with Arlena Gibson)
Boogie in Blue

Fink, Kenneth
Road to Freedom: The Vernon Johns Story

Firstenberg, Sam
Breakin' II: Electric Boogaloo

Ford, John
Judge Priest
Sergeant Rutledge

Fosse, Bob
Pippin

Franklin, Carl
One False Move

Fraser, Harry
Spirit of Youth

Freedman, Jerrold
Native Son (1986)

Freeland, Thorton
Jericho

Freeman, Morgan
Bopha!

Fried, Randall
Heaven Is a Playground

Friedkin, William
Blue Chips
The People vs. Paul Crump

Fukumoto, Hiroshi
Carmen McRae Live

Fuller, Samuel
China Gate

Furie, Sidney J.
Hit!
Lady Sings the Blues

Gardner, Robert
Clarence and Angel

Gerima, Haile
Ashes and Embers
Bush Mama

Gibson, Angus
7-Up in South Africa

Gibson, Arlena (with Flavyn Feller)
Boogie in Blue

Gibson, Brian
The Josephine Baker Story
What's Love Got to Do With It?

Girdler, William
Sheba, Baby

Girod, Francis
L'Etat Sauvage (The Savage State)

Gladstone, Howard (with James Ylisela)
The Race for Mayor

Goldberg, Franck
Franck Goldberg:Sampler

Goldstein, Allan
The House of Dies Drear (Wonderworks)

Goldstone, James
Brother John

Gordon, Robert
The Joe Louis Story

Gordy, Berry
Mahogany

Gowers, Bruce
Eddie Murphy "Delirious"

Graham, William A.
Get Christie Love

Greaves, William
Black Power in America: Myth or Reality?
Booker T. Washington: The Life and the Legacy
From These Roots
Frederick Douglass: An American Life
Deep North
Just Doin' It

Green, Guy
Patch of Blue

Green, Alfred
The Jackie Robinson Story

Greene, David
Roots

Greville, Edmond
Princess Tam Tam

Griffith, D.W.
  The Birth of a Nation

Gutierrez Alea, Tomas
  Last Supper

Hackford, Taylor
  An Officer and a Gentleman

Hampton, Henry
  Eyes on the Prize
  Eyes on the Prize II

Harries, Andrew (with John Percival, Mike Csaky, Christopher Ralling)
  Africa, Part I: Different But Equal / Mastering A Continent
  Africa, Part II: Caravans of Gold / Kings and Cities
  Africa, Part III: The Bible and the Gun / This Magnificent African
  Africa, Part IV: The Rise of Nationalism / The Legacy

Harris, Jr., Wendell B.
  Chameleon Street

Harris, Leslie
  Just Another Girl on the I.R.T.

Head, Helaine
  You Must Remember This (Wonderworks)

Henzell, Perry
  Harder They Come

Herzog, Werner
  Herdsmen of the Sun

Heywood, Donald
  Black King

Hickox, Douglas
  Zulu Dawn

Hill, Jack
  Coffy
  Foxy Brown

Hill, Walter
  48 Hours
  Another 48 Hours
  Brewster's Millions
  Trespass

Hiller, Arthur
  See No Evil, Hear No Evil
  Silver Streak

Hook, Harry
  Kitchen Toto

Hooks, Kevin
  Passenger 57
  Roots: The Gift

Hopper, Dennis
  Colors

Hudlin, Reginald
  Boomerang
  House Party

Hughes Brothers, USA, 1993, 97 mins.
  Menace II Society

Hunter, Tim
  The Saint of Fort Washington

Hyams, Peter
  Running Scared

Ichaso, Leon
  Sugar Hill

Irving, David
  Faith Ringgold: The Last Story Quilt

Irving, Richard
  The Jesse Owens Story

Iscove, Robert
  Puss 'n Boots (Faerie Tale Theatre)

Jackson, George (with Doug McHenry)
  House Party 2: The Pajama Jam

Jewison, Norman
  In the Heat of the Night
  Jesus Christ, Superstar
  A Soldier's Story

Jimenez, Neal (with Michael Steinberg)
  The Waterdance

Jordan, Nei
  The Crying Game
  Mona Lisa

Julien, Isaac
  Looking for Langston

Kadar, Jan
  Freedom Road

Kahn, Richard C.
  Bronze Buckaroo
  Harlem Rides the Range
  Two-Gun Man From Harlem

Kartemquin Films
  Kartemquin Films, Vol. 3: Trick Bag

Kawachi, Kaname
  Keith Jarrett Last Solo Standards II
  Tribute to John Coltrane

Kazan, Elia
  Pinky

Keighley, William (with Marc Connelly)
  The Green Pastures

Kelljan, Bob
  Scream, Blacula, Scream

Kemp, Jack
  Miracle in Harlem

Kidder, Miles
  B.B. King Live at Nick's

King, Jr., Woodie
  Malcolm X: Death of a Prophet
  Torture of Mothers: The Case of the Harlem Six
  Love to All, Lorraine (with Elizabeth Van Dyke)

Koff, David
  Blacks Britannica

Koff, David (with Anthony Kowarth)
  Black Man's Land Trilogy, Vol. 1, White Man's Country
  Black Man's Land Trilogy, Vol. 2, Mau Mau
  Black Man's Land Trilogy, Vol. 3, Kenyatta

Korda, Zoltan
  Cry, the Beloved Country
  Sanders of the River

Korty, John
  Autobiography of Miss Jane Pittman

Korwath, Anthony (with David Koff)
  Black Man's Land Trilogy, Vol. 1, White Man's Country
  Black Man's Land Trilogy, Vol. 2, Mau Mau
  Black Man's Land Trilogy, Vol. 3, Kenyatta

Kramer, Stanley
  Guess Who's Coming to Dinner
  Defiant Ones

Krasilovsky, Alexis (with Baldwin Rickey)
  Beale Street

Landis, John
  Coming to America
  Trading Places

Lane, Charles
  True Identity

Laneuville, Eric
  The Mighty Pawns (Wonderworks)

Lasseur, Dominique (with Catherine Tatgel)
  Beyond Hate Trilogy: Hate on Trial
  Beyond Hate Trilogy: Beyond Hate

Lathan, Stan
  Almos' a Man
  Beat Street
  Go Tell It on the Mountain
  The Sky Is Gray
  Uncle Tom's Cabin (1987)

Lee, Spike
  Do The Right Thing
  Joe's Bed-Stuy Barbershop: We Cut Heads
  Jungle Fever
  Malcolm X
  Mo' Better Blues
  School Daze
  She's Gotta Have It

Legon, Gary
  The Temptations

Leonard, Arthur
  Boy! What A Girl!
  Devil's Daughter
  Sepia Cinderella

Lerner, Carl
  Black Like Me

Lesage, Julia
  In Plain English

Levin, Meyer
  Falashas

Livingston, Jennie
  Paris Is Burning

Loeb, Janet (with Sidney Meyers)
Quiet One

London, Jerry
Kiss Shot

Lowe, Felix C.
Benjamin O. Davis, Jr.: American

Lowney, Declan
Time Will Tell: Bob Marley

Lumet, Sidney
The Pawnbroker
The Wiz

Luyat, Jean-Caude
Four Days of the Masai

Lynn, Jonathan
Distinguished Gentleman

Macartney-Filgate, Terence
Fields of Endless Day

MacDonald, Peter
Mo' Money

Magnoli, Albert
Purple Rain

Malone, Adrian
Millennium: Tribal Wisdom and the Modern World

Mann, Abby
King

Mann, Ron
Twist

Mansouri, Lofti
L'Africaine

March, Alex
Firehouse

Margolis, Jeff
Richard Pryor: Live in Concert

Marks, Arthur
Bucktown
Friday Foster
Monkey Hustle

Marsh, Ray
The Color of Love

Martin, D'Urville
Dolemite
Fass Black

Martinez, Jr., Rene
The Guy from Harlem

Matmor, Daniel
Urban Jungle

McClanahan, Preston
Chester Zardis: The Spirit of New Orleans

McHenry, Doug (with George Jackson)
House Party 2: The Pajama Jam

McLeod, Norman Z.
Panama Hattie

Mendizza, Michael
The Master Musicians of Jahjouka

Metter, Alan
Moving

Meyers, Sidney (with Janet Loeb)
Quiet One

Meza, Eric
House Party 3

Micheaux, Oscar
Body and Soul
Girl from Chicago
God's Step Children
Lying Lips
Murder In Harlem
Swing
Veiled Aristocrats
Within Our Gates

Miller, George
Mad Max Beyond Thunderdome

Miller, Peter (with John Valadez)
Passin' It On

Minnelli, Vincente
Cabin in the Sky

Moore, Rudy Ray
Avenging Disco Godfather
Rude

Morais, Leroy (with Bob Walsh)
Freedom Man

Moses, Gilbert
Runaway (Wonderworks)

Moses, Harry
Assault at West Point

Moss, Carlton
Portraits in Black

Mueller, Denis (with Deb Ellis)

FBI's War on Black America

Mulcahy, Russell
Ricochet

Mulligan, Robert
Clara's Heart
To Kill a Mockingbird

Murphy, Dudley
Emperor Jones

Murphy, Eddie
Harlem Nights

Nair, Mira
Mississippi Masala

Neal, Peter
Jimi Hendrix: Experience

Nelson, Ralph
A Hero Ain't Nothin' But a Sandwich
Lilies of the Field
The Wilby Conspiracy

Newfield, Sam
Harlem on the Prairie

Nierenberg, George
Say Amen, Somebody

Noble, Nigel
Voices of Sarafina!

Nolte, William
Duke Is Tops

O'Brien, John (with Gordon Eriksen)
The Big Dis

O'Neal, Ron
Superfly TNT

O'Steen, Sam
Sparkle

Oliver, Ruby
Love Your Mama

Ove, Horace
Playing Away

Pagliero, Marcel (with Charles Brabant)
Respectful Prostitute

Pakula, Alan J.
Pelican Brief

Palcy, Euzhan
A Dry White Season
Sugar Cane Alley

Palumbo, Dominic
The "Rodney King" Case: What the Jury Saw in California v. Powell

Parker, Alan
Fame
Mississippi Burning

Parks, Gordon
Half Slave, Half Free, Part 1
Leadbelly
Shaft
Shaft's Big Score
The Learning Tree

Parks Jr., Gordon
Superfly

Pasolini, Pier Paolo
Notes for an African Orestes

Pearce, Richard
Dead Man Out
The Long Walk Home

Peerce, Larry
The Court Martial of Jackie Robinson

Penn, Leo
A Man Called Adam

Pennebaker, D. A.
Chuck Berry: Rock and Roll Music
Little Richard: Keep on Rockin'

Percival, John/Christopher Ralling/Andrew Harries/Mick Csaky
Africa, Part I: Different But Equal / Mastering A Continent
Africa, Part II: Caravans of Gold / Kings and Cities
Africa, Part III: The Bible and the Gun / This Magnificent African
Africa, Part IV: The Rise of Nationalism / The Legacy

Peregini, Frank
The Scar of Shame

Petranto, Russ
Uptown Comedy Express

Petrie, Daniel
Raisin in the Sun (1971)

Petsch, Hans-Klaus
Modern Jazz Quartet

Phillips, Maurice

Another You

Pilafian, Billy
Jimi Plays Berkeley

Poitier, Sidney
Buck and the Preacher
Ghost Dad
Let's Do It Again
A Piece of the Action
Stir Crazy
Uptown Saturday Night

Pollack, Sydney
The Slender Thread

Pollard, Sam (with Sheila Bernard)
Ain't Gonna Shuffle No More / A Nation of Law?

Pollard, Bud
Beware
The Big Timers
Look Out Sister
Tall, Tan and Terrific

Popkin, Leo
Gang War

Preminger, Otto
Carmen Jones

Pressman, Michael
And the Children Shall Lead (Wonderworks)
Some Kind of Hero

Prince
Graffiti Bridge
Sign O' The Times
Under the Cherry Moon

Pryor, Richard
Jo Jo Dancer, Your Life is Calling

Rafelson, Bob
Mountains Of The Moon

Ralling, Christopher (with John Percival, Andrew Harries, Mike Csaky)
Africa, Part I: Different But Equal / Mastering A Continent
Africa, Part II: Caravans of Gold / Kings and Cities
Africa, Part III: The Bible and the Gun / This Magnificent African

Africa, Part IV: The Rise of Nationalism / The Legacy

Ray, Bernard B.
Broken Strings

Rich, Matty
Straight Out of Brooklyn

Richards, Lloyd
Paul Robeson
Roots: The Next Generations (with John Erman, Charles S. Dubin and Georg Stanford Brown)

Rickey, Baldwin (with Alexis Krasilovsky)
Beale Street

Ripp, Artie
Shindig! Presents Soul

Ritchie, Michael
The Golden Child

Ritt, Martin
Great White Hope
Paris Blues
Sounder

Roberts, Darryl
How U Like Me Now
Sweet Perfection

Robinson, Richard
Black Vengeance

Robson, Mark
Home of the Brave

Roemer, Michael
Nothing But a Man

Rogosin, Lionel
Come Back, Africa

Romero, George A.
Dawn of the Dead
Night of the Living Dead

Roodt, Darrell
City of Blood
Place of Weeping
Sarafina!

Roquemore, Cliff
Dolemite 2: The Human Tornado

Rose, Bernard
Candyman

Ross, Herbert
California Suite

Rouch, Jean
Jaguar
Les Maitres Fous

Lion Hunters

Rydell, Mark
The Reivers

Santee, Clark and Delia Gravel Santee
Alberta Hunter: Jazz at the Smithsonian
Art Blakey and the Jazz Messengers: Jazz at the Smithsonian
Art Farmer: Jazz at the Smithsonian
Benny Carter: Jazz at the Smithsonian
Joe Williams: Jazz at the Smithsonian

Saville, Philip
Mandela

Sayles, John
Brother From Another Planet
City of Hope
Matewan
Passion Fish

Schenkel, Carl
The Mighty Quinn

Schepisi, Fred
Six Degrees of Separation

Schoendorffer, Pierre
Anderson Platoon

Schrader, Paul
Blue Collar

Schroeder, Barbet
General Idi Amin Dada

Schultz, Michael
Car Wash
Carbon Copy
Cooley High
Disorderlies
For Us, the Living: The Story of Medgar Evers
Greased Lightning (with Melvin Van Peebles)
Krush Groove
Last Dragon

Scott, Tony
Beverly Hills Cop 2

Scott, Oz
Bustin' Loose

Seiden, Joseph
Paradise in Harlem

Seig, Matthew
Lady Day: The Many Faces of Billie Holiday

Shah, Krishna
River Niger

Shearer, Jacqueline (with Judith Vecchione)
The Keys to the Kingdom / Back to the Movement

Shelton, Ron
White Men Can't Jump

Sherin, Ed
The Father Clements Story

Shore, Sig
The Return of Superfly

Siegel, Don (with Robert Totten)
Death of a Gunfighter

Silberg, Joel
Breakin'
Rappin'

Singleton, John
Boyz N The Hood
Poetic Justice

Sirk, Douglas
Imitation of Life

Smallcombe, John
An African Dream

Smight, Jack
Roll of Thunder, Hear My Cry

Smith, Bruce
Bebe's Kids

Smith, Loretta
Where Did You Get that Woman?

Smith, John N.
Sitting in Limbo

Spangler, Larry
Joshua

Spielberg, Steven
The Color Purple

Sporn, Michael
Jazz Time Tale

Starr, Steven
Joey Breaker

Starrett, Jack
Cleopatra Jones

Staudte, Wolfgang
The Threepenny Opera

Steen Jr., Harald Heide
Monk in Oslo

Steinberg, Michael (with
Neal Jimenez)
  The Waterdance

Sternberg, Scott
  *Chuch Berry at the
  Roxy*

Stevens, Jr., George
  Separate But Equal

Stevenson, Robert
  King Solomon's Mines

Stone, Andrew
  Stormy Weather

Strand, Paul
  Native Land

Swackhamer, E. W.
  Man and Boy

Swanson, Donald
  *The Magic Garden (The
  Pennywhistle Blues)*

Tatgel, Catherine (with
Dominique Lasseur)
  *Beyond Hate Trilogy:
  Hate on Trial*
  *Beyond Hate Trilogy:
  Beyond Hate*

Tavernier, Bertrand
  *Coup De Torchon
  (Clean Slate)*
  'Round Midnight

Teague, Lewis
  T Bone N Weasel

Thomas, Marlo
  Free to Be...You and Me

Thompson, Robert
  *Words by Heart
  (Wonderworks)*

Thompson, J. Lee
  *Huckleberry Finn
  (1974)*

Thurling, Peter
  African Story Magic

Totten, Robert (with Don
Siegel)
  Death of a Gunfighter

Townsend, Robert
  Eddie Murphy: Raw
  The Five Heartbeats
  Hollywood Shuffle
  Meteor Man

Trent, John
  The Bushbaby

Ulmer, Edgar G.
  Moon Over Harlem

Uys, James
  Dingaka
  *The Gods Must Be
  Crazy*
  *The Gods Must Be
  Crazy II*

Valadez, John/Peter
Miller
  Passin' It On

Van Dyke, Elizabeth (with
Woodie King, Jr.)
  Love to All, Lorraine

Van Peebles, Melvin
  *Greased Lightning
  (with Michael Schultz)*
  *Story of A Three Day
  Pass*
  *Sweet Sweetback's
  Baadasssss Song*
  Watermelon Man

Van Peebles, Mario
  Posse
  New Jack City

Vasquez, Joseph B.
  *Hangin' with the
  Homeboys*

Vecchione, Judith
  *Eyes on the Prize I
  Prog. 1: Awakenings*
  *Eyes on the Prize I
  Prog. 2: Fighting Back*
  *The Keys to the
  Kingdom / Back to the
  Movement (with
  Jacqueline
  Shearer)*

Verona, Stephen
  Pipe Dreams

Vidor, King
  Hallelujah!

von Radvanyi, Geza
  *Uncle Tom's Cabin
  (1969)*

Vorhaus, Bernard
  Way Down South

Walsh, Bob (with Leroy
Morais)
  Freedom Man

Watkins, Peter
  The Journey, Volume 4.

Wayans, Keenan Ivory
  *I'm Gonna Git You
  Sucka*

Weissbrod, Ellen
  *Listen Up: The Lives of
  Quincy Jones*

Wellman, William
  Good-Bye, My Lady

Wendkos, Paul
  A Woman Called Moses

Whale, James
  Show Boat (1936)

White, Lois
  *Images: Tribute to
  Harold Washington*

Williams, Jr., Spencer
  Blood of Jesus
  *Dirty Gertie From
  Harlem*
  Girl in Room 20
  Go Down Death
  Juke Joint
  Marching On
  Son of Ingagi

Williamson, Fred
  Adios Amigos

Wills, J. Elder
  Song of Freedom

Wimhurst, Jolyon
  Masters of Tap

Wolfe, Leanna
  Running with Jesse

Wyler, William
  *Liberation Of L.B.
  Jones*

Yates, Peter
  *Mother, Jugs and
  Speed*

Ylisela, James (with
Howard Gladstone)
  The Race for Mayor

Young, Terence
  The Klansman

Zucker, Jerry
  Ghost

Zwick, Edward
  Glory

Major Performers Index

Joe Adams 6

Eddie Rochester
Anderson 4, 5, 11

Louis Armstrong 5, 16,
19, 126, 193, 198, 204

Josephine Baker 53, 102,
106, 110

Pearl Bailey 6, 184

Angela Bassett 60, 85

Louise Beavers 1, 10, 13

Harry Belafonte 6, 34, 84,
115, 141

Halle Berry 32

Avery Brooks 47, 73, 84

Clarence Brooks 5, 12, 18

Lucius Brooks 5, 12

LeVar Burton 28, 52, 73,
113, 172

Adolph Caesar 37, 77, 148

Diahann Carroll 6, 19,
44, 51

Nat King Cole 6, 15, 141,
198

Bill Cosby 35, 46, 58, 60,
64, 68, 84, 111, 113,
126, 132

Scatman Crothers 89, 93

Ice Cube 32, 83

Dorothy Dandridge 6, 24

Keith David 82

Ossie Davis 16, 39, 42,
45, 54, 55, 58, 73, 74,
154

Sammy Davis, Jr. 16, 82,
109, 126, 184, 198

Ruby Dee 13, 34, 39, 42,
46, 51, 54, 70, 73, 87,
117, 148, 201

Tamara Dobson 91

Charles Dutton 42, 61,
62, 118, 132

James Edwards 12

Lola Falana 55, 58

Antonio Fargas 52, 91, 92

Tyra Ferrell 69, 86, 120

Stepin Fetchit 14, 17,
126, 198

Redd Foxx 39, 48, 122

Sheila Frazier 97

Morgan Freeman 32, 42,
46, 56, 72, 115, 118, 154

Robin Givens 32, 70, 87

Danny Glover 32, 37, 40,
41, 57, 58, 60, 70, 71,
74, 82, 113,
114, 116

Whoopi Goldberg 36, 37,
45, 55, 58, 59, 74, 76,
85, 117, 213

Louis Gossett, Jr. 34, 42,
44, 65, 71-73, 87

Teresa Graves 93

Dick Gregory 81, 141

Pam Grier 47, 69, 91-93,
95, 96

Robert Guillaume 57, 97,
120

Moses Gunn 47, 48, 55,
95, 96, 116

Arsenio Hall 38, 48, 212

Kadeem Hardison 29

Dorian Harewood 52, 55,
73, 79

Edna Mae Harris 16, 18,
19, 23

Robin Harris 49, 63, 113

Monte Hawley 8, 16, 24

Isaac Hayes 51, 69, 95,
141

Juano Hernandez 13, 16,
17, 20, 71

Gregory Hines 70, 74, 81,
82, 118

Lena Horne 4, 5, 7, 8, 19,
23, 86, 191, 198

Rex Ingram 11

Samuel L. Jackson 29,
53, 61

Eartha Kitt 17, 32, 93,
184

Yaphet Kotto 18, 31, 58,
93, 94

Charles Lane 69, 83, 84

Ted Lange 93

Martin Lawrence 32, 81

Joie Lee 63

Spike Lee 42, 52, 54, 60,
63, 74, 75, 193

Cleavon Little 39, 42, 77

Moms Mabley 2, 4, 15

Pigmeat Markham 5, 14

D Urville Martin 90, 92,
96

Hattie McDaniel 1, 22

Lonette McKee 33, 54, 79

Butterfly McQueen 1

Zakes Mokae 43, 70, 109

Juanita Moore 12

Melba Moore 48

Rudy Ray Moore 89, 92,
94, 95, 212

Mantan Moreland 9, 12,
16, 23-25, 198

Joe Morton 33, 36

Ethel Moses 10

Eddie Murphy 27, 28, 30,
32, 38, 42, 48, 83, 139,
211, 212 Clarence
Muse5, 23, 25

Carmen Newsome 10, 23

Ron O Neal 45, 78, 97

Brock Peters 6, 20, 24,
111, 118, 134

Sidney Poitier 7, 10, 11,
13, 15, 17, 19, 24, 34,
46, 58, 68, 70, 75, 77,
79, 84, 86, 141

Oscar Polk 11

Prince 47, 69, 84, 185

Richard Pryor 27, 28, 31,
33, 35, 47-49, 53, 56,
64, 75-77, 79, 82, 84,
94, 212

Beah Richards 11, 47, 60

Paul Robeson 4, 8, 13, 15,
21-23, 67, 134, 141,
143, 148, 193

Bill Robinson 23, 126

Charles P. Robinson 90

Chris Rock 32, 65, 212

Esther Rolle 43, 51, 62,
71

Howard Rollins 116

Diana Ross 56, 60, 86,
182

Hazel Scott 4

Wesley Snipes 41, 54, 63,
65, 66, 80, 85, 86

Woody Strode 22, 69

Robert Townsend 44, 49,
61, 62, 212

Lorenzo Tucker 25

Cicely Tyson 16, 29, 35,
49, 55, 72, 78, 87

Leslie Uggams 90

Ben Vereen 52, 68, 118

Fredi Washington 8, 12

Ethel Waters 1, 5, 20,
126, 134, 189

Damon Wayans 52

Keenan Ivory Wayans 51,
52

Forest Whitaker 31, 70,
101

Fred Williamson 27, 89,
91, 93

Dooley Wilson 1, 23

Paul Winfield 33, 38, 46,
49, 51, 55, 78, 142

Oprah Winfrey 37, 65, 87

Alfre Woodard 31, 46, 60,
66, 78, 118

Richard Wright 18, 137

Title Index

48 Hours 27

7-Up in South Africa 157

Abbey Lincoln: You Gotta Pay the Band 193

Adios Amigos 27

Aesop's Fables 111

Africa 157, 158

Africa (The Dream Awake) 131

Africa Comeback: The Popular Music of West Africa 170, 171

Africa Speaks to the World 158

African Dream, An 99

African Journey 111

African Story Magic 111

African-American Art: Past and Present 121

Afro-Classic Folk Tales Vol. I 112

Afro-Classic Folk Tales Vol. II 112

Afro-Classic Mother Goose 112

After Hours 193

Ailey Dances 208

Ain't Gonna Shuffle No More (Eyes on the Prize II) 153

Ain't Scared of Your Jails (Eyes on the Prize I) 152

Airmail Special (Harlem Hotshots) 197

Al Green on Fire in Tokyo 171

Al Green...Everything's Gonna Be Alright 171

Albert King 187

Alberta Hunter (Jazz at the Smithsonian) 199

Alberta Hunter: My Castle's Rockin' 193

All American Newsreel, The (Rare Black Short Subjects) 146

Allen T.D. Wiggin 172

Almos' a Man 28

Along the Old Man River (Out of the Blacks Into the Blues) 192

Always for Pleasure 121

American Songster, An 188

America's Music Gospel 172

Amistad, Crispus Attucks, Harriet Tubman and the Emancipation Proclamation 131

Amos 'n' Andy: Anatomy of a Controversy 121, 122

Anansi 113

Anatomy of a Riot 122

And the Children Shall Lead 112, 113

Anderson Platoon 122

Angelic Gospel Singers 172

Another 48 Hours 28

Another You 28

Anything For Jazz 193

Archie Shepp: I Am Jazz...It's My Life 194

Ariadne auf Naxos 206

Art Blakey and the Jazz Messengers (Jazz at the Smithsonian) 199

Art Farmer (Jazz at the Smithsonian) 199

Art of Living, The (Millennium) 140

Art of the Dogon 159

Arvis Strickling Jones: From the Inside Out 172

Ashes and Embers 28

Assassination of Martin Luther King, Jr., The 151

Assault at West Point 28, 29

Aswad Live 186

At the Threshold (Millennium) 140

Autobiography of Miss Jane Pittman 29

Avenging Disco Godfather 89

Awakenings (Eyes on the Prize I) 152

B.B. King Live at Nick's 188

Back to the Movement (Eyes on the Prize II) 153, 154

Bagdad Cafe 29

Beale Street 188

Beat Street 29

Bebe's Kids 113

Ben Webster: The Brute and the Beautiful 194

Benjamin E. Mays: Mentor of Martin Luther King, Jr. 122, 123

Benjamin O. Davis, Jr.: American1 22

Benny Carter (Jazz at the Smithsonian) 199

Bento 123

Best of Blank, The 194

Best of Eddie Murphy Saturday Night Live 211

Betrayed 30

Betye and Alison Saar 123

Beulah Show, The, Vol. 1 1

Beulah Show, The, Vol. 2 1

Beverly Hills Cop 30

Beverly Hills Cop 2 30

Beware 1, 2

Beyond Hate 124

Beyond Hate Trilogy 124

Bible and the Gun, The (Africa)158

Big Bang Boogie (Harlem Swings) 198

Big Ben: Ben Webster in Europe 194

Big City Blues 188

Big Dis, The 30

Big Timers, The 2

Bill Cosby's Picturepages: Numbers 113

Bill Cosby's Picturepages: Words and Letters 113

Bingo Long Traveling All-Stars & Motor Kings, The 30, 31

Biography: Jackie Robinson 124

Bird 31

Birth of a Nation, The 2, 3

Bishop Jeff Banks/Revival Mass Choir 173

Black American Literature 124

Black Americans of Achievement, The 125

Black Americans: Artists, Entertainers and More 133

Black Americans: Political Leaders, Educators, Scientists 133

Black and Tan (Black Artists Short Subjects) 126

Black and White in Color 99

Black Artists Short Subjects 126

Black Arts, The (The Dream Awake) 131

Black Athlete, The 126

Black Belt Jones 89

Black Brigade 31

Black Caesar 89, 90

Black Cowboy, The (The Dream Awake) 131

Black Gestapo 90

Black Godfather, The 90

Black Heritage Holidays (Black Studies: Then and Now) 128

Black Heroes: Builders, Dreamers and More 133

Black Heroes: Freedom Fighters, Cowboys & More 133

Black History: Lost, Stolen or Strayed 126

Black King 2

Black Like Me 3

Black Man 's Land Trilogy 159, 160

Black Military Experience, The 126

Black Orpheus 100

Black Panthers: Huey Newton/Black Panther Newsreel 127

Black Power in America: Myth or Reality? 127

Black Profiles 127

Black Quartet, The (The Dream Awake) 131

Black Sister 's Revenge 90

Black Studies: Then and Now 127, 128

Black Vengeance 90

Blackboard Jungle 3

Blacks Britannica 128, 129

Blood of Jesus 3

Blue Chips 31

Blue Collar 31, 32

Blues Accordin ' to Lightnin ' Hopkins 188, 189

Blues Like Showers of Rain 189

Blues Masters 189

Blues Summit in Chicago 189

Bo Diddley and the All Star Jam Show 190

Boardinghouse Blues 4

Body and Soul 4

Boogie in Blue 190

Boogie in C (Harlem Hotshots) 197

Boogie Woogie Dream (Black Artists Short Subjects) 126

Booker T. Washington (Black Americans of Achievement) 125

Booker T. Washington: The Life and the Legacy 129

Boomerang 32

Bopha! 32

Born Musicians (Repercussions) 184

Boy! What A Girl! 4

Boyz N The Hood 32

Breakin ' 32, 33

Breakin ' II: Electric Boogaloo 33

Breathe On Me: Rev. James Cleveland 173

Brer Rabbit and Boss Lion 114

Brer Rabbit and the Wonderful Tar Baby 114

Brewster 's Millions 33

Bridge to Freedom (Eyes on the Prize I) 152, 153

Broadway Rhythm 4

Broken Strings 5

Bronze Buckaroo, The 5

Bronze Buckaroo, The (Harlem Swings) 198

Brother From Another Planet, The 33

Brother Future 114, 115

Brother John 33

Brother With Perfect Timing 169

Brown Bomber (Black Artists Short Subjects) 126

Buck and the Preacher 34

Bucktown 91

Built By Hand: String Trio of New York 195

Buried Treasures 181

Burlesque in Harlem 5

Bush Mama 34, 34

Bushbaby, The 34

Bustin ' Loose 35

Cabin in the Sky 5

Caldonia (Harlem Swings) 198

California Suite 35

Candyman 35

Car Wash 35

Caravans of Gold 158

Carbon Copy 36

Caribbean Crucible (Repercussions) 170

Carmen Jones 6

Carmen McRae Live 195

Carnegie Hall Salutes The Jazz Masters 195

Cavalleria Rusticana 206, 207

Celebrating Bird: The Triumph of Charlie Parker 194, 195

Chameleon Street 36

Check and Double Check 6

Chester Zardis: The Spirit of New Orleans 195, 196

China Gate 6

Chocolat 100

Chuck Berry at the Roxy 181

Chuck Berry: Rock and Roll Music 181

Circle of Recovery 129

City of Blood 100

City of Hope 36, 37

Clara 's Heart 36

Clarence and Angel 37

Clark Sisters 173

Clean Slate 100

Cleopatra Jones 91

Cleopatra Jones and the Casino of Gold 91

Clouds of Joy 173

Coffy 91

Colin Powell (Black Americans of Achievement) 125

Colin Powell: A General 's General 129

Color of Love, The 129

Color Purple, The 37

Colors 38

Come Back, Africa 160

Coming to America 38

Commissioned in Concert 173

Connection, The 6

Conrack 38

Consuming Hunger 130

Conversation with Gwendolyn Brooks, A 130

Conversation with Magic, A 130

Cooley High 38

Cotton Comes to Harlem 39

Coup De Torchon (Clean Slate) 100

Court Martial of Jackie Robinson, The 39

Creole Giselle: Dance Theatre of Harlem 209

Cry Freedom 39

Cry, the Beloved Country 101, 101

Crying Game, The 101

D.F.W. Mass: I Will Let Nothing Separate Me 173

Dance at Court (Dancing) 210

Dance Black America 209

Dance Theater of Harlem 209

Dancing 210

Dark City 101

Daughters of the Dust 39, 40

Dawn of the Dead 40

Dead Man Out 40, 41

Deadly Drifter 41

Death of a Gunfighter 7

Deep Cover 41

Deep North 131

Defiant Ones 7

Demolition Man 41

Devil 's Daughter 7

Diana Ross Live 182

Different But Equal (Africa) 157

Different Drummer: Elvin Jones 196

Dingaka 102

Dirty Gertie From Harlem 7

Disco Godfather 92

Disorderlies 41

Distinguished Gentleman 42

Divine Horsemen: The Living Gods of Haiti 132

Dizzy Atmosphere (Harlem Hotshots) 197

Dizzy Gillespie196

Dizzy Gillespie: A Night in Chicago 196

Dizzy Gillespie: A Night in Tunisia 197

Dizzy Gillespie: Live in London 197

Do The Right Thing 42

Dolemite 92

Dolemite 2: The Human Tornado 92

Don Redman and His Orchestra with Red and Struggle 198

Don 't Look Back: The Story of Leroy "Satchel" Paige 42

Double Deal 8

Down Memory Lane: Rev. James Cleveland 173

Dr. Charles G. Hayes and the Cosmopolitan Church of Prayer 174

Dr. Martin Luther King, Jr. (Black Americans of Achievement) 125

Dr. Martin Luther King, Jr. (Black Studies: Then and Now) 128

Dr. Martin Luther King, Jr.: A Historical Perspective 151

Dreadlocks and the Three Bears 114

Dream Awake Complete Set, The 131

Dream Awake, The 131

Driving Miss Daisy 42, 43

Drums of Dagbon, The (Repercussions) 170

Dry White Season, A 43

Duke Is Tops 8

Ebony/Jet Guide to Black Excellence 132

Ecology of Mind, An (Millennium) 140

Ed & Chester Bible Stories 114

Ed & Chester Show 115

Eddie Jefferson 197

Eddie Murphy: Delirious 212

Eddie Murphy: Raw 212

Emperor Jones 8, 9

Entertainers, The (Ebony/Jet Guide to Black Excellence) 132

Entrepreneurs, The (Ebony/Jet Guide to Black Excellence) 132

Ernie Andrews: Blues For Central Avenue 197

Evening with Alvin Ailey and the American Dance Theater, An 209, 210

Eyes on the Prize I 151, 152, 153

Eyes on the Prize I and II: The Commemorative Edition 154

Eyes on the Prize II 153, 154

Fact Is Stranger Than Fiction 51

Fair Weather Friend, The (Human Race Club) 116

Faith Ringgold: The Last Story Quilt 132

Falashas 160

Fame 43

Famous Black Americans 133

Fass Black 92

Father Clements Story, The 44

Faure/Poulenc Concert 207

FBI's War on Black America1 33

Fields of Endless Day 134

Fighting Back (Eyes on the Prize I) 152

Firehouse 44

Five Heartbeats, The 44

Florida Mass Choir: Higher Hope 174

Florida Mass Choir: Now I Can See 174

Folks Like Us 161

Follow the Drinking Gourd 115

Following Fidel (Portrait of the Caribbean) 144, 145

For Us, the Living: The Story of Medgar Evers 43, 44

Four Days of the Masai 161

Foxy Brown 92

Franck Goldberg: Sampler 134

Frederick Douglass (Black Americans of Achievement) 125

Frederick Douglass: An American Life 134

Free to Be...You and Me 115

Free, White, and 21 45

Freedom Man 45

Freedom Road 45

French Way, The 102

Friday Foster 93

From Sun-Up 161

From These Roots 134

Gang War 9

General Idi Amin Dada 161

George Washington Carver (Black Americans of Achievement) 125

Georgia Mass Choir: I Sing Because I'm Happy 174

Get Christie Love 93

Getting the Story (Consuming Hunger) 130

Ghost 45

Ghost Dad 46

Gift of Amazing Grace, The 16

Gift of the Black Folk (Portraits in Black) 146

Girl from Chicago 9

Girl in Room 20 10

Glimpses of West Africa 161, 162

Glory 46

Glory of Gospel 174

Go Down Death 10

Go Tell It on the Mountain 46

Gods Must Be Crazy, The 102, 103

Gods Must Be Crazy II, The 102

God's Step Children 10

Golden Child, The 46

Good Mornin' Blues 190

Good-Bye, My Lady 10

Gordon Parks' Visions 135

Gospel Keynotes Live 175

Gospel's Best From Saturday Night Sing 175

Graffiti Bridge 47

Greased Lightning 47

Great Black Baseball Players 135

Great White Hope 47

Greatest Week In Gospel1 75

Green Pastures, The 11

Grover Washington, Jr. in Concert 182

Guess Who's Coming to Dinner 11

Guitar Legends 182

Guy from Harlem, The 93

Haiti: Killing the Dream 135

Hale House: Alive With Love 135

Half Slave, Half Free, Part 1 47

Half Slave, Half Free, Part 2: Charlotte Forten's Mission 48

Hallelujah: A Gospel Celebration 175

Hallelujah! 11

Hangin' with the Homeboys 48

Harder They Come 103

Harlem Hot Shots (Harlem Swings) 198

Harlem Hotshots 197

Harlem Nights 48

Harlem on the Prairie 12

Harlem Rides the Range 12

Harlem Swings 198

Harriet Tubman (Black Americans of Achievement) 125

Hate on Trial 124

Have a Good Time (Harlem Hotshots) 197

Heaven Is a Playground 48

Herbie Hancock Trio: Hurricane! 198

Herdsmen of the Sun 162, 162

Hero Ain't Nothin' But a Sandwich, A 49

Hezekiah Walker and the Love Fellowship Crusade Choir 175

Hi-De-Ho 199

Hi-De-Ho (Black Artists Short Subjects) 126

Hi-De-Ho (Harlem Swings) 198

Hit! 49

Hollywood Shuffle 49

Home Feeling 135

Home of the Brave 12

Homecoming 176

House of Dies Drear, The 116

House Party 49, 50

House Party 2: The Pajama Jam 49, 50

House Party 3 50

How the Leopard Got His Spots 116

How U Like Me Now 50, 51

Huckleberry Finn 51

Hum 255 (Kartemquin Films) 138

Human Race Club: A Story About Making Friends/A Story About Prejudice 116

Human Tornado, The 92

I Know Why the Caged Bird Sings 51

Ida B. Wells 136, *136*

Illusions 51

Images: Tribute to Harold Washington 136

Imitation of Life 12

In Motion: Amiri Baraka 137

In Plain English 137

In the Heat of the Night 13

Individual and Tradition, The (Dancing) 210

Introduction to Richard Wright's Fiction 137

Intruder in the Dust 13

Intruder, The 75

Inventing Reality (Millennium) 140

Iron in the Soul (Portrait of the Caribbean) 144

I'm Gonna Git You Sucka 51, 52

Jackie Robinson (Black Americans of Achievement) 125

Jackie Robinson Story, The 13

Jackson Southernaires 176

Jacob Lawrence: The Glory of Expression 137

Jaguar 163

James Brown & Guest B.B. King 187

James Brown: The Lost James Brown Tapes 187

Jammin' the Blues (Black Artists Short Subjects) 126

Jazz at the Smithsonian 199, 200

Jazz Hoofer Baby Lawrence 210

Jazz in Exile 200

Jazz Time Tale 117

Jazz: Earle Hines and Coleman Hawkins 199

Jericho 13

Jesse Jackson (Black Americans of Achievement) 125

Jesse Owens Returns to Berlin 138

Jesse Owens Story, The 52

Jessye Norman: A Christmas Concert 207

Jessye Norman: Live 207

Jesus Christ, Superstar 52

Jesus Paid It All 176

Jimi Hendrix: Experience1 182

Jimi Plays Berkeley 182

Jo Jo Dancer, Your Life is Calling 53

Joe Louis Story, The 14

Joe Louis vs. Max Schmelling (Black Artists Short Subjects) 126

Joe Williams (Jazz at the Smithsonian) 200

Joe Williams: A Song Is Born 200

Joey Breaker 53

Joe's Bed-Stuy Barbershop: We Cut Heads 52

John Henry 117

Johnny Taylor Live in Dallas 190

Josephine Baker Story, The 53

Joshua 93

Journey, The, Volume 4 163, 164

Judge Priest 14

Juice 53

Juju Music: King Sunny Ade 169, 170

Juke Joint 14

Junction 88 14

Jungle Fever 54, 54

Just Another Girl on the I.R.T. 54

Just Doin' It138

Karibu 163

Kartemquin Films, Vol. 3: Trick Bag 138

Kasarmu Ce: This Land Is Ours 103

Kathleen Battle at the Metropolitan Museum 207

Keep Punching 15

Keith Jarrett Last Solo 200

Kenny Drew Live 200

Kenyatta (Black Man's Land Trilogy) 159, 160, *160*

Keys to the Kingdom, The (Eyes on the Prize II) 153

Killer Diller 15

Killing Floor, The 55

Kilroy Was Here (Rare Black Short Subjects) 146

King 55

King Solomon's Mines 15

King: Montgomery to Memphis 154

Kings and Cities (Africa) 158

Kiss Shot 55

Kitchen Toto 103, 104

Klansman, The 55

Koi and the Kola Nuts 117

Koko Taylor: Queen of the Blues 190

Krush Groove 56

L. Barnes & Red Budd Choir: So Satisfied 176

L.A. All-Stars 201

L.A. Mass Choir 176

La Grande Illusion (Portrait of the Caribbean) 144

Ladies Sing the Blues 191

Lady Day: The Many Faces of Billie Holiday 201

Lady Sings the Blues 56

Last Dragon 56

Last Supper 104

Leadbelly 56

Leaders, The (Ebony/Jet Guide to Black Excellence) 132

Leaders, The: Jazz in Paris 1988 201

Lean on Me 56, 57

Learning Tree, The 57

Legacy, The (Africa) 158

Legends of Rhythm and Blues (Repercussions) 184

Les Maitres Fous 163

Les McCann Trio 201

Let the Good Times Roll 183

Lethal Weapon 57

Lethal Weapon II 57

Lethal Weapon III 58

Let's Do It Again 58

Liberation Of L.B. Jones, The 58

Life and Times of Deacon A.L. Wiley, The 58

Lilies of the Field 15

Lion Hunters 164, 165

Lions of Dakar 169

Listen Up: The Lives of Quincy Jones 183

Little Richard: Keep on Rockin' 183

Long Walk Home, The 58

Look Out Sister 16

Looking for Langston 138

Lord of the Dance, The (Dancing) 210

Lou Rawls Show with Duke Ellington 201

Love to All, Lorraine 59

Love You Like Mad (Harlem Hotshots) 197

Love Your Mama 59

Lucky Ghost 16

Lying Lips 16

L'Africaine 208

L'Etat Sauvage (The Savage State) 104

Mack 94

Mad Max Beyond Thunderdome 59

Madame C.J. Walker (Black Americans of Achievement) 125

Made in America 59

Magic Garden, The (The Pennywhistle Blues) 104

Mahalia Jackson :Give God The Glory 176

Mahogany 60

Malcolm X 60

Malcolm X (Black Americans of Achievement) 125

Malcolm X: Death of a Prophet 154, 155

Mama Florence and Papa Cock 139

Man and Boy 60

Man Called Adam, A 16

Mance Lipscomb and Lightnin' Hopkins (Masters of Comic Blues) 191

Mandela 60, 61

Mandela in America 139

Mandela: The Man and His Country 164

Marching On 16, 17

Mark Naftalin's Blue Monday 191

Mark Of The Hawk 17

Martin Luther King Commemorative Collection 154, 155

Martin Luther King, Jr.: Legacy of a Dream 155

Martin Luther King: I Have a Dream 155

Martyrs, The (The Dream Awake) 131

Marvin Gaye 183

Masks from Many Cultures 164

Master Musicians of Jahjouka, The 170

Mastering A Continent (Africa) 157, 158

Masters of Comic Blues 191

Masters of Tap 210, 211

Matewan 61

Mau Mau (Black Man's Land Trilogy) 159

McDonald's Gospelfest 177

Me Yu an' Mi Taxi 105

Mean to Be Free: John Brown's Black Nation Campaign 139

Menace II Society 61

Meteor Man 61

Mighty Pawns, The 117

Mighty Quinn, The 62

Millennium: Tribal Wisdom and the Modern World 139, 140

Mills Brothers Story, The 201

Mingus 202

Miracle in Harlem 17

Mississippi Burning 62

Mississippi Masala 62

Mississippi Mass Choir 177

Mississippi Mass Choir: God Gets The Glory 177

Mississippi: Is This America? (Eyes on the Prize I) 152

Mistaken Identity 17

Mistaken Identity (Millennium) 140

Mister Johnson 62, 63, 63

Modern Jazz Quartet 202

Mona Lisa 105

Monk in Oslo 202, 203

Monkey Hustle 94

Moon Over Harlem 17

Mother, Jugs and Speed 64

Mountains Of The Moon 64

Moving 64

Mo' Better Blues 63, 64

Mo' Money 63

Mr. Rogers: Music and Feelings 117

Muddy Waters 191

Muhammad Ali vs. Zora Folley 140

Murder In Harlem 18

Murder in Swingtime (Harlem Swings) 198

Murder on Lennox Ave 18

Music Hath Harm (Black Artists Short Subjects) 126

Nat "King" Cole Musical Story, The (Harlem Swings) 198

Nat "King" Cole Story, The 141

Nation of Law?, A (Eyes on the Prize II) 153

Nationtime, Gary 141

Native Land 141

Native Son (1951) 18

Native Son (1986) 65

Negro in Entertainment, The (Black Artists Short Subjects) 126

Negro in Industry, The (Black Artists Short Subjects) 126

Negro in Sports, Entertainment and Industry, The 146

Negro in Sports, The (Black Artists Short Subjects) 126

Negro Soldier 141

New Jack City 65

New Jersey Mass Choir 177

New York Restoration Choir: Thank You Jesus 177

Newsreel Library of America in Sports, A 142

Night of the Living Dead 65

Nightline: Louis Farrakhan 142

Nightline: Nelson Mandela 142

Nightline: South African Debate 165

No Easy Walk (Eyes on the Prize I) 152

No Fear, No Die 105

Notes for an African Orestes 105

Nothing But a Man 18

Obeah Wedding 106

Officer and a Gentleman, An 65

Oh Happy Day 177

On the Battlefield (Repercussions) 184

Once Upon a Time 165

One False Move 66

Only the Ball Was White 142

Open the Door Richard (Harlem Swings) 198

Ornette: Made in America 192

Out of Africa (Portrait of the Caribbean) 144

Out of the Blacks Into the Blues 192

Panama Hattie 19

Parade of Stars 178

Parade of Stars: Live Gospel 178

Paradise in Harlem 19

Paradise Lost (Portrait of the Caribbean) 144

Paris Blues 19

Paris Is Burning 142

Passenger 57 66

Passin' It On 143

Passion Fish 66

Pastime 66, 67

Patch of Blue 19

Paul Laurence Dunbar (Portraits in Black) 145

Paul Robeson (Barnett) 143, 143

Paul Robeson (Richards) 67

Pawnbroker, The 19, 20

Pelican Brief 67

Penitentiary 94

Penitentiary II 94

Penitentiary III 94

Pennywhistle Blues, The 104

Pentecostal Community Choir with Minister Keith Pringle 178

People Under the Stairs, The 67

People vs. Paul Crump, The 144, 145

Perfect Model, The 81

Petey Wheatstraw 95

Philadelphia 67, 68

Pie Pie Blackbird (Harlem Swings) 198

Piece of the Action, A 68

Pilgrim Jubilees 178

Pinky 20

Pipe Dreams 68

Pippin 68

Place of Weeping 106

Playing Away 106

Poetic Justice 68, 69

Poor Man Shames Us All, A (Millennium) 140

Portrait of Jason 145

Portrait of the Caribbean 144, 145

Portrait of the Caribbean Complete Set 145

Portraits in Black 145

Posse 69

Power! (Eyes on the Prize II) 153

Princess Tam Tam 106, 107

Promised Land, The (Eyes on the Prize II) 153

Purdy's Station 69

Purple Rain 69

Puss 'n Boots 118

Putney Swope 70, 70

Quiet One 20

Quilombo 106, 107, 108

Quincy Jones: A Celebration 183

R.C.M. Productions, Inc. Presents Louis Armstrong and His Band 198

Race for Mayor, The 146

Rage in Harlem 70, 72

Raisin in the Sun (1971) 70, 71

Raisin in the Sun (1989) 71

Rappin' 71

Rare Black Short Subjects 146

Real Malcolm X, The: An Intimate Portrait of the Man 155, 156

Rebels and Abolitionists (Black Studies: Then and Now) 128

Reed Royalty 202

Reivers, The 71

Repercussions 170, 172, 184

Respectful Prostitute 107

Resurrection City and the Children (The Dream Awake) 131

Return of Superfly, The 95

Rev. Clay Evans: I'm Going Through 178

Rev. Ernest Davis, Jr. and the Wilmington Chester Mass Choir: H 178

Rev. F.C. Barnes and Co. 178

Rev. Gary Davis and Sonny Terry (Masters of Comic Blues) 191

Rev. James Cleveland and the L.A. Gospel Messengers 179

Rev. James Moore: Live With The Mississippi Mass Choir 179

Rhapsody in Black and Blue, A (Harlem Swings) 198

Rhythms of Resistance 171

Richard Pryor: Live in Concert 212

Rick Grundy Chorale 179

Ricochet 71

Right On!: Poetry on Film 184

Rise of Nationalism, The (Africa) 158

River Niger 72

Road to Freedom: The Vernon Johns Story 72

Robert Coles: Teacher 146

Robert Colescott: The One-Two Punch 146

Rock 'n Roll Revue with Duke Ellington (Harlem Swings) 198

Roll of Thunder 118

Roll of Thunder, Hear My Cry 72

Ron Carter Live Double Bass 202, 203

Roots 73

Roots of Gospel 179

Roots, Rock, Reggae 186

Roots: Salute to the Saxophone 203

Roots: The Gift 73

Roots: The Next Generations 73

Round Midnight 107

Roy Ayers Live 203

Rude 212

Rufus Jones For President (Black Artists Short Subjects) 126

Rufus Jones for President (Harlem Swings) 198

Runaway 118, 119

Running Scared 74

Running with Jesse 147

Saint of Fort Washington, The 74

Salif Keita: Destiny of a Noble Outcast 171

Sanders of the River 21

Sarafina! 74

Savage State, The 104

Savior Is Born, The 118

Say Amen, Somebody 179

Scar of Shame, The (Facets) 20, 21

Scar of Shame, The (Smithsonian/Library of Congress) 20, 21

School Daze 74

Scream, Blacula, Scream 95

Search for Robert Johnson, The 192

See No Evil, Hear No Evil 75

Selling the Feeling (Consuming Hunger) 130

Sensational Nightingales, The: Ministry In Song 179

Sentimental Journey 184

Separate But Equal 75

Sepia Cinderella 21

Sergeant Rutledge 22

Shades of Freedom (Portrait of the Caribbean) 144, 145

Shaft 95

Shaft's Big Score 96

Shaka Zulu 108

Shame (The Intruder) 75

Shaping the Image (Consuming Hunger) 130

Sheba, Baby 96

She's Gotta Have It 75, 76

Shindig! Presents Soul 187

Shindig!: Legends of Rock 'n' Roll 185

Shirley Horn: Here's to Life 203

Shirley Verrett 208

Shock of the Other (Millennium) 139

Show Boat 22

Sign O' The Times 185

Silver Streak 76

Sippie: Sippie Wallace 204

Sister Act 76

Sister Act II: Back in the Habit 76

Sit Down and Listen: The Story of Max Roach (Repercussions) 184

Sitting in Limbo 147

Six Degrees of Separation 77

Sky Is Gray, The 77, 78

Slavery and Plantation Life (Black Studies: Then and Now) 127

Slender Thread, The 22

Slow Poke (Black Artists Short Subjects) 126

Slow Poke (Harlem Swings) 198

Sojourner Truth (Black Americans of Achievement) 125

Soldier's Story, A 77

Some Kind of Hero 77

Something New Out of Africa 147

Son of Ingagi 22

Song of Freedom 23

Sons of Bwiregi 165

Sophisticated Gents, The 78

Soul Vengeance 96

Sound: Rahsaan Roland Kirk and John Cage 208

Sounder 78

South Central 79

Space Is the Place 96, 97

Sparkle 79

Speeches of Martin Luther King, The 156

Spirit of Youth 23

Standards II 204

Stanley Turrentine in Concert (Jazz at the Smithsonian) 200

Stations of the Elevated 204

Stir Crazy 79

Stormy Weather 23

Story About Making Friends, A 116

Story About Prejudice and Discrimination, A 116

Story of A Three Day Pass 79

Straight Out of Brooklyn 80, 80

Strange Relations (Millennium) 139

Street Wars 80

Streetmother 165

Studio Films Inc. Presents Lionel Hampton, Sarah Vaughan, Martha 198

Sugar Cane Alley 108

Sugar Hill 80

Sunday Sinners 23

Super Soul Brother 97

Superfly 97

Superfly TNT 97

Sweet Love, Bitter 81

Sweet Perfection 81

Sweet Sweetback's Baadasssss Song 98

Swing 23

Symphony in Black (Black Artists Short Subjects) 126

Symphony in Black (Harlem Swings) 198

T Bone N Weasel 81

Taking Care of Terrific 118

Tales From Africa (Central) 119

Talkin' Dirty After Dark 81

Tall, Tan and Terrific 24

Tallest Tree in the Forest, The 148

Tamango 24

Tap 82

Temptations and The Four Tops, The 185

Temptations, The 185

Tenor Titans 204

Texas Tenor: The Illinois Jacquet Story 204, 205

The Rodney King Case: What the Jury Saw in California v. Powel 147

They Live 82

This House of Power 148

This Magnificent African Cake (Africa) 158

Threepenny Opera, The 108, 109

Thurgood Marshall (Black Americans of Achievement) 125

Tightrope of Power, The (Millennium) 140

Time Has Come, The (Eyes on the Prize II) 153

Time Will Tell: Bob Marley 186

Tina Turner: The Girl from Nutbush 185, 186

To Kill a Mockingbird 24

To Sir, With Love 24

To Sleep with Anger 82, 83

Toni Morrison: Profile of a Writer 148

Torture of Mothers: The Case of the Harlem Six 148

Touching the Timeless (Millennium) 140

Toy, The 82, 83

Trading Places 83

Tramaine Hawkins 180

Treemonisha 208

Trespass 83

Tribute to Alvin Ailey, A 211

Tribute to Bill Evans, A 205

Tribute to John Coltrane 205

Trick Bag (Kartemquin Films) 138

True Identity 83, 84

Trumpet Course with Clark Terry 206

Twist 211

Two Centuries of Black American Art (Portraits in Black) 145

Two Societies (Eyes on the Prize II) 153

Two-Gun Man From Harlem 25

T'ain't Nothin Changed 180

Uncle Tom's Cabin (1903 & 1914) 25

Uncle Tom's Cabin (1969) 109

Uncle Tom's Cabin (1987) 84

Under the Cherry Moon 84

Unforgettable Pen Pal, The (Human Race Club) 116

Untold West, The: The Black West 148, 149

Uptown Comedy Express 212

Uptown Saturday Night 84

Urban Jungle 98

Veiled Aristocrats 25

Virginia, Georgia and Caroline (Harlem Swings) 198

Voices of Sarafina! 84, 85

Walter Hawkins and Love Alive IV 180

Wanda Nero Butler: New Born Soul 180

Waterdance, The 85

Watermelon Man 85

Way Down South 25

Way to Escape the Ghetto, A (Out of the Blacks Into the Blues) 192

What the Fuck Are These Red Squares (Kartemquin Films) 138

What's Love Got to Do With It? 85

Where Did You Get that Woman? 149

White Man's Country (Black Man's Land Trilogy) 159

White Men Can't Jump 86

Whoopi Goldberg: Fontaine...Why Am I Straight? 213

Why the Sun and the Moon Live in the Sky 120

Wilby Conspiracy, The 86

Wild Style 86

Williams Brothers: I'm Just A Nobody 180

Willie Banks and the Messengers 180

Willie Dixon 192

Willie Neal Johnson and the New Keynotes: The Country Boy Goe 180

Winans, The: Live in Concert 181

Winans, The: Return 181

Within Our Gates 26

Wiz, The 86

Woman Called Moses, A 87

Women of Brewster Place, The 87

Words by Heart 119

World of Strangers, A 109

Worlds Apart (Portrait of the Caribbean) 144, 145

Xica 109

You Must Remember This 120

Young One, The 110

Zebrahead 87

Zora Is My Name! 87

Zou Zou 110

Zulu Dawn 110

Zydeco Gumbo 193